Race and America's Long War

Race and America's Long War

NIKHIL PAL SINGH

UNIVERSITY OF CALIFORNIA PRESS

University of California Press, one of the most distinguished
university presses in the United States, enriches lives around
the world by advancing scholarship in the humanities, social
sciences, and natural sciences. Its activities are supported by
the UC Press Foundation and by philanthropic contributions
from individuals and institutions. For more information,
visit www.ucpress.edu.

University of California Press
Oakland, California

Parts of chapter 1 first appeared in *American Quarterly* 66, no.
4, (2014): 1091–99. Copyright © 2014 American Studies
Association. Chapter 3 was originally published in *South
Atlantic Quarterly* 105, no.1 (2006): 71–93. Copyright 2006,
Duke University Press. All rights reserved. Reprinted by
permission of the publisher. www.dukeupress.edu.

Library of Congress Cataloging-in-Publication Data

Names: Singh, Nikhil Pal, author.
Title: Race and America's long war / Nikhil Pal Singh.
Description: Oakland, California : University of California
    Press, [2017] | Includes bibliographical references and
    index.
Identifiers: LCCN 2017023301 (print) | LCCN 2017025293
    (ebook) | ISBN 9780520968837 (Ebook) |
    ISBN 9780520296251 (cloth : alk. paper)
Subjects: LCSH: Racism—United States—History. | National
    characteristics, American—History. | Political culture—
    United States—History. | United States—Social conditions.
    | United States—Politics and government.
Classification: LCC E184.A1 (ebook) | LCC E184.A1 S613 2017
    (print) | DDC 305.800973—dc23
LC record available at https://lccn.loc.gov/2017023301

Manufactured in the United States of America

26   25   24   23   22   21   20   19   18   17
10   9   8   7   6   5   4   3   2   1

You tell me that hitler
Is a mighty bad man.
I guess he took lessons
from the ku klux klan.

You tell me mussolini's
Got an evil heart.
Well, it mus-a been in Beaumont
That he had his start—

Cause everything that hitler
And mussolini do,
Negroes get the same
Treatment from you.

> Langston Hughes, "Beaumont to
> Detroit," 1943

The road which leads from the Indian massacres of the last century
to the Pentagon and another from the oppressive slave plantation
to the ghetto are the major conjunctive highways running through
the very center of U.S. life and history.

> Jack O'Dell, "The July Rebellions and the
> Military State," 1967

War and incarceration are supposed to bring good things to the
places destroyed in the name of being saved; the devastation
wrought overseas in Iraq and Afghanistan is both prefigured and
shadowed by the history and current experience of life in the
United States itself. The convergence of theory and technique come
into view in the construction of the perpetual enemy who must
always be fought but can never be vanquished.

> Ruth Wilson Gilmore, "Race, Prisons, and War," 2008

CONTENTS

The United States developed its forms of democratic politics and capitalist economics from processes of imperial expansion, colonial dispossession, and racial domination. To observe this is to state a banal truth, yet one that is dimly acknowledged, disavowed, or defensively protested across large swaths of the country. Dispute over the meaning and interpretation of such basic facts gives rise to intense political and ideological struggles over the boundaries of civic belonging and recognition and distributions of material harm and benefit. From abolitionism to the modern labor, civil rights, and black power movements, these struggles have produced exacting visions of solidarity in opposition to racial division and inequality (less so to colonial dispossession) and engendered ever more subtle and intractable forms of accommodation to, and collective reinvestments in, racial and colonial ordering. Until recently, the last point might have been controversial, for many people, perhaps the majority, now reject or condemn slavery, Indian removal, Jim Crow, and racially based immigration and naturalization restrictions, and doubt that similarly extreme forms of exclusion actively shape current U.S. political culture and policy. The successful presidential campaign of Donald Trump shows, however, that no one should be surprised by the resilience of racism's historical legacies and current appeal.

To conceptualize the reanimation and reinvention of racism as more than attitudinal, but rather as a publicly sanctioned ordering of social and economic life along the lines of group inequality and enmity, is no simple matter. An inevitable temptation in the face of its recurrence and disavowal is to lament stubborn continuities of history or deficits of human nature. Racism's manifold extensions from small-scale failures of interpersonal recognition to consequential aggregation and differentiation of group vulnerabilities and privileges is similarly vexing: it can seem omnipresent, yet located nowhere in particular. The great black intellectual and activist W. E. B. Du Bois famously described racial division as "the problem [that] cuts across and hinders the settlement of other problems." Du Bois's relentless mastery of discipline after discipline and his scrutiny of local, national and global contexts showed how presumptions of racial hierarchy structured the broad field of what could be known and what could be valued in the modern world. Examining how forces of white supremacy prevailed following the Civil War and Reconstruction, he observed the specific role played by scholars who made a "propaganda of history," one in which the testimony of emancipated slaves and their descendants remained "barred from court."[1]

The intellectual and political struggles of the past century have lifted some, but not all, of these epistemic blinders. Invariably, racism returns in the double guise of sanctioned violence and sanctioned ignorance that Du Bois identified. Many contemporary antiracists argue that racial violence, and antiblackness in particular, is the ongoing, constitutive basis of U.S. civil and civic organization. A little more than a century ago, the white supremacist, political theorist, and historian John Burgess affirmed this exact point, insisting that any consideration of the rights of "barbaric populations" was "petty and trifling in comparison with the transcendent right and duty to establish political and legal order everywhere."[2] In a country that arrests, deports, and incarcerates millions of people each year— disproportionately black people and people of color—and which, in the name of collective security, engages in police and military action all around the world, including summary assassinations of anonymous enemies who possess no rights that Americans are bound to respect, we must ask how far we have progressed from the modes of racial dominance out of which the wealth of modern nations grew.

Those of us who are committed to contesting and overcoming these historical legacies make a mistake, however, when we regard the manifest continuities of racial hierarchy as a sign of its strength and permanence. Collective efforts of reparation, reconstruction, and resistance by and for the enslaved, segregated, undocumented, colonized, and dispossessed—that is, people generationally burdened by socially antagonistic and fragmenting violence—have provided cognitive and moral resources for a different account and accounting. To remain transfixed at the point of racial abjection and brokenness, repeatedly bearing witness to the bareness of life stripped of well-being, rights, and physical protection, can lead to intellectual solipsism and political paralysis, rendering us oblivious to variation and contingency and to the difference made by struggles for survival, political transformation and collective world making. As a regime of power, racial ordering betrays political weakness. Since it must continually secure and even coerce compliance and also prevent defection among perpetrators, it is unstable and ideologically fragile. Dependent upon morally discomfiting public force, it is subject to continual delegitimation. If there is a lesson that I hope to convey, it is not the inexorability of racial domination but the record of social failure that its defectors, critics, opponents, and survivors have illuminated.

Amid racism's historical ruins and contemporary wreckage, it is not easy to balance understanding of continuity and change. A central claim of this book is that we are living in a period in which the structural violence of racial division and animus has been renewed and renovated under the sign and aegis of war. The frontier wars, the wars of the early U.S. empire, and the twentieth century's world wars all illuminated affinities between war making and race making, activating or reanimating distinctions between friend and enemy along an internal racial border. "We have two enemies to contend with," announced the mayor of Richmond, Virginia, during the war of 1812: "the one open and declared; the other nurtured in our very bosoms." In a dispatch from the Philippines in 1899, Marine sergeant Howard McFarland recounted his desire to "blow every nigger into a nigger heaven," confirming the observation of an unnamed black soldier who thought that U.S. counter-insurgency was an extension of "home treatment for colored people."[3] After the racial pogroms in several U.S. cities during World War I, a disillusioned Du Bois wondered, "How could America condemn in Germany that which she commits, just as brutally, within her own borders?" "Our life is a war, and I have been a traitor all my born days, a spy in the enemy's country, ever since I give up my gun back in the Reconstruction," Ralph Ellison's protagonist notes in the opening pages of *Invisible Man,* recalling his grandfather's deathbed revelation. Following the U.S. invasion of Vietnam, James Baldwin observed that black and brown people in the central city also lived in occupied territory: "The meek Southeast Asians, those who remain, shall have their free elections. The meek American Negroes—those who survive—shall enter the great society."[4]

Ellison and Baldwin wrote in the milieu of the rising black-freedom movement that developed in a contentious dialectic with U.S. globalism. From its inception after World War II, U.S. global power rested on the pillars of an aspirational racial liberalism and economic growth. Through the expansion of international circuits of resource extraction, trade, finance, and manufacturing, economic growth was the medicine that would forestall communist "slavery" and cure international capitalism of its colonial hangover. The cold war was also the crucible for fundamental concessions to black civil rights and political participation and rejection of national origin as a criterion for immigration and naturalization. Domestic racial injustice was magnified by the global claims and staging of U.S. power. Internal racial conflict, in turn, became a lens for viewing U.S. military engagement overseas and adjudicating whether it represented a departure from or an extension of colonial domination, and for examining an internal colonial divide within the affluent society. Following the passage of successful national civil-rights legislation and intensifying urban black protest, Martin Luther King Jr.'s indictment of the Vietnam War for foreclosing the promise of a generous, inclusive, full-employment welfare state at home brought these issues together in a uniquely powerful way. It also highlighted a widening gulf between a national, institutionalized black politics, whose fortunes were now tied to the liberal-pluralist distributive order, and internationalist black radicalisms, fragmented and denuded in battles with repressive state power.

From the 1970s onward, the imagined fulfillment of the black civil-rights imperative and public claims to a new national standard of racial inclusivity suggested progress beyond the old, tortured dialectic of the inner and outer war. Instead, the dialectic was entering a new phase. The pacification process directed at black and third world radicalisms after the 1960s, in particular, was a seedbed from which new conceptions of inequality were realized and practiced in trials by violence: the wars on crime, drugs, and now terror. Through the 1990s, the success of neoliberal policies that rolled back welfare-state protections and market regulations in the name of austerity, efficiency, and individual responsibility carried a similarly sharp racial edge as they sought to separate the deserving from the threatening poor. At the same time, as it settled into orthodoxy, neoliberalism came to represent a paradoxical bifurcation of the racial order, with promises of upward mobility linked to values of racial diversity and market- and investor-friendly public policy, and widening states of economic precariousness managed through de facto racial profiling, criminalization, and ever stingier, means-tested assistance for the poor.

Much as Gilded Age capitalists claimed title to the abolitionist legacy against the backdrop of lynch law and the small wars of U.S. empire, neoliberal exponents of market progressivism appropriated liberal antiracism and civil rights discourse in the shadow of the carceral state and the launching of the global war on terror. In this context, commonplace pronouncements about the end of racism and racial divisions strike a discordant note. Some on the political Left (historically committed to struggles for racial justice), for example, have argued that under the terms of neoliberal order, talk of racial disparity has come to obscure fundamental material deprivation and class violence, including a convergence of market-induced debilities—stagnant wages, joblessness, homelessness, and ill health—for the black and nonblack poor alike.[5] In the decades following World War II, publicly subsidized, racially discriminatory suburban housing markets and transportation infrastructures contributed to stark, multigenerational disparities between black and white household wealth. Since the 1970s, flat wages and the steady loss of manufacturing jobs have widened economic inequalities across the board. Greater black access to private home ownership (often financed by subprime mortgages), preceded the great recession of 2008. In that year alone, more than $7 trillion in household equity evaporated, dramatically eroding the financial standing of the (aspiring) middle class as a whole and leading to the highest numbers of people in poverty in the United States in almost half a century.[6] In a society that protects ever-narrower bands of wealth and privilege against the needs of the many, the race line and the class line follow increasingly similar contours.

What the renewed attention to class division and class struggle overlooks, however, is how technologies of sequester, confinement, and partition—informed by a long history of white supremacy and imperial citizenship—also expanded decisively during this period, despite declining rates of crime. Today, forms of militarized police enclosure—from gated communities to carceral spaces—represent a kind of generalized protective custody—

a broad and flexible modality of class rule that augments and conjoins police and military power as necessary to managing capitalism's unevenness across borders and within populations, and reanimates racial despotism as a vector of community protection. The primary casualties and victims of the new regime of racial sequester, black men of prime working age, have been removed from public life in staggering numbers.[7] No less significant, though less visible, is the removal of several million undocumented migrant workers since the 1990s.[8] In the wake of these trends, the response to the attacks of September 11, 2001, engendered a sweeping expansion and reorganization of the security state. Today sharply differentiated zones of affluence and dereliction, militarized policing, and criminal stigma have been substituted for urban and suburban racial geographies, the legal dualism of Jim Crow, and the overt racial stereotyping of the previous racial regime. Emerging alongside the liberalization of market action and tolerance for racial diversity is a society of walls, cages, and endless war.

The commonsense view that overt, racially targeted state-sanctioned violence is now unacceptable and a social problem leads to assessments that deem such violence—for example, police shootings of unarmed black men and women—as arising from justified fear, accident, or individual error, rather than a structured and structuring public mechanism and investment.[9] Racial differentiation, however, persists as a specific type of social relation precipitated in and through the state and the public sanctioning of violent exceptions to consensual politics under cover of law—in the service of material inequality and collective security. This past history of race making has yielded vast territories of exception drawn around hollowed-out central cities, border zones, impoverished suburbs, agricultural deserts, and carceral corridors that run from urban schools to rural prisons.

In the context of a global history of imperial and colonial capitalism, in which the liberalism of metropolitan centers was little more than a pale shadow, race making also develops through forms of national aggression and predation that produce new racist assemblages. The socially created artifact of racism, race is a fungible assemblage rather than a coherent, preconstituted entity. Not only is there no singular racism, but, like any complex collectivizing or aggregating figure (like class), race is heterogeneous, and it also works through heterogeneity. Gender, religion, economic conditions, sexuality, dis/ability and other key markers of social and embodied difference are the modalities in which race is lived; they are also selectively accented in processes of ascribing racial characteristics to groups, especially ideas about deviant sexuality, mental incapacity, moral deficiency, and behavioral threat. Rather than illuminating racism's uniformity and constancy, the ebb and flow of animus against migrants, the more recent rise of Islamophobia, or the periodically renewed ambit of antiblackness from slavery and Jim Crow to mass imprisonment, illustrate change as well as constancy in racial orders.

It is often observed that the experience of national belonging requires citizens to forget the founding violence that lies at the origins of modern nation-states. For the most part, however, forgetting and disavowal remain the prerogative of dominant states and national insiders. Those outside this charmed circle have been marked as fair game. Race is a product of racism, but it is not imposed only from the outside. Predatory violence against people presumed to be lacking in sovereignty or unfit for self-government has imprinted and burdened individual bodies, intergenerational kinship relations, and spatially demarcated contact zones with memories and expectations of stress, vulnerability, and proximity of death. Memories and identifications form narrative enclosures and conceptions of "linked fate" and common struggle for affected groups, whose differentiation by both traumatic and quotidian violence is recast by the very society that depends upon but disavows such violence in official stories about inherent group deficiencies and threats. Such is the discursive weave (and the only real and substantive basis) of racial differentiation.[10]

Race, in short, is a modality of group domination and oppression. Yet it requires a story (whether biological, sociological, anthropological, or historical) explaining how and why such practices persist and can be justified. Paradoxically, to be counted as an ethical and reasonable person within contemporary society requires the rejection of race as a legitimate mode of ascription. Where racism is overt, it is often met with opprobrium (though this and other features of the post-civil rights era liberal order may be giving way). Historical indexes of racial domination, including group-differentiated vulnerabilities to violence, poverty, punishment, and ill health, are in this view, thought to be vestigial, unsystematic, unintended, and lacking in social authorship, and their elimination is considered socially desirable. Deepening the paradox is that for elite institutions, evidence of nontransformative racial diversification is the surest proof of racism's vestigial character—up to and including electing a black president.

Arguably it was at this very moment when the shadow lineage reasserted itself. By 2008, the containment of race talk by a color-blind, postracial consensus, enlivened with a little diversity, was falling apart. Racist talk, thought to have been banished, reemerged with a vengeance. When it lamented loss of country and Muslim/socialist/illegal alien/terrorist-sympathizer occupants of the White House, it was ridiculed as fringe. But decades of torture, abuse, murder, deportation, and imprisonment of black and brown men and women, by police and military forces of the United States—from Guantanamo to Abu Ghraib and Bagram to the streets of Chicago, St. Louis, Baltimore, New York City, and beyond—suggested otherwise. The idea that the toxicity of race is consigned to the past is similar to the denial that humans have made the planet hotter and less habitable.

The essays in this book take the imperial, settler-colonial, and slaveholding provenance of the United States as their starting point. They consider race making as an artifact and product of this history, its economies of extraction and expansion, affluence and precariousness, dispossession and security. They reject an oft-told story in which the Indian Wars were tragic, inevitable, and consigned to the past, and the "original sin" of slavery was redeemed in successive American wars of liberation from bondage.[11] Exploring the interrelationship between the inner and outer war over a wide swath of American history, they point to a more violent and corrupt set of origins for today's endless wars in the interior of U.S. society and in its imperial history. They suggest that the "long peace" after World War II—the supposedly virtuous circle linking liberal internationalism overseas and liberal (racial) reform at home—was not only shaped by the cold war but shadowed by the wars on America's internal racial border.

These essays were written over several years and influenced by many people working on common fronts. The premise that guides them is that labors of egalitarian social transformation will fail if they do not frontally address the forms of human sacrifice and sundering of human commonality effected by state-sanctioned violence. *Race and America's Long War* trespasses on terrain explored more deeply and more fully by many able scholars and writers. Particularly influential on my thinking in this book is the work of historians and theorists of the carceral state; studies that examine the postcolonial history of the U.S. empire; the recent and powerful resurgence of indigenous and critical theoretical accounts of North American settler colonialism; scholarship on the global lineaments of counterinsurgency and police power; and work in African American studies that tracks the afterlives of Atlantic slavery.[12] In the interests of brevity and accessibility, I do not expressly engage with this secondary literature or probe the work of individual scholars for lines of agreement or disagreement. In no way should this approach be considered a diminution of my debts to them or an indication of their agreement with me.

I thank the individuals and collectives who have sustained me and helped me to develop many of the ideas presented here. During a decade at the University of Washington in Seattle, I learned to think about U.S. race and empire with a remarkable group of scholars that included Chandan Reddy, Moon Ho Jung, Jonathan Warren, Vicente Rafael, Sanjeev Khagram, Stephanie Smallwood, Alys Weinbaum, Bruce Burgett, Keith Feldman, Anoop Mirpuri, Georgia Roberts, and Simeon Man. A number of inspirational colleagues, including Matthew Frye Jacobson, Ruth Wilson Gilmore, Kimberlé Crenshaw, George Lipsitz, David Roediger, Robin D. G. Kelley, Penny Von Eschen, Robert Vitalis, Howard Winant, Avery Gordon, Michael Dawson, Dylan Rodriguez, Barnor Hesse, Andrew Friedman, Paul Gilroy, Joshua Clover, and Laleh Khalili have set the standard for the critical study of race, capitalism, and colonialism in their respective scholarly fields. I can only hope that this modest contribution lives up to their example.

I thank those who commissioned or commented on parts of this work in previous iterations, including Andrew Friedman, Asma Abbas, Robert Reid-Pharr, Eric Lott, Melvin Rogers, Daniel HoSang, Laura Pulido, Oneka LaBennett, Joe Lowndes, Dana Nelson, David Kyuman Kim, Tavia Nyong'o, Neferti Tadiar, Anupama Rao, Harry Harootunian, Casey Primel, Alex Lubin, Gaye Theresa Johnson, Richard Seymour, Colin Beckett, Richard Drayton, and Cynthia Young. I especially thank Niels Hooper at the University of California Press, who believed in and encouraged me to pull this collection together quickly when I had my doubts.

Since moving to New York University in 2008, I have been lucky to teach with two of the most luminous scholars and thinkers of my generation. In my graduate course with Ruth Wilson Gilmore "Race, Prisons, War," I first tested many of these ideas under the watchful eyes of a visionary teacher and renowned activist scholar. In our undergraduate course "Slavery, Race, and Radicalism," Jennifer Morgan pushed me to rethink everything I thought I knew about gender, race, and slavery, and in doing so posed questions that I will grapple with long into the future.

Charting new terrains of theory and research, Monica Kim's forthcoming book on the interrogation rooms of the Korean War is a profound work of scholarship that will change our understanding of the cold war and the U.S. approach to decolonization. Likewise, Stuart Schrader's forthcoming book on U.S. counterinsurgency and professional policing will make it difficult for anyone to consider U.S. global military empire as distinct from the expansion of police power and the fashioning of domestic racial order after World War II. Both Monica and Stuart have been generous readers of my work. I also want to recognize one of the most spirited cohorts of graduate students I have had the good fortune to work with, including Emma Shaw Crane, Maya Wind, Jackson Smith, Cos Tollerson, and Sam Markwell, who stuck it out with me for a two-year graduate seminar, "Security and Freedom in the U.S. in the World." Special thanks are due to Rachael Hudak and the staff of the NYU Prison Education Program for their support during the period when completing this work competed for my time. Finally, I am grateful to Shira Mogil, Dore Brown, and Erika Bűky for their fine work preparing the manuscript for publication.

From the time we first met in 2005, Jack O'Dell and Jane Power shared with me their home and their vistas of activist memory and practical experiences of movement building. My time with them left an indelible imprint on how I think about race and class, egalitarian struggle, and transformational politics. Since I moved back to New York City, Jennifer Morgan and Hermann Bennett have been generous friends and trusted confidants. I attribute much good fortune in the academic profession to the invisible hand of the incomparable Andrew Ross, a comrade for a very long time. Last, there are the immeasurable debts to my loving family: my amazing daughters, Myha and Anhna, and my brilliant and lovely wife and partner, Thuy Linh Tu, whose good sense is my North Star.

Introduction

The Long War

America has never been an empire. We may be the only great power in history that had the chance and refused.

George W. Bush, "A Distinctly American Internationalism," 1999

We don't seek empires, we are not imperialistic, we never have been. I don't know why you would ask the question.

Donald Rumsfeld, press conference, 2003

The United States has now been at war for almost two decades. Initiated in Afghanistan in response to the terrorist attacks of September 11, 2001, and extending to Iraq and the greater Middle East, the war, sometimes framed as a single "global war on terror" and sometimes as a series of discrete military campaigns, has left hundreds of thousands dead and hundreds of thousands more maimed, displaced, diseased, and traumatized.[1] Marred by military atrocities, torture scandals, fiscal waste, toxic exposure, popular opposition, and public disgust, the U.S. invasion of Iraq induced a regional death spiral and inspired new terrorist networks of the kind that the war was ostensibly fought to vanquish. Even as the active U.S. military presence has decreased, there have been repeated calls to return large-scale U.S. combat forces to the region and renewed panic about "Islamic" terrorist infiltration of the U.S.

"homeland."[2] The longest U.S. war to date, this conflict has taken on an aura of permanence that is extraordinary by any measure.[3]

A few years after the 2003 invasion of Iraq, U.S. Secretary of Defense Donald Rumsfeld predicted "a long war" lasting generations. "Just as the cold war lasted a long time, this war is something that is not going to go away. It is not going to be settled with a signing ceremony on the USS *Missouri*. It is of a different nature."[4] Though Rumsfeld and others inside the George W. Bush administration regularly invoked the cold war as a precedent, most commentators have struggled to make sense of this "war of a different nature." The unilateral decision to invade Iraq—a contentious and rule-breaking event that provoked wide dissent—abandoned historical and legal commitments to international order that had been developed over more than half a century.[5] U.S. war planners struggled to justify the Iraq invasion because of the tenuousness of the claims of an imminent threat to U.S. national security and the consequent failure to attain international legitimacy for an attack through the sanction of the United Nations Security Council.[6] Against the backdrop of shuffling pretexts for the war, the return of terms like *empire* and *imperialism* to the pages of elite opinion-forming publications, like *Foreign Affairs* and the *New York Times,* acknowledged the role of the United States as the world's most militarily dominant state but also flirted with more unsettling reconsiderations of the meaning of U.S. global power.

The conventional story told about the rise of the unparalleled military power of the United States typically forecloses the question of empire. In this view, U.S. power and diplomacy serve to guarantee and secure a peaceful world order, defined by mutually beneficial multilateral trade and national sovereignty. After World War II, the United States went to great lengths to promote and realize the vision of a world governed by international rules, mediated by global institutions, and underwritten by the promise of consensual political order and economic growth and development. Formal opposition to imperialism and colonial domination and a growing commitment to universal human rights—delinked from race, religion, and national origin—were core features of the U.S. understanding of itself and its role in the world.

The militarized cast of the cold war compromised this liberal internationalist vision, but it did not fundamentally alter its core commitments. Complicating the defensive justifications for war, the cold war institutionalized affirmative use of U.S. military power in the name of the security and functioning of capitalism itself. The United States engaged in continuous covert and overt military interventions between 1946 and 1989, including involvement in the overthrow of popular or democratically elected governments in Guatemala, Iran, the Congo, Brazil, Indonesia, Chile, Nicaragua and Grenada; devastating, total wars in Korea and Vietnam; interventions in civil wars and support for counterinsurgencies in Greece, the Philippines, Lebanon, Laos, the Dominican Republic, Vietnam, and Thailand; and proxy wars in Central America, the Middle East, Angola, and Afghanistan. The U.S. intervention in the longstanding colonial and civil war in Vietnam (extending into Cambodia), resulted in several million deaths and the chemical poisoning of the land and people that lingers fatally half a century later.

One of the contradictions of the American empire—if indeed we decide to settle on that term—is that the period identified as "a long peace" and an economic golden age was also an epoch in which the United States engaged in continuous and accretive wars all over the world—some named, almost all formally undeclared—whose toll of violence has been excluded from the balance sheet of moral, political, and material costs and benefits. U.S. military incursions overseas (when avowed) were said to be welcomed, even actively sought, by weaker or emerging states. They were formalized in multiple and bilateral regional security compacts and mounted under the strictures of Congressional war powers and international law and its primary institutions, particularly the United Nations. Even in Vietnam, U.S. military intervention genuflected to nation-state sovereignty, multilateral rules and norms that supposedly limited and decentered U.S. coercive power as an exclusive agent of global ordering.

At the end of World War II, Henry Stimson, the last important secretary of war before the position was recast to oversee a sprawling national security project, made the case for the cold war while also cleaving to the postwar promise of building "a world peace, not an American peace." Heralding what he called a "new interrelation of American life with the life of the world," Stimson cautioned against "the childishness of parochial hopes and un-American fears" and especially the temptations of launching a "preventive war" against the Soviet Union. The realm of foreign affairs, Stimson argued, was now "an intimate domestic concern." In consequence, domestic policy and politics were also subject to the exacting standards of global leadership. Against the backdrop of the devastating firebombing of Tokyo and the nuclear annihilation of Hiroshima and Nagasaki, Stimson affirmed a need to offer the world "leadership towards . . . life" by helping to reconstruct those parts "closest to us in history, politics and economics" and by recognizing our indivisible "connections with . . . life everywhere."[7]

During and after World War II, U.S. elites claimed the mantle of cosmopolitanism and universalism as the strategic and ideological requisite of global leadership. "The forces which have all but annihilated longitude and latitude," the black intellectual Alain Locke wrote in 1942, made it impossible to avoid reckoning with the fundamental partitioning of the world by race. With "the unresolved problem of the Negro in America," Locke wrote, "the Achilles of the West has a dangerously vulnerable heel."[8] Commentators like Gunnar Myrdal highlighted what Stimson left implicit: American universalism meant modeling a form of global power capable of engaging the emerging "darker nations," whose rising power he called "axiomatic." In 1950, the Republican senator Henry Cabot Lodge found himself elevating a metaphor of wartime black radicalism, describing the long shadow of U.S. racial domination as "our Achilles heel before the world." Running for the presidency in 1960, vice president Richard Nixon explained the geopolitical stakes to a white Southern voter: "I am deeply concerned with the impact of racial division in terms of world power. Most of the people of the world belong to the colored races. They deeply resent any slurs based on race. If we of the United States are considered racists, then we may lose to the Communist camp hundreds of millions of potential friends and allies. That would leave us disastrously isolated in a hostile world."[9]

Framed as a moral aspiration and driven by political realism about the balance of forces in the world, the vision of a global, American-centered, racially inclusive world, one organized around formally equal and independent nation-states, was a controlling fiction that for several decades has been unraveling. The causes of its dissolution are complex. The long and disastrous Vietnam War shattered illusions that U.S. power was arrayed on the side of a just and peaceful decolonization. Domestic opposition to the war radicalized the civil rights, black power, and peace movements, advancing a sharply revisionist view of the United States as a new kind of empire, internally riven by racial crisis and disorder. Defeat in Vietnam inspired official handwringing, including Congressional efforts to limit executive power and rein in overseas military action. Public hunger to turn away from a legacy of U.S. war crimes in Vietnam brought to the fore a more definitive emphasis on the importance of human rights in U.S. foreign policy.

This uneasy period of reflection and ambivalence ceded to a renewal of cold war conflict by the 1980s. What some historians have called "the second cold war" was something of a shadow play, behind which the terms of global economic and political order rapidly shifted, as evidenced by Nixon's unilateral decision to break from the gold standard and float the dollar against other currencies and by the opening to China in 1972.[10] Strained by military defeat and fiscal crisis, U.S. hegemony, which was based not only on a preponderance of military force but also on the conviction among international partners that the United States was a stable and reliable guarantor of the international order (a justification for fighting the Vietnam War in the first place), was under severe strain. The Carter administration's ratcheting up of the cold war, in response to the Soviet war in Afghanistan, was a response to this situation. The success of Ronald Reagan's more muscular foreign policy and the securing of a U.S.-Soviet nuclear arms control agreement seemed to signal a decisive restoration of an American-centered world order.

In retrospect, the signal crisis of an imperial foreign policy and domestic racial division that had emerged during the Vietnam War remained unresolved. The phenomenon of globalization itself—a concept that emerged at the end of the cold war—represented a widening distribution of capital accumulation on a global scale, but one that coincided with enduring challenges to Western prosperity, rising inequality, and, beginning in the 1970s, low productivity and slowing economic growth within the United States.[11] Although the end of the cold war presented the possibility of a "peace dividend" and solidified commitments to liberal internationalism and human rights under U.S. leadership, what happened instead was a renewed emphasis in national security circles on the costly maintenance of an absolute preponderance of U.S. military power, including prerogatives to use military and police power preemptively, and a gradual withdrawal of U.S. investments in the global balancing of forces and respect for international public opinion.[12]

The long civil rights movement that benefited from superpower competition and decolonizing pressures during the cold war, and struggled to widen circles of inclusion with respect to race and national origin in the United States, was a casualty of this shift. Following the extension of the formal rights of liberal democracy to African Americans and the end of national-origin strictures in U.S. immigration policy in 1965, the U.S. government defined fighting crime as a core feature of national security, a project announced by Lyndon Johnson in 1967 as "a war within our borders" and labeled by his successor, Richard Nixon, as a "war on crime." "If there is one area where war is appropriate," Nixon declared, "it is in the fight against crime." Nixon's rhetoric erased a wide array of local and regional social and economic determinants of criminal acts that were viewed under the rubric of poverty amelioration. According to one of his closest aides, H. R. Haldeman, "Nixon recognized the fact that the whole problem is really the blacks, you have to devise a system that recognizes this without appearing to. [He] pointed out that there has never in history been an adequate black nation."[13] As the juxtaposition suggests, for Nixon, African Americans were domestic in a foreign sense, tied to the "darker nations," but subject (like them) to a new political calculus.

In the wake of Vietnam and black urban unrest, U.S. policy makers not only reasserted the value of force and violence over rule and consent in foreign policy but also recast the use of force in the pursuit of domestic order. When U.S. army forces were sent in alongside the National Guard and state police to quell the 1967 riots in Detroit, it became clear that war on the home front was not a metaphor. Nixon's rhetorical emphasis on criminalizing nonprescription drug use was followed by Ronald Reagan's declaration of a "war on drugs." This too was war, and it marked the start of equipment transfers from military to police forces, the extensive use of special weapons and tactics (SWAT) forces in drug arrests, and the authorization of Pentagon oversight of and National Guard assistance with drug interdiction that contravened longstanding prohibitions on the domestic deployment of military forces. As the North American Free Trade Agreement spurred an economic crisis in rural Mexico and increased migration to the United States, U.S. policy makers responded by militarizing the southern border and criminalizing immigration violations. Most significant was the widening ambit of criminal punishment in general: the unprecedented investment in state capacity to cage, control, and punish populations deemed dangerous to the U.S. body politic, numbering approximately 370,000 in 1970, 1.1 million in 1990 and 2.3 million in 2000—the majority black and brown, and poor.[14]

The metastasization of a carceral state of walls and cages directly paralleled the weakening of the support mechanisms of the social-welfare state. Together, these phenomena represent the most significant political and institutional development in American life since the late 1960s.[15] More specifically, widening the ambit of criminal stigma eroded equal protection with respect to nationality and citizenship (both actual and prospective). Limned by post-1960s figurations of welfare queens, street terrorists, and illegal aliens, the carceral state, to paraphrase Ruth Wilson Gilmore, blossomed as a state-sanctioned regime of group-differentiated dishonor, dispossession, and premature death—one that was less reliant on formal racial ascription and categorization than on the inflation of the public and moral salience of crime and the enhancement of practical means to identify criminal enemies located within (and outside) the body politic. Bluntly dubbed the "new Jim Crow" by a popular chronicler, this was perhaps the clearest warning signal that post–New Deal democratic politics and its progressive liberal firmament had entered a period of terminal crisis.[16]

Scholars of U.S. diplomacy and international relations typically separate questions of global power from domestic politics. I suggest instead that foreign policy and domestic politics develop in a reciprocal relationship and produce mutually reinforcing approaches to managing social conflict. The corruption of globalist ideals exposed by the Vietnam War, as Martin Luther King Jr. predicted, had a domestic analogue. The criminal burglary and scandal that brought down the Nixon administration are better remembered than the international crimes that initiated them, especially the illegal bombing of Cambodia but also the administration's support for Pakistani military atrocities in Bangladesh and sponsorship of the coup that led to the overthrow of the socialist government of Salvador Allende in Chile.[17] Just as Secretary of State Henry Kissinger pronounced that the democratic affairs of Chile were too important to be left to Chilean voters, influential policy analysts like Samuel Huntington, friendly to the U.S. government, expressed concerns about "a crisis of democracy" at home, fueled by rising demands for rights and inclusion by formerly passive groups and constituencies.[18]

By the end of the 1970s, the racial crisis of poverty and spatial isolation, the health crisis of drug addiction, and the economic downturn precipitated by oil shock and stagflation had yielded a military revolution in policing at home. Riot control in particular had emerged as a major field for the transfer of ideas and technology between military operations and domestic policing. During this period, the urban space itself was being reconceptualized as a zone that needed to be expressly pacified and reclaimed for commercial and propertied interests. In 1978, a key campaign adviser to Ronald Reagan, William Casey, cofounded the Manhattan Institute, an influential think tank that was at the intellectual forefront of these trends. Its projects included neoliberal visions for reducing welfare-state tax requirements and entitlement commitments while augmenting policing capacities and techniques of surveillance and spatial control. Daryl Gates, the chief of the Los Angeles Police Department, who presided over the militarization of one of the nation's bellwether urban police forces, voiced the folk wisdom that animated the new dispensation: "The streets of America's cities had become a foreign territory."[19]

To grasp the importance of these developments for our own period, we must follow the storylines of both the inner war and the outer war. When we think about the outer war today, it is tempting to think that history began anew on 9/11. Members of the Bush administration viewed the terrorist attacks that occurred on that day as an "opportunity" to awaken the martial appetites of a wary public and to realize long-held aspirations to bring unilateral military supremacy to bear against a host of potential threats, adversaries, and combinations of adversaries for the foreseeable future. But the intellectual and political reflexes that led to this moment were developed over a longer period. One of the engineers of the Iraq invasion, Paul Wolfowitz, was a member of the infamous group of hard liners known as Team B, assembled by Central Intelligence Agency director George H. W. Bush and reporting to Dick Cheney and Donald Rumsfeld, President Gerald Ford's chief of staff and secretary of defense. Team B prepared a "worst-case" assessment of the Soviet threat to rival the one that had been put forth by the CIA's National Intelligence Estimate in 1975. In response to what they viewed as a waning of cold war resolve, a new generation of prodefense conservatives (later known as neoconservatives), which included the future President Reagan), had revived the early postwar Committee on Present Danger. Prominently inserting themselves into the national security debate, they enthusiastically embraced Team B. Subsequently criticized for overestimating the Soviet threat, the report laid the groundwork for reanimating the enmity-driven politics of the cold war as the baseline of responsible national security stewardship against disarmament efforts, making sure that movement towards détente with the Soviets (and Chinese) would not hinder offensive U.S. military preparedness and planning.[20]

A key aim for these government insiders was to restore a flexible mandate for aggressive U.S. military intervention, including forms of executive and covert action that they believed had been compromised by the Vietnam War and its boggy aftermath of Congressional investigation, increased oversight, and public skepticism. They sought a renewal of cold war interventionism in the developing world, seeing the United States "in opposition" to hostile postcolonial states whose international significance and rights of sovereign protection they increasingly derided as a cover not only for communism but also for criminality, corruption, and state failure.[21] Important figures in the Reagan and first Bush administrations (wrongly) claimed that the Soviets were engaged in a large-scale military buildup and were sponsoring revolutionary violence and international terrorism around the world.

Under Reagan, "cowboys" in the CIA and the National Security Administration were given lease to arm the Afghan mujahideen and their Islamist allies in an effort to "bleed the Soviets white," as it was put by the man installed as Reagan's CIA director, William Casey. Under Casey, the CIA became involved in an illegal, covert trade involving drugs, arms, and American hostages in Iran to support right-wing paramilitaries and Central American death squads. Winning the cold war—Reagan's crowning achievement of international arms control and unchallenged U.S. global military supremacy—dominates retrospective hagiography and is credited for overcoming a Soviet challenge that was already long in remission. This narrative fails to capture the scope of a new violent dispensation in formation that resulted in another major political scandal rooted in foreign policy malfeasance: Iran-Contra. With Casey in the White House bunker, this period marked the beginning of a conscious return to older colonial models of small wars and proxy wars, with an eye toward the circumvention of public scrutiny and Congressional oversight of military affairs and helping to seed the wars of the future.[22]

Cheney, Rumsfeld, and Wolfowitz resurfaced in the presidential administration of George H. W. Bush, where they launched Operation Just Cause against Panama and helped to forge the international consensus and financial support for the first Gulf War to discipline and punish the cross-border aggression of the former U.S. ally Saddam Hussein. The invasion of Panama was literally a police action, mounted to serve an arrest warrant for Manuel Noriega, a former CIA asset turned drug dealer. Though undertaken in the name of toppling a dictator and promoting democracy, the invasion was a reversion to the old hemispheric police power in which national sovereignty was a relative value weighed against U.S. claims to administer justice. In Iraq, President Bush claimed that with this, the first large-scale demonstration of U.S. military force since the Vietnam War, the United States had finally "kicked the Vietnam syndrome," ushering in nothing less than a "new world order." The implication was that restraints on muscular and morally righteous uses of American military power—imposed by technologically inferior insurgents, antiwar moralists, dovish internationalists, and calculating realists—had finally been overcome. Those who supported the first Gulf war on these terms, however, were dejected by a venture they viewed as too cautious by half. Watching the nascent Iraqi uprising crushed by Saddam Hussein's forces under the terms of the U.S. cease-fire, Wolfowitz casually drew from the lexicon of urban crime, describing U.S. inaction as comparable to "idly watching a mugging."[23]

During the 1990s, Iraq was subject to a murderous blockade, causing hundreds of thousands of fatalities. As many Iraqi children died in these years as in the fires of Hiroshima. Expressing less than complete satisfaction with the status quo, President Bill Clinton's U.N. ambassador, Madeleine Albright (later secretary of state), flashed her irritation with the architect of the cease-fire, General Colin Powell, in a famous quip: "What is the point of having this superb military you are always talking about if we can't use it?"[24] While genocide raged in Rwanda, the NATO bombing campaign spurred by Serbia's ethnic cleansing presumed a new international legal mandate for humanitarian intervention. More decisive was the bipartisan passage of the Violent Crime and Law Enforcement Act (1994) and the Anti-terrorism and Effective Death Penalty Act (1996), that enshrined crime and terrorism at the center of national security thinking. Largely forgotten (against the backdrop of Clinton's impeachment scandal) was another round of sordid military misadventures, culminating in the firing of fourteen cruise missiles into the Al Shifa pharmaceutical factory in Sudan in 1998 in retaliation for the Al Qaeda embassy bombings in Kenya and Tanzania. The factory, which was Sudan's largest producer of medical products, including antimalarial drugs, was taken out on the grounds—later discredited—that it was a chemical weapons facility with links to Osama Bin Laden.[25]

These were a few signs of the longer-term atrophy of American thinking about the balancing of force and consent and the relationship between military coercion and sustainable political order, both at home and abroad. Today's wars were still the tentative plans of nongovernmental operatives in Southwest Asia and in Washington, DC, think tanks (like the Project for a

New American Century). The astute British military historian Michael Howard discerned the decisive turn early on, one that ran against the tenor of cosmopolitanism and universalism that had been central to the post-1945 conception of world order: "When global organization began to appear possible and necessary, the image that came to many American minds was not that of balancing power between states, but of protecting law and order against its disturbers, the protection to be provided by a sheriff with his *posse comitatus*. If human corruption and inefficiency made this impossible, it must be provided by the efforts of a few good men following the dictates of a moral law within . . . [an] American populist belligerence, termed by some historians 'Jacksonian.'"[26]

George W. Bush's swaggering declaration of a "global war on terror" (initially called Operation Infinite Justice) appeared to be the apotheosis of this tendency. Bush described the war as a "crusade" against a new kind of "evil" loosed upon the world. His starkly dichotomous moral rhetoric, evocative of a long history of Western incursions into Muslim lands under the banner of Christian piety and a civilizing imperative, was soon rejected as unsuitable for wars that would require the cooperation of "good" Muslim allies to defeat "bad" Muslim enemies.[27] Instead of proclaiming a "clash of civilizations"—the prospect offered by disenchanted policy intellectuals like Samuel Huntington as a new paradigm for post-cold war conflicts—the administration defaulted to the vocabulary of cold war American universalism. The people of the world, Bush argued, were menaced by "a new totalitarian threat," its perpetrators akin to those "who once killed in the name of racial purity or class struggle." He depicted the new enemy as engaged in a "conspiracy against our liberty"—this time motivated not by radical political ideology but by "false religious purity."[28]

Bush's rhetoric retained fidelity to the normative insistence on ascribing to U.S. military power noble aspirations toward racial, religious, and international comity. Even as Muslims, Arabs, and South Asians were suddenly subject to new forms of racial profiling, vigilante attacks, immigration scrutiny, and biometric screening, the new wars were proclaimed as a defense of freedom itself—defined as a secular liberal order in which Christians, Jews, *and* Muslims stood united in the capitalist marketplaces and tourist meccas of the world.[29] Following the 9/11 attacks, the *New York Times* even reported a lowering of long-simmering interracial mistrust—including, most improbably, expressions of sympathy between black communities and the New York City Police Department (NYPD), despite raw memories of the police killing and torture of unarmed black criminal suspects such as Amadou Diallo and Abner Louima in the late 1990s. The hip-hop artist Talib Kweli added a note of skepticism, drolly remarking: "We saluting flags, wrapping them around our head, when niggaz ain't become Americans till 9/11."[30]

When it came to the public symbolism of racial and ethnic division, the interrelation of American life with the life of the world that Henry Stimson called for remained a demanding proposition. On the eve of the invasion of Iraq, the Canadian intellectual and politician Michael Ignatieff offered one of the most important liberal defenses of the project, arguing that the United States had achieved global ascendancy after World War II by refraining from conquest and restraining unilateral military action, despite a history of "significant lapses in our own hemisphere." He acknowledged that the power of the U.S. military —with its thousand military bases in eighty countries around the world—might warrant the use of the term *empire*. What legitimated the U.S. recourse to coercive force, however, was that it was "unlike empires past, built on colonies, conquest and the white man's burden."[31] Noting that liberal internationalism and its peaceably ordered "security community" seemed to be intact on the one-year anniversary of the invasion, John Ikenberry affirmed the judiciousness of the initial assessment: "If the United States is an empire . . . it is like no other before it."[32]

In retrospect, we might detect a note of fear and plaintiveness in these pronouncements, like the person who hopes to restrain a violent fellow by reminding him of his better self. Although a few pundits like Niall Ferguson and Max Boot were willing to identify the new era of global war as a return to pre-World War II liberal imperialism, marked by the West's militarized governance over disordered and benighted peoples, such commentary met with stern rebukes. Writing after 9/11, John Lewis Gaddis, the dean of U.S. diplomatic historians, admitted more frightening precedents, but he downplayed their salience. In the United States, "apart from two glaring exceptions—the persistence of slavery and the persecution of Native Americans—there was no compelling desire to construct a formal empire against the wishes of those to be included within it. The acquisition of the Philippines half a century later did, to be sure, violate this principle; but that event proved to be an anomaly, not a pattern for the future."[33]

Lurking just beneath the surface of these legitimating treatises was a pressing counterpoint: the possibility that "the long war" marked this specific *recrudescence*—neither a "clash of civilizations" nor the embrace of active, imperial administration recommended by a few outlying pundits, but a reengagement with the more primal terms of American race war and the fantasy of national social and economic regeneration through (frontier) violence. Amid the claims of existential defense and emancipatory ends used to justify the Afghanistan and Iraq wars, the administration's war policy conjured a host of less salutary, historically disavowed racial and imperial precedents. "Look back on the Philippines around the turn of the century," observed Jay Garner, the first administrator of Iraq. "They were a coaling station for the navy, and that allowed us to keep a great presence in the Pacific. That is what Iraq is for the next new decades: our coaling station that gives us great presence in the Middle East."[34] In the face of stiffening Sunni resistance and insurgency after defeat of Iraqi military forces, Robert Kaplan enjoined U.S. planners and publics to remember the bloody U.S.-Philippines War of 1898 for the lessons it provided as "the most successful counterinsurgency fought by a Western army in modern times." Efforts to rebrand strategy and tactics drawn from a host of brutal, morally and politi-cally discredited counterinsurgency wars from the late colonial era became the stock-in-trade of a rising cohort of warrior-intellectuals predicting a future defined by "small wars" of pacification and de facto imperial logics of indirect rule.[35]

In the very text in which he describes U.S. empire as anomalous, Gaddis doubles back, framing the Bush administration's national security policy in terms of U.S. territorial expansion: the global frontiers of liberal society, threatened by terrorists and other nonstate actors, are like those once besieged by "native Americans, pirates, marauders, and other free agents." Likewise, for Kaplan, "'Welcome to Injun Country' was the refrain I heard from troops from Colombia to the Philippines, including Afghanistan and Iraq. . . . The War on Terrorism was really about taming the frontier. But the fascination was never meant as a slight against Native North Americans."[36] From within the war zone, the Marine Corps chronicler Bing West described the Sunni com-batants in Fallujah, who were besieged and burned alive with the white phos-phorus that U.S. forces once used on the Vietnamese, as a "strange, sullen, wild-eyed" people with a "rough analogy" to "American Indian tribes in the nineteenth century, sharing a hostility toward settlers while launching raids at different times for different reasons."[37] A member of the illegal, hatchet-wielding Seal Team 6 (the outfit credited with killing Osama Bin Laden, dubbed Geronimo, in 2011) made such connections vivid: "Our job is to ensure that we conduct ourselves in a way befitting the American people and the American flag. The hatchet says, 'We don't care about the Geneva Conven-tions' and that 'we are above the law and can do whatever we want.'"[38]

The prison camp at Guantanamo Bay, Cuba, a space governed by the sus-pension of international laws of war and U.S. constitutional protections, emerged as perhaps the most baleful symbol of U.S. impunity. Populated by means of the rendition and torture of "enemy combatants," it owes its very existence and status as an offshore prison to the hemispheric intervention of

1898 in support of limited Cuban independence from Spain.[39] Writing about his many years of confinement beginning in 2002, the Mauritanian detainee Mohamedou Ould Slahi called Guantanamo the "place where the law has nothing to say." His torture there, he writes, in a text heavy with black redaction marks, was "a thick line drawn between my past and future." Rebuking his captors, he observes that it was "not the first time [Americans] kidnapped Africans and enslaved them."[40] Critical commentators have interpreted the events at Baghdad's Abu Ghraib prison in a similar vein, observing that the stacking and arrangement of bodies and celebratory photographs of naked, tortured, and sexually abused prisoners was reminiscent of a lynching party.

No less than on the troublesome frontier, the aggravating presence of blacks in the body politic haunts contemporary U.S. wars. Many of the military police and guards involved in the torture got their start in onshore U.S. prisons, infamously rife with abuse. Richard Zuley, Slahi's principal torturer in Guantanamo, was an important figure in the Chicago police unit that established the equivalent of a black site in the city, where predominantly African American criminal suspects were sent for interrogation, without being charged with specific offenses. If spaces like Guantanamo have remained "foreign in a domestic sense," to use the language of the Insular Cases that governed the annexations and occupations of 1898, we might say that the Chicago precincts where Zuley, John Burge, and others tortured predominantly African American criminal suspects over a generation are domestic in a foreign sense, in the wake of slavery and its afterlife.[41]

Given our history, these examples should not shock or surprise, and yet they do. Rather than appearing as anomalies or exceptions, these occurrences, and the histories of slavery, Indian wars and hemispheric interventions that they evoke and extend, raise a different possibility. Instead of the idea that "the United States has never been an empire," we confront the proposition that the United States has only ever been a kind of empire.

Taking this idea as the point of departure, the chapters that follow suggest a different set of political and historical reference points for understanding the recent period of U.S. military violence. They call into question the claims of forward-strategic thinking, ideological self-confidence, and renewed commitments to universalism among U.S. defense and policy intellectuals and planners. They suggest that the many labored rhetorical and historical efforts to fit the global war on terror into the threadbare garments of postwar and cold war internationalism—including official stances against racism and imperialism—protest too much. The open-ended authorization of militarism by the executive branch that underwrites our era of war thus represents a substantive devolution. Walter Benjamin famously argued that the unresolved violence of the past has a way of erupting in moments of emergency. It should not be surprising that in a moment when the U.S. government deploys an increasingly malleable sense of law and retrofits it to purposes of war, we also find ourselves in the midst of a renewed delimitation of civic politics through idioms of racialized dishonor and dispossession.

In an insightful observation after 9/11, but well before he became president, Barack Obama hinted at the new and dangerous alignments of the inner and outer wars, writing that the conflict between "worlds of plenty and worlds of want twists the lives of children on the streets of Jakarta or Nairobi in much the same way as it does the lives of the children on the South Side of Chicago." Failing to comprehend this dynamic, the powerful needlessly intensify a destructive spiral with their "dull complacency[,] . . . unthinking applications of force[,] . . . longer prison sentences and more sophisticated military hardware."[42] Obama advanced his successful presidential campaign by characterizing the Iraq War as a grievous error on the grounds of its departure from strictures of multilateral diplomacy; its traducing of U.S. and international law, particularly with regard to policies of torture and rendition; and the manner in which its excessive emancipatory claims about democracy and nation building strained domestic political, fiscal, and military capacities. Seizing the mantle of civil rights and racial inclusivity as an extension of his personal narrative and political success, Obama called on the nation to "choose our better history," one in which persistent struggles—for abolition, racial equality, and full citizenship—was expressly tied to American ecumenicism and consensus building around the world.[43]

Obama's appeal to racial inclusivity in defense of the American realm was part of a worn-out body of thought and action—one that was already on life support. In 2005, after Hurricane Katrina, scenes of black bodies adrift, shivering in ship holds and herded into stadiums, brought the contradictions of the inner and outer wars to a head. In response to an event that occasioned comparisons to the unfolding disaster of torture and insurgency in Iraq, the Bush administration dispatched its highest-ranking black official, Secretary of State Condoleeza Rice, to the Gulf Coast to replaster the crumbling ideological facade. Rice sounded a familiar theme and went further still: "Across the empire of Jim Crow, from the upper Dixie to the lower Delta, the descendants of slaves shamed our nation with the power of righteousness and redeemed America at last from its original sin of slavery. . . . By resolving the contradiction at the heart of our democracy, America finally found its voice as a true champion of democracy beyond its shores."[44] In one awkward turn of phrase, Rice conjoined "empire and Jim Crow" as the polar opposite of the American global ideal. The problem, as Hurricane Katrina laid bare, was that Jim Crow was as American as cherry pie.

Rice adeptly drew on the rhetoric of "cold war civil rights," in which domestic advances against racial oppression were heralded (against a similar litany of public racial atrocities) as proof of the superiority of American democracy and the legitimacy of U.S. global leadership in the struggle against communism.[45] Indeed, Rice's was a mature, even hyperbolic, example of this discourse: she enlisted her own position as a senior cabinet official as a sign of definitive racial progress, labeling the scenes of black abjection in

New Orleans a "vestige" of the old South. Much as Gaddis marked out the broad sweep of U.S. history before 1950—defined by settler colonial expansion, indigenous extermination and removal, racial slavery and Jim Crow, gunboat diplomacy and overseas colonization—as exceptional to an otherwise consistent anti-imperialist stance, Rice externalized Jim Crow and white supremacy as an imperial form, alien to American democracy.

The question raised, of course, was the depth and persistence of the contribution of "the empire of Jim Crow" to the U.S. vision of world order, both past and present. Writing soon after World War II, Hannah Arendt observed that European imperialism worked in part by drawing a strict boundary between "colonial methods and normal domestic politics." The rise of Nazi power in Europe had illuminated the folly of believing that the separation really held and presaged what she described as a "boomerang effect . . . [or] the introduction of colonial methods into European affairs . . . [and with it] the temptation to deprive all citizens of legal status and rule them with omnipotent force."[46] But in the United States (whose history Arendt understood poorly), extreme police measures were always in use in a targeted manner along the inner, racial border. Even as Rice was pronouncing on the vestigial nature of race and empire in the American South, Louisiana governor Kathleen Blanco issued her directive to the National Guard troops brought in to restore civic order and protect private property from "looters" (a racial code word): "These troops are fresh back from Iraq, well trained, experienced, battle-tested, and under my orders to restore order in the streets. . . . They have M-16s and they are locked and loaded. . . . These troops know how to shoot and kill, and they are more than willing to do so if necessary, and I expect they will."[47]

In New Orleans, the redemptive national narrative—of racial progress, common citizenship, and militarized foreign policy in the service of emancipatory ends overseas—turned violently on itself, like a snake eating its own tail. The corruption and cronyism that had been on display in Iraq emerged again here, with no-bid, multimillion dollar contracts for reconstruction awarded to the firm Kellogg, Brown and Root (a subsidiary of Halliburton, the security and oilfield-services company once led by Dick Cheney). Many of the private mercenaries from the Blackwater Corporation who roamed Kabul and Basra with impunity were employed under the Department of Homeland Security contracts to secure New Orleans's higher ground against predation from the newly homeless, most of whom were African Americans. As Baghdad was being ethnically partitioned by U.S. forces, plans were hatched to permanently rezone the new swamplands of New Orleans to make the city's historically black ninth ward safer, smaller, and whiter. Disaster capitalism consistently brought home unsettling comparisons with the theater of war. With a few notable exceptions, most commentators failed to observe that the social contexts of racial(izing) division at home and civil(izing) war overseas were more than uncanny, parallel universes: they were parts of the same economic, cultural, political, and societal condition.[48]

African American collective existence has long manifested and negotiated the proximity of racism and war. Participation in the nation's wars has been understood as one of the surest routes to full citizenship, from the Civil War's famous black regiment to the frontier war's Buffalo soldiers to promised rewards for black participation in the twentieth century's world wars, best epitomized by W. E. B. Du Bois's call to "close ranks" during World War I. Yet black communities have just as frequently conceived warfare abroad in an intimate relationship to a persistent, ongoing, undeclared race war at home. Thus, even as military service has represented a means to imagine and enact a shift from racial to national belonging, it has just as frequently amplified the disjuncture of the two. Thousands of slave men and women fled to the British side during the Revolutionary War. Indian country held the promise of freedom from slavery for those who dared to cross its threshold. A century ago, black publics viewed the Philippine insurgency through the lens of domestic racial subjection. Bitter memories of the post–World War

I red scare and racial pogroms led black activists to call for a "double victory" against racism at home and fascism abroad during World War II.

World War II exhibited the full range of contradictory conjunctions of race and war for African Americans. Antiblack riots and strikes rocked the home front even as a heightened emphasis on cultural pluralism and modest efforts at domestic racial reform sought to highlight the difference between democracy and fascism. By the 1960s, the sense of the intimate proximity of violent racial abjection, of race making at home and war making overseas, had become integral to black critical discourse. Radical activists such as Jack O'Dell argued that the contempt bred by America's familiarity with ongoing, sanctioned violations of black life and limb was the link that connected "Selma and Saigon." Martin Luther King Jr. observed that the promises of Johnson's Great Society had been shot down on the battlefields of Vietnam, expressing his regret that "my own country is the greatest purveyor of violence in the world today."[49] Twenty years on, when George H. W. Bush was kicking the "Vietnam Syndrome" in Iraq, the rapper Ice Cube tied it to the violence of the drug war, memorably describing the first Gulf War as a giant "drive-by shooting." The acquittal of the New York City police officers who killed an unarmed black man, Sean Bell, in a hail of gunfire in 2007 prompted the family's minister to remark, "Here it's just like Iraq, we don't have any protection."[50]

These commentaries illustrate how black collective life in the United States has been viewed from within as indistinct from a situation of war. They illuminate in a more concrete and compelling manner Michel Foucault's inversion of Clausewitz's famous maxim, "War is the continuation of politics by other means," suggesting how (racial) politics remains indelibly imprinted with the logic of war:

> While it is true that political power puts an end to war and establishes or attempts to establish the reign of peace in civil society, it certainly does not do so in order to suspend the effects of power or to neutralize the disequilibrium revealed by the last battle of war. According to this hypothesis, the role

of political power is perpetually to use a sort of silent war to reinscribe that relationship of force, and to reinscribe it in institutions, economic inequalities, language, and even the bodies of individuals. . . . What is at work beneath political power is essentially and above all a warlike relation.[51]

Foucault associates the development of the modern concept of race with wars of conquest. The violence of war constitutes a traumatic line of division in a population that comes to share a single sphere of political representation. We might say that race becomes the name for manifestations of divided collective experience that are, as he puts it, "anchored in a certain relationship of force that was established in and through war at a given moment that can be historically specified."[52]

But what if the actual history of race war is even more proximate and considerably less silent than we think? Before it became a figure for science, law, and biopolitical regulation, racial difference was conceptualized as a domain of recurrent and continuous warfare. American thinking about space and power has returned again and again to the elimination or sequestration of "savages" as the grounds of a story whose reiterated violence fortifies the national body and thus, we are told, should be neither grieved nor redressed but instead renewed. It has long been possible to acknowledge the fundamental injustice of the Indian wars while asserting their necessity and inevitability. "Who is there to mourn for Logan?" Thomas Jefferson asked in *Notes on the State of Virginia* (1787), referencing the Indian chief, the last of his slaughtered kin, whose natural freedom Jefferson claimed to admire. "Not one," was his answer. Andrew Jackson viewed Indian removal as the progress of civilization: "What good man would prefer a country covered with forests and ranged by a few thousand savages to our extensive Republic, studded with cities, towns, and prosperous farms embellished with all the improvements which art can devise or industry execute, occupied by more than 12,000,000 happy people, and filled with all the blessings of liberty, civilization and religion?"[53] Theodore Roosevelt mocked the anti-imperialists of his day who opposed U.S. counterinsurgency wars in the Philippines and Cuba as sentimentalists who would give Arizona back to the Apaches. More than half a century later, General Maxwell Taylor made the dismantling of the Vietnamese countryside legible to the U.S. Senate by observing, "It is hard to plant the corn outside the stockade when the Indians are still around. We have to get the Indians farther away in many of the provinces to make good progress."[54]

Metaphors of "Indian country" routinely emerge in the rhetoric of U.S. militarism overseas, from the Philippines at the start of the twentieth century to the Pacific battlefields of World War II to Vietnam in the cold war and Afghanistan and Iraq today.[55] Even the most famous U.S. scholarly reconsideration of the theory of the just war, written in part in response to the injustice of the Vietnam War, preserved this reasoning. Justifying Israel's preemptive first strike in the 1967 war that led to the occupation of the West Bank, the Golan Heights, and the Gaza Strip, Michael Walzer suggests the "analogy" of "an unstable society like the Wild West of American fiction," in which "a state under threat is like an individual hunted by an enemy who has announced his intention of killing or injuring him. Surely such a person may surprise his hunter if he is able to do so." In the context of the current wars, Gaddis echoes Roosevelt's dismissal of those who might be squeamish about the violence required to subdue a continent: "Would you want to give it all back?" Another prominent Iraq War supporter, Paul Berman, makes the more categorical and telling assertion that "if you reject the Indian Wars, you reject America." This is something considerably more than the common injunction against litigating injustice long past. In every case, even when tragedy or excess is admitted, the Indian Wars are redeployed as an ideal for regulating and directing attitudes toward U.S. state violence in the present. Part of what this shows, to paraphrase the important theorist of settler colonialism Patrick Wolfe, is that in the United States, (and other settler colonies), invasion, occupation, and territorial dispossession constitute not a singular event but a structure of reasoning, feeling, even imagination (*pace* Walzer's fictive Wild West), one that demands fealty and that orients attitudes toward the present and future.[56]

If recursive yet generally disavowed violence marks the national mythos concerning Indians, the nation's other others have often been invited into the orbit of settler freedom. During the twentieth century, particularly after World War II, the abolition of slavery and the overcoming of Jim Crow were used to legitimate U.S. world power in the eyes of nonwhite peoples and to link it to their own aspirations. Similarly, diverse histories of immigration have been used to lay claim to an idea of the United States as the "universal nation" and a "nation of nations." Less savory continuities, deriving from a long internal history of antiblack insurrectionary fear—from the patrolling of racial borderlands to the criminalization of black life and its subjection to paramilitary policing (the precursor to the militarized policing and hyperincarceration of our own time)—are largely downplayed. Likewise, the formative histories of "enemy aliens," internment, surveillance, and deportation that have routinely come to the fore, especially in times of war, are largely disregarded as constitutive elements of the U.S. national security landscape that consistently worries and confuses whether the greatest "foreign" threats come from the inside or from the outside. An intranational problematic of race and alien status in this way has informed domestic political contention over U.S. foreign relations and has also given shape to a comparative racial and imperial politics along widening arcs of U.S. global involvement.

Today it is rarely acknowledged that histories of enslavement, frontier violence, and coerced migration continue to trouble the United States in the present. One prominent study recognizes the long influence of federal Indian policy in shaping U.S. views on governing "third world" places, polities, and peoples, and slavery and its abolition in shaping an emancipatory narrative of U.S. world power, but it presents these histories only as background to the main story.[57] The history of territorial expansion that required more than a century of wars with hundreds of indigenous polities, scattered over 80 percent of the continent in 1776, is forgotten or else quietly inscribed as a lasting achievement of U.S. nationhood.

The centering of the Indian Wars in the U.S. historical experience marked the elevation of the violent prerogatives of the executive through undeclared wars or police actions in a manner that sought to directly oppose popular local will to legal protections and treaty obligations that offered support for indigenous title to land. The influence of these "wars," including support for local sovereign initiatives, states' rights, and sanctioned homicide, echoes through Frederick Jackson Turner's account of the glorious history of U.S. democratic self-fashioning: the advancing of the line of American civilization in its ceaseless confrontation with savagery (a narrative in which he tellingly describes slavery as "but an incident.") As John Grenier writes, "The 205 years between the first Indian war in Virginia in 1609 and the end of the Creek War in 1814 were the seedbed from which the rest of U.S. military history grew." The military tradition conferred by the Indian wars included practices of "extirpative war" that observed no distinction between combatants and civilians, combined with the adoption of forms of exemplary, extravagant violence said to have been learned from the savages themselves, such as scalping. Settler frameworks, in turn, consciously blurred the lines between war and policing, investing ordinary citizens with an expansive police power.[58]

Savage war and race war have been closely related as antitheses of a consensual order based on the peaceful disquisitions of contract and property. Claims about the Indians' fundamental injustice or "wickedness" drew their greatest force from the notion that Indians placed no limit on violence and observed no established forms of reciprocity in war. Indians were similarly regarded as incapable of establishing ordered civil relations, despite considerable historical evidence about the precontact ritual limitation of warfare and the establishment of robust and far-reaching indigenous networks of kinship and trade. This view is concretely expressed in the U.S. Declaration of Independence, with its representation of "merciless Indian Savages, whose known rule of warfare, is an undistinguished destruction of all ages, sexes and conditions."[59] Wars of extirpation against Indian tribes were represented as just, defensive, and retributive in the face of Indian atrocities, regardless of political disputes over territory that might have been the proximate cause. Adding to the difficulty, insofar as warfare was defined as the prerogative of sovereign states (that is, "the law of nations"), settlers engaged in violent conflicts with native peoples used the term *war* inconsistently and often eschewed it altogether, rendering indigenous counterviolence illegitimate or illegible from the outset.

If U.S. settler freedom was defined in opposition to Indians, it came to linger in complex ways on blacks and blackness. Blackness cultivated and reproduced under the slave regime remained a permanent threat. The African presence—central to capital accumulation through agricultural development and trade—presented an unwanted and ongoing reminder of hierarchy, heterogeneity, and imperial subjection. By contrast, natives, in spite of their resistance and survival, were slated for historical obscurity. The two populations represented different but interrelated threats: if Indians in the state of nature were "jurally minimalist creatures who were to a greater or lesser extent at war with one another," slaves were by nature criminals harboring murderous wishes and intentions that needed to be held permanently in check.[60] As I argue in chapter 1, both populations featured in the development of a racialized narrative of security, one that invested every white person with the sovereign right to kill and blurred the lines between military and police action, as citizen militias and slave patrols were functionally equivalent in many parts of the nation.[61]

What arguably makes the United States distinctive among modern imperial states is a sustained ambiguity and conflict over the boundaries of political membership and the delineation of territorial borders. Throughout its history the United States has been both an "imperial nation" and an "empire state," in which commitments to democratic self-government and coercive subjection within a domestic realm are intertwined with anti-imperial affirmations of sovereign protection and independence, and military conquest of foreign peoples and territories.[62] Imperatives of expansion and emancipation are politically and discursively yoked together, but with contradictory implications for the heterogeneous populations that are party to these encounters. Intertwined in a complex skein of legalism and myth, material accumulation and moral disavowal, a national narrative of ever-expanding freedom has oscillated against commonsense and institutional commitments to permanent yet unpredictable violence that is viewed both as freedom's instrument and as its guarantor. Continuously weighing calculations of prosperity against the necessary attrition of life elsewhere, the people of the United States have arguably never been at peace. In this respect, as the historian Richard Hofstadter sharply puts it, "Americans certainly have reason to inquire whether, when compared with other advanced industrial nations, they are not a people of exceptional violence."[63]

Violent contestations of physical frontiers and internal borders gave shape to a conception of foreign relations insular in its knowledge and understanding of peoples elsewhere and at the same time boundless in its sense of an entitlement to involve itself with those peoples and their lands, markets, and resources—what might be termed an effort to domesticate or annex the foreign, unknown world. The mirror and analogue of this process has been the development of a civic and political culture that is characterized by a similarly paradoxical combination of high levels of quotidian violence and long-term expansion of infrastructures and bases of centralized authority—what might be termed the normalization of civil insecurity as a feature of national belonging.

Most consequential, struggles over the boundaries of national belonging—particularly the legacies and ongoing practices of antiblack domination, anti-indigenous frontier warfare, and anti-alien immigration restriction—have never been removed from questions of the state's foreign policy: that is, military intervention and debates over the proper frontiers of U.S. state action, especially coercive and violent state action, wars both declared and undeclared. Engagement with imperial forms of rule, most fundamentally government without consent of the governed—by way of police and military action—has characterized U.S. involvement at the local, regional, continental, hemispheric, and global scales.

Putting questions of race and violence at the center of the story of American empire does not displace motives of capitalist profit, the expansion of circuits of wealth accumulation, or class division. Rather, as I argue in chapter 2 by way of a reading of Marx's *Capital, Volume I*, it suggests tightly woven connections between racism, war, and liberalism in the development of capitalist power and material accumulation. If the American road to capitalism circumvented the encrustations of a landed aristocracy and the densities of urban class stratification and accommodation, it also marked a dramatic compression of the time and space between money, violence, and materially consequential decision under terms that Marx described as "primitive accumulation," that is, an ability both to purchase and seize land and to purchase and command labor. The relatively low protection costs and the dispersed, decentralized aspects of the settlement project meant that the direct application of force and violence in the service of property ownership and productive investment has played a far more direct role in American historical development than is generally acknowledged.

What the historian Sven Beckert terms "war capitalism" was central to the development of modern imperialism, overseas colonization, and slavery around the world as well. But what distinguishes the American form of empire is the intensive development of infrastructures of violence—made up of segregated and carceral spaces, suburban idylls and racialized ghettos, militarized green zones and internment camps—to manage a population sharply divided along multiple racial lines. This development has achieved wide public sanction and evolved alongside a form of governance that privileges the pursuit of private wealth and property. To quote Hofstadter, "the primary precedent and primary rationale for violence has come from the established order itself."[64] As its own mode of valuation and risk assessment, racial judgment developed along with processes of capital formation and accumulation. We cannot understand the commingling of expansively consensual visions of U.S. nationhood as self-government and private contract, and the coercive subjections of U.S. racism and empire, without understanding the nexus of race and capital formation that has been integral to its history.

One of George W. Bush's favored locutions was that fighting terrorists "over there" was a kind of preventive medicine, a way to forestall having to fight them "at home." In this framing of global military engagement, the American nation, or people, remained at a reassuring distance from the United States' extensive and violent global project, its strategic planning, its network of military bases and multiple theaters of military operation. As I suggest in chapter 3, it is tempting to view the moral and ideational separation of the U.S. domestic and overseas realms—with American civilians enjoined to shop and conduct business as usual as its military specialists struck at enemies faraway and unseen—as a strange, contemporary mutation of an American way of war, a peculiar prophylaxis whose signal figures are the stealth operatives and remote warriors, the drone operators working in unmarked trailers, and the special-ops commandos whose names we will never know. But perhaps the active disconnect between the foreign and the domestic is where we must look if we are to understand the evolution of empire in the U.S. global age—not the refusal of the temptations of empire but the equally persistent claim never to have been one.

An unmistakable result of the military responses to 9/11—the launching of two long, large-scale wars—was to give war making a sense of normalcy and permanence. The idea that we live in an age of permanent war now appears to reverberate indifferently across a chain of iconic signifiers, historic military calamities, and rallying cries, from the U.S. frontier wars with Native Americans and Mexico, the Spanish-American War (particularly in the Philippines), World War II (especially in the Pacific theater), and the cold war in Asia: the Alamo, Wounded Knee, Pearl Harbor, and (more often invoked as things deteriorated in Iraq), the "quagmire," Vietnam. Each of the following chapters represents an effort to take the measure of the shadow cast by the long war, in some cases tentatively, by considering how America's outer wars—that is, exercises of externalized state violence focused on threats from beyond its borders—emerge from and remake our society and its history.

American war craft remains perennially bound to American race craft as the politics of fear and lineaments of enemies without and within morph together, intertwine, and mutually inform and at times reinforce one another.[65] Following the unilateralist military departures of the war on terror came a rejection of those parts of the post–World War II international order most definitively identified with rule-boundedness, consensus, and inclusivity. It was further accompanied by the erosion of fundamental and universal personal protections; the Bush administration's public embrace and legal defense of torture; extralegal rendition; the abrogation of ancient rights of habeas corpus; and an insidious reassertion of an integral relationship between national origin, biophysical marking, threat potential, and subjection to extreme police measures. As I argue in chapter 4, in an examination of the changing contours of U.S. racial formation in the post–civil rights era, one of the important effects of the long war has been a renewal of forms of *state racism*, either long since pronounced dead or thought to be in remission, across the political spectrum.

The election of Barack Obama in 2008, and his promised, partially successful efforts to scale back the officially sanctioned violence and rhetoric of the war on terror, augured a return to normative antiracism and consent-based internationalism. Obama quietly lowered the volume on the bellicose rhetoric and lightened the military footprint of the long war. He moved the mass deportation of undocumented migrants back into the shadows and inaugurated modest reforms of the drug wars and the mandatory sentencing guidelines that have been key to expanding the criminal punishment complex. Nonetheless, Obama strengthened the interrelationship between the inner and outer wars, as well as their legal and institutional basis. By expanding the use of unmanned, armed drones in targeted assassinations, Obama also added a new and terrifying dimension. The arrogation of the right of the U.S. president to kill anyone anywhere in the world without due process suggests a government that regards itself above and beyond the law. According to one study, as of 2015, U.S. attempts to kill forty-one individuals resulted in more than one thousand deaths. Another study of a period of five months of drone strikes in Afghanistan in 2015 revealed a 10 percent success rate. Even if assassination by drone were somehow deemed acceptable, these assessments suggest a level of operational failure, a lack of transparency and accountability, and a disregard for human life that call for redress.[66]

The rise of Donald Trump, who in his campaign for U.S. president promised to bring back waterboarding and racial profiling, increase deportation, and require Muslim registration—and who, despite his belated opposition to the Iraq misadventure, prioritizes violent and unilateral state action in foreign affairs—grimly suggests another terrible turning of an infernal gyre. My final chapter offers an early assessment of the rise of Trump in the context of the broader arguments presented here. Though Trump indicated a rejection of liberal internationalism in the name of nonintervention, his stated admiration of Andrew Jackson—a favored reference point for his chief adviser, Steve Bannon—might also be viewed as a signal of renewing what one historian terms an "imperialism beyond the liberal variant."[67] Jacksonianism has a number of important valences in U.S. domestic and international relations. Among the most important is its justification of territorial expansion and extraterritorial jurisdiction in support of the economic prerogatives and security claims of a settler polity. The Seminole War, which Jackson prosecuted against both Southern tribes and the fugitive slaves who had found refuge among them, provided a U.S. model and precedent for later nineteenth-century depredations by colonial powers in Asia and Africa by affirming the right to designate racial exceptions to the protections of natural law.[68]

By the start of the twentieth century, the United States was the world's leading model of a society founded on colonial settlement, and the world's "leading racist jurisdiction." Its history was invoked as a precedent for the Nuremberg laws and during World War II by Nazi officials seeking to justify territorial annexations in eastern Europe.[69] Though openly legalized racism has faded, the settlement precedent lives on. In his infamous 2003 memo defending executive action and torture in the war on terror, John Yoo tellingly cited the 1873 case of Modoc Indian prisoners as precedent for an exemption from the Geneva Conventions as well as domestic statutes on the grounds that "the strictures that bind the Executive in its role as a magistrate enforcing civil laws have no place in constraining the President in waging war." As the relevant passage from the 1873 case states, the "laws and customs of civilized warfare may not be applicable to an armed conflict with Indian tribes on our Western frontier," since Indians obey no "recognized laws of war." To paraphrase the Chickasaw scholar Jodi Byrd, this suggests that anyone who is "made Indian" can be killed with impunity, even as violence on the part of "Indians" is always already criminalized—that is, outside the realm of legitimate politics or rational grievance.[70]

The term that most succinctly defines the articulation of sovereignty as a right of exclusion, with a claim that binds kinship and nationality to an ideology of freedom, is *racial nationalism;* Jacksonianism was one of its formative and most coherent expressions. To be more specific, we might identify how the Jacksonian tradition of "small wars" and "police actions" against savages reproduced a distinctive (and fictive) "American" ethnicity and mode of government action that furthered the development of the United States as a racial state by transforming a vision of blood spilled in battles against racial enemies into the empowering abstractions and material gains promised by inclusion in a protected and privileged domain of national subjectivity. This is why the Indian wars remain an Ur-text for framing U.S. war making: they have been a basis for an inclusive, even at times a racially alchemical, conception of U.S. nationality. In historical terms, however, and against the backdrop of the rising power of American capitalism, Jacksonianism was always a defense of slavery: it was directed equally toward racial enemies within and those without.[71] When these traditions are invoked today, therefore, they are not only metaphorical: they also refer to ongoing struggles over appropriation and dispossession, and to populations whose very existence is deemed an affront within shrinking kingdoms of Western prosperity. As a consequence, they pose for the United States questions thought settled: who is an object of dread and elimination, and who is a subject of rights and inclusion?[72]

CHAPTER ONE

Race, War, Police

[For] preventing the many dangers and inconveniences that may arise from the disorderly and unlawful meetings of Negroes and other slaves, patrols should be established.

    Georgia General Assembly, 1818

The police power is the counterpart . . . to the realm of individual liberty.

    John Burgess, 1899

Once the classic method of lynching was the rope. Now it is the policeman's bullet.

    Civil Rights Congress, 1951

FROM WAR TO POLICE

It is common to speak of the militarization of policing, and the blurring of the boundaries between war and police in the United States today. In the context of the long history of U.S. racial formation, policing has arguably never been distinct from a kind of civil warfare. Criminal assignment has linked presumptions about individual and group propensities to antisocial behavior and threat to embodied stigma and subjection to sanctioned violence that exceeds the logic of civil compact. Policing makes race and race has defined the objects of police at the point where relations of force take primacy. W. E. B. Du Bois famously observed this race making dynamic, writing that a black person is someone who must "ride Jim Crow in Georgia."[1] Extending this point, we might now say that to be black is to be a target of sanctioned force that often takes on an extrajudicial or arbitrary character, a force that reaffirms rightlessness as a shadow law written with violence upon the body.

At the founding of the United States, more than 20 percent of the entire population were slaves. Blackness had already come to identify the enslaved and enslavable: that is, it was constructed within the ambit of property law. The transformation of the armed seizure of black bodies and the theft of black labor into bills of lading and acts of sale, however, covered up a crime that made severe demands on the body politic. A key challenge for founding U.S. statesmen was to reconcile the creation of a legal order with support of a criminal enterprise. The inability to resolve this contradiction introduced a slippage, in which the plunder of black bodies was transferred to the natural criminality of the enslaved. The slave was "by nature a thief," Benjamin Franklin, argued, later amending this assertion to argue that a propensity for thieving was a consequence of slavery as an institution. Thomas Jefferson claimed that the emancipation of slaves would threaten U.S. society itself, leading to the need for a permanent sequester of freed people far from U.S. shores. Blacks unable to forget the terrible wrongs done to them would nurse murderous wishes and intentions, while whites would live in a state of anticipatory fear that urged preemptive violence, resulting in a likely "extermination of the one or the other race," that is, race war.[2] Regardless of its ascribed source or etiology (oppression from whites or the nature of blacks), the racial line constructing civil life marked a materially and existentially consequential mistrust born of criminal acts.

A similar logic can be observed in justifications of land appropriation. Like the black presence within, "the red men" on the border, to paraphrase James Madison, presented an obstacle to the perfection of the republic. Although Indians were also enslaved in the early colonial period, U.S.

settlement was predicated on a presumption of (limited) Indian freedom, including title to land that could be transferred only to the new nation-state, under federal authority. The problem, as John Jay complained to Jefferson in 1776, was "Indian affairs have been ill managed. . . . Indians have been killed by our People in cold blood and no satisfaction given, nor are they pleased with the avidity with which we acquire their lands."[3] The killing Jay deplored was on the order of extrajudicial murder and therefore problematic for those who worried about the dispositions of stable, centralized governance and legal order. Yet punishing these actions as crimes risked an even more destabilizing settler revolt. Jay's framing of Indian killing as a managerial problem and with respect to those denoted as "our People" demonstrated that such killing retained an implicit government imprimatur.[4]

At both the local and the individual scale, the ideal of freedom as self-rule was directly linked to a moral and legal right to murder or sequester racial outsiders—designated as savages and slaves—in the name of infrastructure development, collective security, and private accumulation.[5] The production of the normatively and legally valorized white citizenry was the basis of national sovereignty. Defined by statute, white status carried with it the presumption of innocence, protection, and fair dealing for those inside its civic ambit. Over time, and as its boundaries grew, it conferred a set of distinct yet conjoined social, political, and economic "freedoms" across a social order based on sharply unequal levels of private accumulation.

Insofar as slavery and settlement were defined by laws of property, whiteness has been rightly discussed as akin to private property or self-possession. But whiteness did not issue directly from ownership of property, let alone slave property. Rather, it emerged from the protection of private property and the interests of its holders in relation to those who were thought to have no property and thus no calculable interests, and who were therefore imagined to harbor a potentially criminal disregard for a social order organized on this basis.[6] Whiteness, in short, was designed as an intermediary status distinction that worked to extend, fortify, and equalize the government of public life in a world dominated by private property holders whose possessions included other human beings and lands already inhabited, but unframed by claims of legal ownership.

Slave owners and large landholders were a distinct minority in the new nation. Asserting whiteness as its own peculiar form of property, allowed them to offer a quasi-democratizing stake in an order that supported land- and slave-owning interests. Whiteness suggested a relationship between the differential valuation of human beings and valuable access to indigenous land and human capital (that is, slaves), and later to skilled jobs and varieties of state support.[7] In the antebellum South's minimal state, the slave tax was a significant source of public revenue, and extraordinary levies on slave property were made by the federal government in times of war (and by the Confederacy during the Civil War).[8] For the majority destined for waged (or wageless) life under capitalism, claiming and asserting whiteness promoted access to public benefits, as well as to the sadistic pleasures and material rewards derived from the management of racial order itself. The racial differentiation of society over centuries has been continuously remade as the quasi-democratic counterpart to the publicly sanctioned accumulation of private wealth and the social costs, divisions, forms of remediation, and crises that it has engendered. The democracy in question, however, foreclosed aspirations toward material equality even as it promoted the idea that policing as a method for regulating and securing the unequal ordering of property relations—was arrogated to white citizens.

Policing has been broadly understood as preventive mechanisms and institutions for ensuring the security of private property within public order, including legal uses of and narrative justifications for coercive force. Policing is anticipatory: it comprises, in Foucault's influential account, those "supervisions, checks, inspections and varied controls, that, even before the thief has stolen makes it possible to identify whether he is going to steal."[9] Where discipline in Foucault's schema seeks to arrest the movement of wrong[doing] bodies in space by means of varieties of artificial enclosure, security enables the proper circulation of people and things across great distances. Policing, in this sense, as John Burgess noted, is the paradigmatic institution for a society founded on individual liberty. It marries juridical consistency with administrative prerogative, coordinates the proportion of carceral space to open space, and balances the necessary use of force with the inherent riskiness of a society dependent upon consent of the governed. Policing further differentiates between the need to arrest and the imperative to develop; it determines, finally, who must be subjected to discipline so that others can pursue their self-interest.

Often overlooked by Foucault-inspired accounts of policing and security is the way the constitution of this predictive, self-aggrandizing power within the United States, as well as in other slave-owning, settler-colonial, and colonizing societies, has been bound to plural forms of racial differentiation against which an elastic and inclusive sense of national belonging coalesced. The American settler colonies' break from British imperial control accelerated independent social, political, and material development through territorial expansion achieved by white settlement. Though ascribed to providence and nature, the design was consciously economic and biopolitical, the product of elite policy formulation that broadened the latitude and democratic basis of settlement by rooting it in private ownership and control of land, and a relatively open and flexible conception of political membership. The homogenization of the nonslave, settler polity (some three-quarters of whom were propertyless) was underlined by the designation "free white persons" quietly inserted into the first U.S. immigration statute, of 1790, which provided a path to citizenship requiring a short two-year residency.[10] Judgments about settler and emigrant sameness, or their capacity to become the same: a "new race of men . . . an American race," in Hector

St. John de Crèvecoeur's memorable formulation, was the basis of a novel ethnology of government.[11]

Demographic engineering and abstractions and simplifications of parceled land jointly produced American national legibility. Benjamin Franklin's famous longing that an "Edenic" North America might become a production hub for the world's "purely white people," though not borne out, was no pious wish: it supported conscious government intervention in the sociobiological constitution of human collectivity across long arcs of migration and encounter. Jefferson viewed the "federative principle," underlined by a homogenizing political anthropology, as unassailable and potentially limitless: "It is impossible not to look forward to distant times, when our rapid multiplication will expand itself beyond those limits and cover the whole northern, if not the southern continent with a people speaking the same language, governed in similar forms and by similar laws," he wrote, in an echo of Franklin. "Nor can we contemplate with satisfaction either blot or mixture on that surface."[12]

The prevention of blot and mixture required more than moral suasion: in a polity founded on slaving and land appropriation, the criminalization of blackness and redness was an indispensable feature of liberal government. The Declaration of Independence, authored largely by Jefferson, constituted the democratic future of those endowed with inalienable rights as vulnerable not only to threats from the despotic powers of the British king, but also to dangers that the crown was accused of inciting: "domestic insurrections" (a code for slave revolts) and alliances with the "inhabitants of our frontiers, the merciless Indian Savages whose known rule of warfare is an undistinguished destruction of all ages, sexes and conditions."[13] This radical view of settler liberty defined the new sovereign nation against a stratified British empire, decried by Thomas Paine as "that barbarous and hellish power which has stirred up the Indians and Negroes to destroy us,"[14] Two decades later, the anti-Federalists advanced the case for the possession of Louisiana on the grounds that French imperial meddling would lead "the tomahawk of the savage and knife of the negro to confederate," an outcome that promised "no interval of peace."[15]

The influential writings of John Locke made a lasting contribution to the argument for colonial settlement in North America: the idea that Indians remained in a "state of war" with a close kinship with beasts of the forest.[16] Locke's *Second Treatise on Civil Government* envisioned an original condition, a benign state of nature comprising "the vacant places of America," that yielded to the rational consent of men of wealth who justly acquired landed property but who agreed to cede their otherwise unlimited natural liberty to form a civil government that precluded the exercise of arbitrary power in their relations with each other. In a second, more concretely historical view of the state of nature, however, Locke foregrounded the threats that motivated civil compact. The state of nature may devolve into a "state of war"—the result of the presence of a vaguely defined "ill nature" and of the persistence of "criminals" and "noxious Creatures," who "declared War against all Mankind, and therefore may be destroyed as a Lyon or a Tyger, one of those wild Savage Beasts, with whom Men can have no Society nor Security."[17]

Classical liberal thinking about war and peace, in this founding vision, opposed an already "moralized" state of nature—whose tendencies toward individual labor and (unequal) private accumulation led automatically toward the development of rational self-interest, civil regulation, and peaceful modes of trade and conflict resolution—against the persistence of zones of wild, uncultivated nature—where the absence of propertied interest promoted a state of war and justified removals, evictions, enclosures, enslavement, and settlement.[18] Settler encroachment, Indian raiding, irregular warfare, and ensuing cycles of revenge and retaliation were the historical backdrop to these reflections, embedding conceptions of the savage enemy deep within the most reflective and progressive thinking of the colonial era. The prospect of feral Indian terror was not only the antithesis of liberal order but also invited an extreme violence, even terror, in response and as a requisite to securing that order. In its meditations on "America," classical liberalism thus discovered a basis for exceptions to the universal applicability of natural law and for limitations on the coercive power of sovereign governments in their relations with each other and their citizens, by preserving and extending an older tradition of the "just war," defined as resisting the irruptions of the state of nature against the state of civil law.[19]

Classical liberalism similarly justified the enslavement of captives. Enslavement was an alternative to killing an enemy in a just war that embedded the power to enslave and to dispose of the life of slaves within modern conceptions of political sovereignty.[20] The links between war and slavery were well understood in the Carolinas, where Locke participated in drafting the Foundational Constitution (1669), Here, warfare with Indian tribes and enslavement of captives existed alongside the African slave trade.[21] The fact that Locke offered arguments for the reconciliation of slavery and natural rights is generally ignored in most commentaries. "Master and servant," Locke writes, "are names as old as history," and bound by contract. "But there is another sort of servant, which by a peculiar name we call slaves, who being captives in a just war are by right of nature subjected to the absolute dominion and arbitrary power of their master. These men having, as I say forfeited their lives and with it their liberties."[22]

The doctrine of war slavery limned the historical convergence of settler expansionism and racial slavery in North America, linking both to the idea of the just war or police action against an "ill nature" that supposedly precedes (but in fact persistently shadows) the establishment of civil order, political consent, and the moral and legal regulation of warfare and state violence inside and between empires and settler polities that claimed the sovereign title of *nations*. As elaborated in an imperial, settler-colonial, and slave-holding context, liberalism's typical "limitation of power" was thus selective and bounded: it paradoxically licensed a flexible and expansive ideology of war at the margins of civic order.[23] Significantly, Locke framed crimes against property, including those that did not threaten physical harm, as warranting punishment up to and including homicide. Despite stating concerns about punishment proportionate to criminal acts, Locke writes, "It is lawful for a man to kill a thief." This is because theft of property de facto entered the criminal, outlaw, or thief into "a state of war" that threatened the natural rights of the individual and the basis of civil government.[24]

Such notions of warfare in the name of settlement and against a specific kind of uncivil and absolute enemy made an important, if generally unrecognized, contribution to the ideological and practical development of racialized police power. The state of peace was said to be unknown to savages and slaves, who in Locke's terms, could not "in that state be considered as any part of civil society, the chief end whereof is the preservation of property."[25] "Absolute dominion and arbitrary power" was considered necessary in relations with those who were constitutively outside and incapable of participating in civil society. Indeed, violence in these terms could be viewed as part of a humanizing endeavor, civilizing process, and security project. Wars and police actions against such uncivil and uncivilized beings—and the land, labor, and other things appropriated from them—was inherently just and bore no resemblance to the emerging diplomatic norms, military practices, and international laws that sought to regulate violent conduct, including war, between civilized adversaries.[26]

Police action, defined as the management and disposal of racial outsiders, developed along a continuum from biopolitical inclusion (graduation into whiteness) to the destruction of entire communities (genocide). The production of the white nationalist subject was an active social process—one that was built on an already given history of racial differentiation but which also worked by generating new distinctions. In racial orders, what changes is as important as what arguably remains the same: change points toward spaces of politics and struggle, resistance and flight. It suggests that even for the dominant insiders, racial orders must be actively institutionalized, that is, managed by personnel who are recruited, invested in, and subjectively constituted for this purpose. Similarly, those who have been racially dominated have been addressed in different terms: The exterminationist approach to relations with indigenous peoples had the character of irregular warfare over plural, unsettled sovereign land claims. The slave-holding regime constructed blackness by way of a biopolitics oriented toward the management of capital and the depletion (and depreciation) of the lives of people whose bodies and labors were essential to its accumulation.

The supposed transparency and legibility of whiteness as a claim to self-rule was never by itself inadequate to assure the internal ordering of a polity marked by divisions of wealth and power, including differential access to land and slaves and the presence of laboring populations of different national origins and colonial histories. The Alien and Sedition Acts of 1798, for example, specifically warned against the importation of "hordes of wild Irishmen" and increased the probationary period for naturalization from two to fourteen years. In doing so, they added a lasting figure, the "enemy alien," to a security lexicon primarily focused on indigenous and racial others. From this point forward, the problem of in-migration of potential enemies added another layer of complexity to quests for national security. The successful opposition to the acts by the Jefferson-led Democratic-Republican Party, including the ouster of the incumbent president, defined them as a threat to Americans as a "free self-governing republican people," and to individual rights secured by "the jurisdictional autonomy of the state-republics."[27] Going so far as to threaten nullification in their respective states, the anti-Federalists demonstrated that the prospect of secession was a far more significant threat to political union than the moral and practical difficulties associated with controlling blacks and Indians. Pan-European settler in-migration and expansive conceptions of civil liberty were thus perennially intertwined as reliable means of producing free white men.[28]

In short, settler freedom and autonomy should be understood as a distinct ethical and practical mandate that shaped the development of American federalism as an imperial form.[29] Just as early U.S. settlers chafed against and broke free from British imperial control, they periodically rebelled against subsequent concentrated assertions of centralized state power. Imperial and settler sovereignties were never mutually exclusive. State and local jurisdictional disputes and controversies over the natural rights and territorial claims of plural indigenous peoples or nations or escaped slaves were decided on the basis of the power exercised by the federal state through its claim of sovereignty over Indian lands and human chattels.[30] The hallmark of state and local sovereignty, in turn, was the direct control exerted by white citizens over indigenous and exogenous others—that is Indians and slaves—through mechanisms of population transfer, confinement, and death enacted by militias, patrols, overseers and frontier soldiers.[31]

Race management, and resistance to it, induced the ongoing slippage between policing and war that visibly characterizes the present.[32] The steady expansion of the application of criminal law to acts of indigenous counterviolence, for example, was a primary means of erasing Indian tribal sovereignty negotiated through warfare and treaty obligations.[33] The slave patrol grew directly from the citizen militia, motivated primarily by fears of slave insurrection. Developing the legal and narrative means to criminalize the actual and imagined counterviolence of dominated peoples was not only central to the institutionalization and legitimation of suppressive force but was also a repression and disavowal of any prior recognition (such as Jefferson's) that enmity, discord, and trauma issued from the violence of white settlers and enslavers. Beneath any ideological or psychological ruminations lay the practical concern of how to both defend and legitimate a social order built on murder and dispossession: that is, the theft of black labor and indigenous lands.

By the late seventeenth century, racial differentiation was already defined through graduated policing and punishment that distinguished blacks and Indians from prospective members of civil society. Under Virginia law, blacks and Indians sentenced to whipping were to be stripped of any protective garment; white Christian servants, by contrast, were allowed to retain the dignity and protection of clothing while being beaten.[34] The fabrication of race through such petty differentiations in the types of violence that could be enacted upon the body illuminates what has often been the paucity of white privilege. It also developed, however, into more salient distinctions between the punished and the punishers. An important mediating institution was the slave patrol, which, in the language of the Georgia General Assembly (and notwithstanding divergent social histories of the indigenous and the enslaved), presumed that "every negro, indian, mulatto or mustizo [sic] . . . is a slave."[35]

John Caphart, a constable and slave catcher in Norfolk, Virginia, in the 1840s, illuminates the distinctive economy of deterrence and prerogative, sadism and reward that governed the fashioning of racial order: "It was part of my business to arrest all slaves and free persons of color, who were collected in crowds at night and lock them up. . . . I did this without warrant and at my own discretion. Next day they are examined and punished. The punishment is flogging. I am one of the men who flog them. . . . I am paid fifty cents for every negro I arrest, and fifty cents more if I flog him. I have flogged hundreds. . . . I never refuse a good job of that kind."[36] Here the link between whiteness as a pivot between individual opportunity and national standing, between access to the wage and access to the public mechanisms of legitimate violence, is clearly laid out.

Caphart's account also highlights how the racial line constructing civil life developed from the longstanding fear that black social life subverted the body politic. In 1802, the U.S. postmaster general warned against hiring "Negro mail carriers," as it might lead to "associating, acquiring and communicating sentiments" about their natural rights under the Constitution, thus "establishing a chain or line of intelligence" and insurrectionary activ-

Race, War, Police

ity dangerous to civic order.[37] The right to bear arms under the Second Amendment—on the grounds of "a well regulated militia being necessary to the security of a free State"— and the defense of the open carrying of weapons—was similarly linked to the preservation of local policing prerogatives and "Southern honor" in the face of black population density, and divided national sentiment over slavery.[38] The infamous Dred Scott decision defending the status of slaves as property throughout the nation cemented these associations by connecting the freedom of fugitive slaves with illegality and reinforcing the idea that blacks, in the words of Supreme Court Justice Roger Taney, possessed no rights that whites anywhere were bound to respect.

In one of the first systematic histories of slavery, an apologia, the white supremacist historian U. B. Phillips observed that "all white persons were permitted and in some regards required to exercise a police power over slaves."[39] Phillips, of course, erased the course of abolitionist and antislavery agitation and underground resistance incited by the Dred Scott decision, which intensified the midcentury crisis over slavery and led eventually to the Civil War. Resistance to slave rendition in the 1850s, for example, led the fugitive-slave commissioner in Boston to decry abolitionists for "levying war on the United States."[40] In truth, resisting slavery was a crime against property that threatened the basis of civic order. Writing two decades before Phillips, Burgess was more circumspect and attuned to how to manage an on-going conflict: "Had the slaveholders made wise use" of the advantages given to them under the Dred Scott decision, he wrote, they would have given "themselves . . . no further occasion for slavery agitation," ceased "to claim the rendition of their fugitive slaves by the general government," and instead turned "their attention to perfecting the police administration in the slaveholding Commonwealths." Here, he recognized the bulwark that federalism [i.e., states' rights], defined by police discretion and jurisdictional autonomy provided when it came to maintaining racial order based on holding people as property.[41]

It is not incidental that the scholarly and public study of police power in the United States emerged in the ascendant period of U.S. white supremacy after the Civil War and Reconstruction. Above all, it pointed out the formless, discretionary, and aggrandizing dimensions of police functions and institutions in a world that appeared to be in rapid racial transition. According to Ernst Freund, "The police power is not a fixed quantity, but . . . the expression of social, economic and political conditions. As long as these conditions vary, the police power must continue to be elastic, i.e. capable of development." Attending to the state and local levels of political sovereignty, Burgess called "the police power . . . 'the dark continent' of our jurisprudence . . . the convenient repository of everything for which our juristic classifications can find no other place."[42] In 1904 in the name of securing public order beyond the nation's borders President Theodore Roosevelt (a former New York City police commissioner), arrogated to the United States an expansive "international police power" to confront "chronic wrongdoing, or an impotence which results in the general loosening of ties of civilized society."[43]

One does not need to read deeply here to notice the elective affinities of policing and race making within a developmental schema that comprised normative visions of public order and the rule of law *alongside* the preservation and cultivation of exceptions permitting the expanding use of discretionary violence. Blackness all but defined a state of biopolitical "impotence" and propensity to "chronic wrongdoing" that for Roosevelt justified an enlarged and broader police function. Blackness was by this time an increasingly thick and naturalized but also fungible means for defining a type of person and a state of being whose relationship to contract was untrustworthy and unstable, and at worst null and void, requiring permanent supervision and sometimes direct domination. Black people at this time were deemed ineligible for insurance because membership in the race was held to constitute an inherent risk of premature death. Actuaries such as Frederick Hoffman, who drew these conclusions, went on to develop methods of compiling crime statistics that provided a positivist validation of black criminal propensity and to modernize police violence as a matrix of racial discipline.[44] The new dispensation of blackness as a negative biopolitics in need of permanent policing was underscored by the U.S. Supreme Court in *Plessy v. Ferguson* (1896), which described legal prohibitions on interracial marriage as a technical interference with "freedom of contract" that was nonetheless justified as an exercise of "the police power of the state."[45]

The closing of the continental frontier, followed by the declaration of the Roosevelt Corollary, suggested that the inwardly focused, racialized vector of police power needed outward testing. As an example of a blackened and disordered space in the racial imagination, the Philippines under U.S. occupation was the major institutional proving ground—the first overseas U.S. counterinsurgency of the new century. In the words of the historian Alfred McCoy, a significant contribution of the U.S.-Philippine war was that it functioned as a "laboratory of police modernity."[46] Here, the development and synthesis of new methods of clandestine operations, information science, photographic identification, demographic research, intelligence gathering, and legal repression far outstripped the capacities of major metropolitan police forces. Such developments were a response to a fierce anticolonial insurgency against U.S. occupation forces. As one U.S. general summarized the consensus opinion of U.S. counterinsurgents: "The keynote of the insurrection among the Filipinos, past, present and future is not tyranny, for we are not tyrants. It is race."[47]

The modern power of police has been correlated to "the Dark Continent" as the domain in which civil order is seen as either being absent or always already suspended. This condition constitutes a permanent state of emergency or exception. From the standpoint of power, it has no knowable properties beyond its criminal propensity and the open-ended threats it poses. In other words, these threats require rigorous and potentially limitless applications of "legitimate" violence. With the rise of nationalist and anti-colonial politics and struggle in the twentieth century, the enhancement of institutional capacities for policing was also intensified by fear of the potential loss of white monopolies on space, resources, and moral right. Supporting Roosevelt's vision of U.S. military "points of vantage" across the Caribbean and the Pacific, the naval strategist Alfred Thayer Mahan specifically warned against the yellow peril, arguing that extension of U.S. maritime forces would be the key to deciding whether "eastern or western civilization is to dominate throughout the earth and to control its future."[48] Responding to both concerns about Asian powers, and to a rising tide of liberal critics of the "white Australia" policy, Prime Minister Alfred Deakin offered a far-seeing judgment that what would ultimately be required were "colorless laws [that could be] administered so as to draw a deep line of demarcation between Caucasians and all other races."[49]

For settler colonies that emerged from the Anglosphere's imperial crucible, asserting boundaries of race and nation trumped the language of empire and assumed an anti-imperial, demotic tone. It is mistaken to think of race making as a contradiction to forms of universal reason we associate with the Enlightenment, including the progressive alignment of the rights of national citizens with human rights. Rather, racial differentiation constituted the grounds on which claims to rationality, rights, self-rule, and national standing were imagined as simultaneously universal and delimited—much like the nation-state itself. Neither blackness nor whiteness are in this sense strictly reducible to phenotype. Rather they, like other modern racial forms, emerged as subject positions, habits of perception, and modes of embodiment that developed from the state-based government of capitalist property relations. Variants of capitalist state and society have developed simultaneously with plural and heterogeneous processes of racial formation around the world. Needless to say, a sharply dualist conception of blackness and whiteness accrued special force with the ascendancy of the Anglo-

American form of capitalism in which slavery and settler colonization were motors of accumulation.

The importance of criminality in race making is exemplified by Deakin's recognition in Australia (whose settler jurisprudence paralleled that of the United States), that the rule of law and formal equality could be effectively welded to racially targeted administrative discretion. Much has been made of the fact that the U.S. Thirteenth Amendment abolished slavery "except as a punishment for crime." Regardless of whether penal administration amounted to a new slavery, the carving out of the exception—like the rulings on "separate but equal," the institution of formally neutral voting restrictions, the selective granting of marriage licenses, and going forward, real-estate steering, racially disparate uses of zoning laws, and what banking interests termed "residential security" (red-lining, discriminatory credit allocation)—made the preservation of racial order subject less to formal legal defense than to the manifold applications of administrative prerogative in the name of public safety and privately held value. Even as the completion of continental expansion and the transition from slavery to freedom appeared to normalize and extend the wage contract to all individuals, it gave rise to new elaborations of and responses to blackness and indigeneity as a temporal lag, a state of exception, a dangerous predicament, and, equally important, a state from which value could be directly extracted, security and threat potentials assessed and acted upon.

The period from Reconstruction to World War I was the high era of white world supremacy. From the perspective of the postslavery U.S. black population, civil war never ended; the postbellum period witnessed the rise of lynching, racial terror, and the broad criminalization of black life, not only in the South. Lynching in particular was defined as the reassertion of the sovereign rights and capacities of white citizens.[50] For native peoples, national reunification unleashed the last, bloodiest, and most one-sided Indian Wars from the Midwest to the Southwest, including the infamous massacres of the

Western Utes and the Lakota Sioux at Wounded Knee. Nativist agitation and periodic pogroms aimed primarily at Asian migrants and at southern and eastern Europeans shaped U.S. immigration policy over subsequent generations. Beginning with landmark immigration restriction targeted at Chinese exclusion, the U.S. Supreme Court linked immigration control, police and war powers. Within a global field understood in racial terms and the rise of nonwhite state powers, immigration was tantamount to foreign aggression. In the words of the court, "foreigners of a different race" were "potentially dangerous to peace and security" even in the absence of "actual hostilities with the nation of which the foreigners are subject."[51]

An astute commentator on the history of U.S. racial conflicts, Carey McWilliams, observed that scenarios of U.S. war with Japan first emerged in 1905, when the presence of Japanese immigrants was associated with the invasion of California by the rising power of the east. From this period dates the initial—if premature—program first articulated by Woodrow Wilson's secretary of state, William Jennings Bryan, of solving the "Oriental" problem by forcibly breaking up and removing Japanese populations from the West Coast and dispersing them in the nation's interior.[52] The passage of the racially exclusive Immigration Act of 1924, which formally established an "Asiatic barred zone," also marked an escalation of skirmishes with Mexican migrants. The institutionalization of a military-style border patrol that year turned the southern border into a site of vast, state-enforced population transfers.

World War I saw the emergence of Wilsonian internationalism as a prospective model for governing the planet on the basis of consensus and comity among leading industrial powers. That vision, of course, was stillborn. Wilson and his European counterparts were committed to the preservation of the "white world order," with its colonial and racial hierarchies now seen as being under threat from revolution, anticolonial agitation, and the rising power of nonwhite nations such as Japan.[53] U.S. attention to the conditions of freedom around the world, including the regulation and limitation of war, remained bound to the development of "international police power" and the ordering of race and space. Much like the U.S. Civil War, the global civil war (as some historians label the two world wars), showed that the containment of race war by inwardly focused police powers of settlement and colonization had reached a limit. As the German sociologist Max Weber observed in 1906, "The historical origin of modern freedom has had certain unique preconditions which will never repeat themselves. Let us enumerate the most important of these . . . the overseas expansions. . . . In our whole economic life even today this breeze from across the oceans is felt, . . . but there is no new continent at our disposal."[54] The stage was set for the North American settler colony to become a global power.

POLICE INTO WAR

Before World War II, the government and people of the United States were hostile to overweening military establishments. The ambit of police—often termed "peace officers"—was always wider than the waging of war. War was viewed as an extragovernmental power exerted by states against a commensurable organized force and against political enemies—that is, other states. Policing was a form of government power exerted against the criminal enemies of the body politic, both within national boundaries and in spaces deemed ungoverned or nonsovereign. Even at the onset of World War II, peace was still defined as a condition specific to states characterized by publicly ordered civic life—that is, a state unknown to savages. More or less continuous violence against the uncivilized was thus thought to be a humanizing endeavor and perhaps a pathway to their civic engagement and material development.

The framing of what we now think of as war by police historically precedes what we often now describe as the militarization of policing, or the conditioning of police by war, which includes both the real and metaphorical inflations of the term *war* to define battles against various domestic ills: poverty, crime, drugs, terror, and the like. After World War II, as colony after colony became a sovereign state, the United States engaged in numerous military interventions overseas. Not a single one of these involved a formal declaration of war, and many, if not all, were labeled as "police actions." Domestically, World War II inaugurated the modern imperative to uphold black civil rights within the nation-state. Yet, it also marked the consolidation of a federal law-enforcement bureaucracy in the interests of national security. The intensive surveillance of political radicals and black social movements after World War I, and the mass deportations and cross-border detainee operations that spiked during the Great Depression, vastly expanded during and after World War II. The Japanese internment illuminated passage between racial alien and alien enemy. After the war, the U.S. military transferred surplus war materiel, including aircraft, to the border patrol. Materially limning the connection between inner and outer race wars, between war and police, 4,500 linear feet of chain-link fencing was delivered to the border patrol from the internment camp at Crystal City, California that once housed Japanese immigrants and their American-born children.[55]

The infamous but insightful Nazi jurist Carl Schmitt lamented that the two world wars had broken the duelists' compact of the *jus publicum europaeum* that had previously governed war between recognized sovereign entities, distinguishing combatants from civilians and ridding war of its criminal and punitive character. Colonial wars and civil wars, Schmitt noted, were "outside this bracketing": hence the tendency in such conflicts for violence to become punitive and for the enemy to be criminalized. The latter conflicts were often not dignified with the name *war*, at least in part so as not to enhance the status of enemy combatants. In this way, colonialism supported a foundational differentiation between the conduct of war between equal sovereigns, as an extension of specific and limited political

Race, War, Police

and state aims, and the means by which imperial sovereigns asserted jurisdiction, seized territory, and exercised a more or less open-ended police power over ungoverned, unproductive, unsettled spaces and the "unfit peoples" who inhabited them.[56] Indeed, Schmitt observed, the effective origins of police action derived from "the old doctrine of just war whose primary result was to create a legal title for land appropriation."[57]

The mastering of nonsovereign, or colonial areas, Schmitt emphasized, was "the spatial element upon which European law is founded."[58] Witnessing the beginning of the end of colonialism, Schmitt doubted that the new era of world affairs would lead to a new bracketing or limitation of war. Instead, he predicted a future in which, under the auspices of dominant powers—and particularly the United States—warfare would devolve into a limitless series of "police actions" and "police bombing" against "troublemakers, criminals, and pests," in which "the intensification of technical means of destruction" would produce new and extreme forms of moral debasement and legal nullification of opponents in war.[59] Schmitt was preoccupied by what had been done to Germany, including the prosecution of German war crimes following World War II. He mostly elided the longer history of asymmetric "small wars" and race wars that were the basis of colonial settlement and overseas colonial administration by major powers, which the Nazis invoked as precedents. Nazi expansionism had explicitly referred to a comparative colonial and racial history. (As a German official reported from the Ukraine front in 1942, "We are here in the midst of Negroes.")[60] As for the United States, the situation of "total war" of World War I and World War II was the exception to the longer period in which the nation exercised international police power in the Western hemisphere or waged wars on its frontier and border that were not understood as either war or conquest.

If the U.S. era of continental settlement progressively translated war into policing and frontiers into borders, the globalization of the U.S. realm translated policing into war and projected the frontier beyond the nation, so that it became possible to think of war at home and police in the world. Crucially, colonial and racial precedents, institutions, and practices remained instrumental to the blurring of these boundaries. Reviewing the history of the use of "dogs in war, police work, and on patrol" in the journal *Police Science* in 1955, the American police professional and scholar Charles F. Sloane argued that the distinction between inwardly concentrated and outwardly tested state violence was traversed by a more fundamental line—one that separated the progressive achievements of human civilization from savage regression. This fact, Sloane argued, not only established the basis for reciprocity and continuity between cross-border war making and domestic crime fighting, but it also gave a controlling seat to police power: "If one gives some thought to the subject, there is but little difference between fighting an enemy in a declared war and fighting an enemy, the criminal, at home on the crime front. Both are comparable battles for the very existence of civilization, for without the thin wall of police protecting the people from criminal depredation, the world would soon revert to savagery and bestiality."[61]

Sloane outlined a series of specific global coordinates and civil precedents for harnessing animal force against criminals, (whom he described as kin to animals). "The English police, the Mounted Police of Canada, Australia, South Africa, and Southern Rhodesia," he argued, "have been most successful in their use of dogs for trailing the spoor of a human. . . . [with the] most famous of police Training Centers for dogs in the world. . . . located [near] Pretoria in the Union of South Africa." Having framed the art of hunting humans as a legacy of the Anglosphere and its settler colonies, Sloane did not fail to note a distinctively American lineage: "The use of dogs in tracking down escaped criminals and slaves," he averred, "has been commonplace in the United States for the past two centuries."[62]

In light of the emerging civil rights movement, Sloane's present-tense juxtaposition of criminal and slave is notable. His essay also emerged just as municipal police forces in the United States were establishing their first K-9 units, led by the cities of St. Louis and Baltimore in 1956. An article in the same journal a few years later, assessing the progress of K-9 policing across U.S. municipalities, solidified the historical chains of racial meaning Sloane took for granted, linking the slave and felon as objects of police violence subjected to the nonhuman force of dogs. "Cities with large slum and deteriorating areas have more need for dogs than suburban communities," the authors noted, with an important exception: "Suburban areas bordering on the central city have used dogs successfully in curbing the city's overflow of crime."[63] Most cities were just starting to experiment with K-9 forces. The city of Birmingham, Alabama, reported that police "dogs were not yet in use, but would be soon."[64] Heavily infiltrated by the Ku Klux Klan, Birmingham's police force, with its beasts unleashed, would soon be at the forefront of white Southern resistance to the civil rights movement.[65]

Charles Sloane served as the police chief of Cortland, New York, before moving to a senior position in the New York State government in Albany, where he developed and oversaw qualifying examinations aimed at professionalizing local police. The year his article on police dogs appeared, his career took another turn: he joined the Michigan State University Group (MSUG) assigned to Saigon, where he was charged with establishing South Vietnam's first police academy, (including the introduction of police dogs). Funded by the U.S. State Department's International Cooperation Administration (precursor to the Agency for International Development) and comprising U.S. police professionals and CIA operatives disguised as Michigan State University professors, the advisory group supported the development of countersubversion, police intelligence, and interrogation techniques and detention facilities to consolidate the Ngo Dinh Diem regime. Working in various police advisory roles, Sloane spent parts of the following decade "in-country," as U.S. soldiers would come to describe Vietnam, a shorthand for "Indian Country."[66]

Sloane's intellectual and professional trajectories illuminate the circuit that connects colonial frontier policing and slave catching to the deadly euphemisms that defined an emerging U.S. cold war imperium. During the John F. Kennedy administration, vast numbers of U.S. police and corrections officers went to ply their trade as advisers in Vietnam.[67] The euphemistically labeled practices of *civic action*, *police assistance*, and *nation building* were enacted on "America's new frontier."[68] Sloane was a bit player in a larger drama in which the overseas projection of U.S. police power was integral to reshaping conceptions and tactics of domestic policing. His career trajectory helps us to chart what Lisa Lowe has termed the "intimacies of continents," global relations defined and redefined by imperial rule and the afterlives of U.S. slavery and settlement. American power during the cold war collapsed the distance between places like Cortland, Saigon, and East Lansing, not only through transportation logistics and applications of massive military force but also through the diffusion and dissemination of distinctive repertoires of racialized governance.

While stationed in Saigon in 1955, Sloane missed a lecture by Los Angeles Police Department chief William Parker, who at that time was one of America's most illustrious policemen. At Michigan State University's School of Police Administration, Parker offered his thoughts on "the police role in community relations."[69] It is possible that in his article on police dogs, Sloane was referencing Parker, who described the police as "a thin blue line of defense . . . that we must depend [on] to defeat the invasion from within."[70] Five years into his tenure as chief, Parker hailed the Los Angeles experiment as proof that "enforced order" was "the first step towards improved community relations."[71] Describing LA as the "white spot of the great cities of America today," he argued that LA's success rested on the pillars of police professionalization, good press, and well-managed public relations.[72] Never one to put too fine a point on matters, Parker argued that police power needed to be concentrated in certain parts of the city because "certain racial groups . . .

commit a disproportionate share of the total crime. . . . If persons of Mexican, Negro, or Anglo-Saxon ancestry, for some reason, contribute heavily to other forms of crime, police deployment must take that into account. From an ethnological point-of-view, Negro, Mexican and Anglo-Saxon are unscientific breakdowns; they are a fiction. From a police point-of-view, they are a useful fiction and should be used as long as they remain useful. The demand that the police cease to consider race, color, and creed is an unrealistic demand."[73]

This must have sounded reasonable in 1955, much as it may sound reasonable today. Acknowledging race as a social fiction has not led to its retirement or obsolescence as a guide to socially consequential action, particularly in the domains of criminal policing and punishment. Whatever its social etiology, Parker argued, disproportionate black and brown criminality (and Anglo-Saxon lawfulness) was simply a fact, and the police needed to "concentrate on effects, not causes." Dimly acknowledging the circularity of this argument about black crime, he was concerned that liberal antiracist norms might strip police of their most indispensable, discretionary tool, (in today's parlance, racial profiling). Although Parker came to be viewed a revanchist on racial matters (particularly after his remarks during the Watts riots), he was already an important police modernizer, as indicated by this conscious effort to square the scientific debunking of racial categorization with an empirical practice of policing that depended upon it.[74]

In her reading of the origins of the contemporary U.S. carceral state, Naomi Murakawa traces it back to the early postwar period, arguing that there was never a dichotomy between a governmental emphasis on law and order and civil rights reform: the right to "the safety and security of the person" against "private and arbitrary violence," as President Truman's Civil Rights Committee put it in 1947, was the first and most "essential" civil right. By virtue of this initial design, it is not surprising that criminal justice imperatives came to outweigh the expansive sense of rights and redress against public, state-sanctioned violence pursued by black social movements during the 1960s.[75] The emphasis on national security, however, has not been fully examined as a vector of this story. It is well known that white Southerners seized on cold war and anticommunist pretexts to repress the emerging civil rights movement. At the same time, policing, as we can see in Parker's writings from the 1950s, was already being refashioned on a more forward-looking and expansive basis, one defined by a mix of concessionary and punitive approaches to black freedom struggles, including efforts to protect local police discretion and prerogatives of institutionalized racism with the veneer of a professional, antiracist ethic. Even though policing and criminal justice remained a social policy backwater, with little claim on federal budgetary largesse before the mid-1960s, police professionals like Parker and Sloane already recognized the boon that the emerging national security discourse offered to their field of enterprise.

Black radicals had no need to invent a "colonial analogy" to describe the situation inside the United States. The Watts riot in particular was a touchstone for a many-sided comparison between domestic and international uses of police and military power. The chair of the commission that studied the riot, former CIA director John McCone (who had been a member of Kennedy's Special Group on Counterinsurgency), warned that in all the recent American riots and overseas insurrections, the issue of police brutality had been raised in order "to destroy effective law enforcement."[76] The *Chicago Tribune* called it "the Los Angeles terror." They quoted Chief Parker, who must have considered his own standpoint vindicated when he pronounced on the third night of upheaval in Watts that "this situation is very much like fighting the Viet Cong. We haven't the slightest idea of when this can be brought under control."[77]

Competing visions of counterinsurgency—hard and soft, outside and inside the nation—had by the late 1960s become increasingly difficult to separate. In 1967, a *Life* magazine spread juxtaposed "the other war"—counterinsurgency in Vietnam—with "the 'Other' Pacification—to Cool U.S. Cities. . . . Here at home the U.S. also has its pacification program, no less urgent than the one in Vietnam." National security adviser Walt Rostow earnestly advanced the same argument in a letter to President Lyndon B. Johnson after Johnson's speech following the 1967 Detroit riots. "I was much struck by the parallels between your formulation of domestic policy and those you have applied to foreign policy. At home your appeal is for law and order as the framework for economic and social progress. Abroad we fight in Vietnam to make aggression unprofitable, while helping the people of Vietnam and all of free Asia build a future of economic and social progress." For Rostow, war in Vietnam was "the equivalent of domestic law and order on the world scene."[78]

Frank Armbruster, policy intellectual who helped to design the most brutal and violent phase of counterinsurgency in Vietnam under the rubric of Civil Operations and Revolutionary Development Support (CORDS), operationalized as the Phoenix program in 1967, noted that insurgency was a "police problem" that needed "specifically designed military activity to provide an environment in which policemen and professional administrators can do their jobs . . . Police work may have to become the tail that wags the dog as far as military planning is concerned." Armbruster doubted that social reforms could be carried out quickly enough to offset the "chaos on which extremists consistently thrived." His example came from close to home and exemplified the collapse of domestic policing and counterinsurgency thinking: "In the United States, one of the demands of the protest leaders in the Watts section of Los Angeles after the disturbances was money to rebuild the commercial area demolished by extremist elements during the riots incited, in part, by this protest movement."[79]

The effort to rout what agents of Operation Phoenix called the Vietcong infrastructure involved widespread interrogation, torture, mass detention, and assassination—all defined as police work—alongside an escalating conventional war. This novel approach produced its own brand of crisis. By the end of the decade, field reports from Vietnam desperately sought support for addressing a growing prison crisis involving hundreds of thousands of detainees. The leading U.S. official in charge of the CORDS Public Safety Division, Randolph Berkeley, attempted to reassure CIA director William Colby in 1971, that, as yet, "no prison in Vietnam has become a disaster such as San Quentin or Attica."[80]

The acknowledgment that brutal conditions within U.S. prisons were worse than those in Vietnam should give us pause. Black radicals pressed the case throughout the 1960s for precisely this kind of reading—not an analogy between the black and Vietnamese situations, but a homology, that is, the recognition that a single mode of rule had been elaborated in different contexts. As Jack O'Dell argued in "A Special Variety of Colonialism," published in *Freedomways* in 1967: "In defining the colonial problem, it is the role of the institutional mechanisms of colonial domination which are decisive."[81] Attempting to stay within the terms of a fracturing liberal consensus, Martin Luther King Jr. spent his last years arguing that violent expressions of black discontent and revolt were the "language of the unheard" and thinking about how to translate the collective anger of dispossession into a collective politics that could create what he called a beloved community.[82] The best that the liberal reformers could offer the urban poor was a vision of "maximum feasible participation," conditioned by choice architectures designed by powerful elites. Many of those same elites were already signaling a willingness to revert to an older model, revoking participation on the grounds that rational state violence was the only language that certain collectivities were capable of hearing. The black journalist Samuel Yette cut to the core issue that both liberal reformers and their conservative antagonists avoided: "In the ghettos, as in Southeast Asia, the need for pacification rises out of a history of colonization—the economic and cultural exploitation of a subject group. An honest determination to relinquish such exploitation would obviate any need to pacify."[83]

Counterinsurgency, in its reminted U.S. iteration, went beyond foreign policy in pursuit of a situation of affirmative governance that could correct the lack of publicly structured and politically organized interiority among formerly subject populations. Its principal doctrinal statement, the Overseas Internal Defense Policy (OIDP) of 1962, is to this day what its primary author called "the most interventionist statement of American policy ever promulgated." It is also striking in its generality and lack of clear boundaries. The OIDP characterized the domestic social patterns and institutions of "underdeveloped nations" as "malleable," "shapeless," and "illogical" and thus subject to "initiatives which . . . cross the line into disorder and violence." Under pressures of social change, isolated rural people "crowd[ed] into the strange environment of cities that lack for them a satisfactory pattern of living." Tempted into dissidence, an uprooted peasantry was "the ultimate and decisive target" of communist insurgency and thus of internal defense programs designed to "assist in the immunization of vulnerable societies" against insurgency. The most salient feature of this document was its emphasis on "potential threat, latent, or incipient" revolt, which required "continuous assessment" and monitoring. In this view, insurgencies in underdeveloped societies were not only an inevitable hazard but also had a particular life cycle: detected early enough, they could be suppressed. The primary agents of detection were the police, which the OIDP called "the first line of defense against subversion and insurgency."[84]

Counterinsurgent policing was imagined as a shift away from large-scale, more violent, less discriminating military intervention. Anticommunism, though it framed the U.S. understanding of the global problem of insurgency, was revealing a decidedly imperial substrate, one in which countering the violence, criminality, and social disorder of formerly subject people was understood to be a hazard of the modernization process. According to Richard Critchfield, an academic embedded in U.S. national security circles, Sir Robert Thompson, the widely revered British architect of the

Malayan counterinsurgency and head of the British Advisory Mission to South Vietnam, viewed the Viet Minh as little more than an "illegal armed civil disobedience movement."[85] The American form of counterinsurgency added an important affirmative dimension to this view: the idea that rural Asians, passive and politically indifferent, had been underserved by central authorities and needed to be more effectively connected to the positive instrumentalities of government.

The perspectives of counterinsurgency experts exhibit uncanny resonances with those of domestic race-relations managers. In *The Negro Family: The Case for National Action* (1965), for example, Daniel Patrick Moynihan argued that "measures that worked for most groups will not work here." The lack of strong patriarchal authority and a concomitant disintegration in "the fabric of conventional social relationships," along with near-total "isolation" from the white world, had created a situation in which "crime, violence, unrest, disorder—most particularly the furious, unrestrained lashing out at the whole social structure . . . is not only to be expected; it is very near to inevitable." Even if the consequences of centuries of white racism (or for that matter, European and U.S. colonialism) was acknowledged, these dynamics, as Moynihan famously remarked, were now perpetuating themselves "without white assistance." The violence that had created these conditions was in effect converted into a potential for antisocial violence that could be curbed only with the exercise of legitimate force. According to Moynihan (in one of the less frequently cited parts of his report), this meant increasing black military service, by which means "a world run by strong men of unquestioned authority" could overcome the social pathology that had been spawned by a "disorganized and matrifocal family life."[86]

As modern-day Lockeans, liberal counterinsurgents viewed themselves as expanding the boundaries of the community of the free without regard to prior racial or colonial status. In the words of McGeorge Bundy, national security adviser and member of the CI Special Group, "There is no safety yet for free men anywhere without us, and it is the relation between this astonishing proposition and the complexities of each part of the world that makes the conduct of our foreign affairs such an overwhelming task."[87] But universal expansion was predicated on the delimitation wrought by racial and colonial violence, including the irresistible translation of social and political debilities into naturalistic terms. At a famous gathering of global counterinsurgents convened by the Rand Corporation in Santa Monica in 1962, Frank Kitson, a British veteran of the brutal Kenyan counterinsurgency, for instance, blithely informed his audience that "the African . . . can absorb an unbelievable amount of lead without taking notice of it." The record of proceedings gives no indication that anyone objected to this blunt racist reassertion of black imperviousness to pain and death.[88]

The fundamental dilemma that the Rand conference participants wrestled with was how to destroy the enemy and win over the population. This, of course, elided the more fundamental problem of how to meaningfully distinguish between the two, when facing popular insurgencies. The OIDP suggested that any restiveness within targeted populations was a potential sign of latent or incipient insurgency. Pacification was therefore, the opposite of politicization. Even if some counterinsurgents viewed excessive repression and violence as counterproductive, their vision was not one of mediation through politics, but of more policing. The OIDP reasoned, "The primary purpose of internal defense programs is to deal with and eliminate the cause of dissidence and violence." Yet it bluntly concluded that the answer was to "bind [the police] more closely to the community"—the same remedy that first brought Charles Sloane to Saigon and that William Parker prescribed for the racialized zones of the city of Los Angeles.

The mandate to achieve "maximum feasible participation of the poor" defined the high-water mark of Lyndon Johnson's "war on poverty," whose implementation was assigned to U.S. undersecretary of defense, Adam Yarmolinsky, also an adherent of the counterinsurgency gospel. The participatory imperative, the brainchild of liberal and progressive defense intellectuals, functioned primarily at the level of affect and perception. It sought to create a feeling of participation rather than to ascribe the poor a role in the design of government authority. This enterprise, characterized by the historian Arthur Schlesinger Jr. in its overseas iteration as the "very American effort to persuade developing countries to base their revolutions on Locke rather than Marx," glossed over the fact that the vision of governance was organized around submission rather than consent.[89]

Conservatives agonized much less than liberals about abuses of power and political representation. Casting his dyspeptic eye on the urban crisis, Edward Banfield observed there "seems to have been a marked increase since the civil rights revolution began in the amount of crime by Negroes." The Kerner Commission's emphasis on "white racism" as a cause "almost certainly made it easier for many Negroes to commit crimes that they would not otherwise have committed. . . . [I]t does not follow that . . . pursuing a more enlightened policy . . . could significantly reduce [crime]."[90] Another who grew skeptical of the value of the elaborate participatory nostrums of counterinsurgency, Samuel Huntington, infamously claimed that the "forced-draft urbanization" produced by the U.S. bombing and rural defoliation campaigns in Vietnam was speeding up the modernization process by default. Yet Huntington too was worried: the "Vietnamese family situation," he argued, was "not altogether dissimilar from that which the Moynihan report found to exist among Negro families in American urban slums. This decay of the family, if it continues, bodes ill for the future stability and economic development of South Vietnam."[91]

When push came to shove, a liberal-conservative consensus prevailed, asserting the necessity of building the future on the exclusions of the past. The problem, in the end, was not too little democratic participation but an "excess of democracy," as Huntington famously described it. A group of influential thinkers, including Banfield, James Q. Wilson, Richard

Herrnstein, and Charles Murray (who did his own counterinsurgency stint in Indonesia), reintroduced arguments about the criminogenic poor and flirted with eugenic discourse. Banfield was unabashed about the necessity to abridge the freedom of "individuals whose propensity to commit crime is so high" that no "feasible incentives" could influence them otherwise. George Kelling—the architect, with Wilson, of broken-windows policing (based on his experience observing beat cops in the black ghetto of Newark, New Jersey)— dimly acknowledged the troubling racial precedence of the "black codes—vague loitering and vagrancy laws" in the new forms of intensive policing practices they were advocating. Like Kitson's racism at the Rand conference, the observation gave his conscience no further trouble.[92]

Some, more disillusioned with the state of affairs at the end of the 1960s, tried to hold onto faith in liberal reform. Retiring to the academy after his stints in the Department of Defense, running the war on poverty, and promoting Bobby Kennedy's tragically foreshortened presidential bid, Yarmolinsky presided over a massive study supported by the Twentieth-Century Fund, *The Military Establishment*. It concluded with a warning that has largely gone unheeded: "The use of techniques applied in foreign wars and in planning for future wars may lead to increased likelihood that certain groups in American society will gradually be regarded as an enemy with action appropriate to that perception. . . . Insensitivity to unwarranted police violence and insensitivity to brutality in military actions—abroad and at home—may be unrelated phenomena, but they cannot escape mutual reinforcement."[93]

This observation was only half true. As we have seen, the two things have been related throughout U.S. history. Racism is the means by which war became normalized as policing, and police action licensed war. More precisely, racial distinctions have been made and renewed in the passage between norm and law, police and war, and the movement of state violence inside and outside its prescribed borders. Policing makes race when it removes normative barriers to police violence. War makes race when it relieves legal barriers to war's limitation.

Few careers illuminate this relationship more clearly than that of the notorious Chicago policeman John Burge. When Burge flunked out of the University of Missouri in 1966, he moved back to live with his parents in a Chicago suburb. The Burge family lived within shouting distance of an area that a few months later became the site of a pitched battle between local residents, mostly white, and civil rights protesters led by Martin Luther King Jr., challenging Chicago's racially discriminatory housing policies. Like most men unable to attend college, Burge faced the prospect of being drafted to fight in Vietnam. Instead he decided to sign up for six years of service, beginning his tour of duty at Fort McClellan in Alabama and moving to the army's military police training school in Georgia. Burge was assigned to the Ninth Military Police Company at a base named Dong Tam ("united hearts and minds"), located fifty miles south of Saigon. This was the heartland of U.S. counterinsurgency operations, which escalated steadily in the late 1960s. When local villagers were suspected of involvement in ambushes that killed U.S. soldiers, their fingers and genitals were wired up to makeshift electric-shock devices built from a crank and a field telephone. As one soldier put it, "We could do pretty much whatever we wanted to them, as long as we didn't leave scars."[94]

Discharged in 1969, John Burge returned to Chicago and joined the police department. Racial unrest was high, spurred by sharp racial turnovers in many Chicago neighborhoods. A number of police officers had also been killed in the line of duty. Over a twenty-year period, Burge presided over a police unit that systematically tortured over one hundred criminal suspects, every single one of them African American. The preferred method was a makeshift black box with two exposed wires and a crank that generated electric shocks. Created on home soil, forged in war, and institutionalized in policing, techniques of brutality and punishment migrated with Burge from

Georgia to Saigon and back to Chicago. From there, they traveled onward. A fellow detective, Richard Zuley, brought his police expertise from Chicago to Guantanamo Bay in the service of the "enhanced interrogation regime" in the current wars.[95]

Vietnam was a laboratory for "counterinsurgency techniques and equipment," as the chair of the Joint Chiefs of Staff, Maxwell Taylor, put it at the start of the war. This idea needs to be taken seriously, with respect not only to the future of overseas U.S. military action but to the future of domestic governance as well. Its harshest manifestations, including the routine use of police dogs and military-grade weaponry, riot control techniques, police intelligence gathering, violent interrogation methods, detention, torture, and assassination were disseminated domestically by the late 1960s in police responses to urban riots and rebellions. In his autobiography, published after the LA uprisings in 1992 that erupted after the acquittal of four police officers who had been taped brutally beating an unarmed black motorist, Rodney King, Daryl Gates recalls that at the end of the 1960s, "without official authorization," he and a few colleagues "began reading everything we could get our hands on concerning guerilla warfare. We watched with interest what was happening in Vietnam. We looked at military training, and in particular we studied what a group of marines, based at the Naval Armory in Chavez Ravine, were doing. They shared with us their knowledge of counterinsurgency and guerilla warfare."[96]

It remains difficult to connect the dots all the way back or to recognize, with Charles Sloane, that the hunting of "human spoor"—ordinary American police work—was developed on the "human terrain" fashioned by slavery, colonialism, and its afterlives. The very idea of distinct domains of foreign and domestic policy is a hindrance to understanding the institutionalized and distinctively renewable violence that constitutes U.S. racial formations after World War II. A focus on processes of domestic racial exclusion and reform obscures the institutional and ideological exchanges and logistical networks that connect, revitalize, and repurpose local and regional racial despotisms within and through the U.S. globalist idiom. The ideational chains, technology, and personnel transfers linking inwardly concentrated and outwardly tested state violence thickened, particularly during the Vietnam era, simultaneously renovating and reinforcing long-held colonial assumptions about group attributes and behaviors that indicate a threat. In other words, it wasn't simply the case that the war overseas came home, or that domestic racial conflicts were externalized: for both national-security and police professionals, home and world were always racially disaggregated spaces. The world as they imagined it was one of "white spots" set against a "darkened" landscape of global, civilizational disorder.

It is perhaps facile to equate "the beat" of the slave patrol with the modern patrol officer's beat. Still, former New York City police commissioner Raymond Kelley (at one time a candidate for director of the Department of Homeland Security) defended the racially discriminatory policy of stop-and-frisk on the grounds that it "instills fear" in the city's criminal element. Encouraged by a "statistics-based performance management system," the NYPD conducted a staggering 5 million stops and some 2.5 million frisks between 2002 and 2012. More than 85 percent of those stopped were black and Latino/a residents, overwhelmingly men. Only 1.5 percent resulted in the discovery of a weapon, and only 6 percent of all stops resulted in summons or arrest. Judge Shira A. Scheindlin, who ruled against this policy (before being removed from the case), noted that "the racial composition of the precinct or census tract predicts the stop rate above and beyond the crime rate" and that the population stopped and frisked is "overwhelmingly innocent."[97]

Policing what comes to be denoted or anticipated as crime—by means ranging from mild correction to justifiable homicide—was the essence of slave and frontier law. The long-standing practice of criminalizing blackness in particular helps us to recognize racial distinction as an obscured mode for instituting society that has been retained across changes in formal racial categories and degrees of inclusion. White supremacy, even as its legitimacy has waned, gave shape to a form of group-differentiated power, pleasure, and social control that accrued value and shaped U.S. institutions over a long period. The racial distribution and directionality of the legitimate violence it has exerted over those regarded as "dangerous and inconvenient" publicly confirmed it and performed its most essential work. "The majority of Negroes are of a plotting disposition, dark, sullen, malicious, revengeful, and cruel in the highest degree," Benjamin Franklin noted toward the end of his life, this time without qualification. In spite of his growing abolitionist sympathies, Franklin doubted that "mild laws could govern such a people," which is to say that he affirmed an existence beyond the civil realm that could only be held in check by violent means.[98]

War shaped the disposition of police power in the early republic. Today it is common to observe that urban policing is a field of war. These are related propositions. Both the recasting of war as policing and the licensing of police to engage in the equivalent of warfare rely on and reproduce the racial construct of an enemy population without substantive rights. In the 1990s, Eric Holder, the first black U.S. attorney for the District of Columbia, was instrumental in implementing Operation Ceasefire, a precursor to stop-and-frisk, to combat the drug trade and its associated violence. The scale of violence during this period routinely occasioned comparisons to war. As one local policeman observed, "This is a jungle; We rewrite the Constitution every day down here."[99] Just over a decade later, during his tenure as President Obama's Attorney General, Holder was called upon to issue an opinion on the use of drones in the global war on terror. Notably, he defended the practice of targeted killing in spite of occasions of collateral victims (often including guests at weddings and funerals), by likening it to the exigencies of the police who not unreasonably "prevent [a suspect's] escape by using deadly force."[100]

With the arrival of Donald Trump in the White House, the emphasis has returned to the inner war—on the border and in the central city. Trump's first executive actions were signals of the power of police discretion in the name of national security. Trump owed his own political rise to a particular kind of racist signaling toward police, from the moment when he called for the execution of the Central Park Five to his support for stop-and-frisk during his election campaign. In commenting on Black Lives Matter protests against police violence, Trump's chief strategic adviser, Steve Bannon, invoked the thinking of Benjamin Franklin, Edward Banfield, and countless others who have ascribed antisocial violence to racial differences: "Here's a thought: What if the people getting shot by the cops did things to deserve it? There are, after all, in this world, some people who are naturally aggressive and violent." Bannon and Trump have similarly defined immigration policy as falling within the ambit of war, with a reassertion of the possibility of national-origins restrictions and the widening of criminal suspicion and administrative prerogative attached to racial alienage. "These are not Jeffersonian Democrats," Bannon remarked in 2016, referring to immigrants from Muslim-majority countries to the United States and Europe. "These are not people with thousands of years of democracy in their DNA coming up here." The arc of settler freedom once again bends along the racial border.[101]

In the contemporary United States, criminal assignment and anticipatory criminalization license ever-widening practices of discrimination, in which the situational debilities and material debts that sometimes lead to unlawful acts against persons and property become the fixed property of persons. An astonishing 11 million arrests were recorded in the United States in 2015, in a period that has been marked by a decline in crime rates.[102] A felony conviction imposes a durable civil liability, blocking access to free movement, employment, education, housing, and in many cases the franchise, even for those who have completed prison sentences. Since 1990, the size of the border patrol and Immigration and Customs Enforcement (ICE) agencies has quadrupled. They now detain more than four hundred thousand people per year, operating a system of capture and mass removal that continues to expand the carceral state.

Criminality is the name given to a type of violence that threatens the social and civic order; policing is the institution that keeps such violence in check. This often appears to be a normalized and unproblematic claim. Yet this presumed normalcy partakes of a shadow lineage in which human incommensurabilities became the means of licensing and retroactively justifying extraordinary violence. Beginning after World War II, overseas war in nominally sovereign, postcolonial nations was routinely described as police action, while U.S. domestic policing was increasingly invested with the ontological urgency and moral equivalence of war. Certain (perceived) somatic and (allegedly) genetic features have long been linked with moral, aesthetic, spiritual, and intellectual defects that fix a person's place in the social hierarchy. Over several decades, antiracist and anticolonial struggles brought naturalized racial stigma under stricter public scrutiny and criticism and even into disrepute. However, inverse to these successes, the expansion of policing and criminal punishment maintained, restored, and expanded the ambit of debilities and penalties that were established long ago at the nexus of race and war.

CHAPTER TWO

From War Capitalism to Race War

Many of the black carpenters were freemen. Things seemed to be going on very well. All at once, the white carpenters knocked off, and said they would not work with free colored workmen. Their reason for this, as alleged, was, that if free colored carpenters were encouraged, they would soon take the trade into their own hands, and poor white men would be thrown out of employment. . . . My fellow apprentices very soon began to feel it degrading to them to work with me. They began to put on airs, and talk about the "niggers taking the country," saying we all ought to be killed.

Frederick Douglass, *Narrative of the Life of Frederick Douglass*, 1845

When we look at social relations which create an undeveloped system of exchange, of exchange values, and of money, or which correspond to an undeveloped degree of these, then it is clear from the outset that the individuals in such a society, although their relations appear to be more personal, enter into connection with one another only as individuals imprisoned within a certain definition, as feudal lord and vassal, landlord and serf etc. or as members of a caste, etc., or as members of an estate etc. In the money relation, in the developed system of exchange (and this semblance seduces the democrats), the ties of personal dependence, the distinctions of blood, education, etc. are in fact exploded, ripped up; . . . and individuals seem independent (this is an independence which is at bottom merely an illusion, and it is more correctly called indifference) . . . The defined-ness of individuals, which in the former case appears as a personal restriction of the individual by another, appears in the latter case as developed into an objective restriction of the individual by relations independent of him and sufficient unto themselves. . . . A closer examination of these external relations shows, however, . . . [that] these external relations are very far from being an abolition of "relations of dependence"; they are rather the dissolution of these relations into a general form; they are merely the elaboration and emergence of the general foundation of the relations of personal dependence . . . in such a way that individuals are now ruled by abstractions. . . . The abstraction, or idea, however, is nothing more than the theoretical expression of those material relations which are their lord and master.

Karl Marx, *Grundrisse*, 1857

The fifth day after my arrival I put on the clothes of a common laborer and went upon the wharves in search of work. . . . I saw a large pile of coal . . . and asked the privilege of bringing in and putting away this coal. . . . I was not long in accomplishing the job, when the dear lady put into my hand two silver half dollars. To understand the emotion which swelled my heart as I clasped this money, realizing I had no master who could take it from me, that it was mine—that my hands were my own, and could earn more of the precious coin—one must have been himself in some sense a slave.

Frederick Douglass, *Notebooks*, 1881

How should we think about the links between human bondage and capitalist abstraction, and subsequent racial differentiation within capitalism? In this chapter, my concern is to complicate a Marxist conception of capitalism as the emergence of a productive regime of superior efficiency through the economic exploitation of wage labor that is structurally separated and historically removed from forms of extraeconomic coercion and modes of accumulation whose lineages are ascribed to noncapitalist, or precapitalist, histories. Based on stories of capitalist "takeoff," this view, despite its historicist bent, often converges with a modernization paradigm. More specifically, it proposes that the development of class and property relationships in the English countryside in the sixteenth century represented a distinctive break with previous modes of accumulation and domination, resulting in the emergence of a new and radical form of market dependency and driving a shift toward radically self-augmenting productivity and capital expansion.[1]

The main problem of this approach is that it discounts contemporaneous modes of economic expansion, particularly slavery and the slave trade.[2] It also supports a wider tendency in Marxist thought to think of slavery as an antecedent to capitalism—a historical stage—thereby glossing over the startling fact, affirmed in much recent historiography, that the chattel slave was a new kind of laboring being and a new species of property born with capitalism.[3] As Sven Beckert writes, slavery, especially on North America's "cotton frontier," was not only a labor regime but also a means of allocating capital that was "tightly linked to the intensity and profits of industrial capitalism" that largely dispensed with the direct coercion of producers (i.e., laborers).[4] Marx's oeuvre, which often compares the labor of workers with that of slaves during this time, exemplifies the problem, on the one hand affirming what W. E. B. Du Bois once called the "slavery character" of capitalism in its Anglo-American ascendancy, yet on the other contributing to a problematic relegation of African slavery to a secondary role in capitalism's development that has haunted radical politics ever since.

An effect of this relegation has been the separation of race, sex, and gender domination from capitalist exploitation, conceptually and in the determination of strategic priorities for working-class unification and struggle. Ironically, this way of constituting anticapitalist struggle not only impedes the kind of solidarity required in a world characterized by "intimate and plural relationships to capital" (in the words of Dipesh Chakrabarty),[5] but it also forfeits a powerful analytic, discernible within Marx's oeuvre, that conceives capitalism as a machine whose productive expansion depends on increasing degrees of appropriation and dispossession.[6] Marx not only describes capitalism as "veiled slavery" but also takes "slave management in slave-trade countries" as a reference point for thinking about capitalism's seizure of vital life processes, including what he calls the wage worker's "premature exhaustion and death."[7] As subsequent anti-Marxist critics have argued, slavery in this register is paradoxically indispensable for thinking about capitalism and as such "unthinkable." Sometimes slavery seems "closer to capitalism's primal desire . . . than wage [labor]," while at other times it seems to have been superseded by an order of oppression whose power rests on a supposed ability to dispense with violent dominion.[8]

Strictly distinguishing between the worker's exploitation and the slave's "social death"—a common move in an important strand of contemporary black critical theorizing known as Afro-pessimism—offers no better answers to this conundrum but merely a kind of inversion in which slavery and the antiblackness that proceeds from it are the excluded ground of politics as such. This approach further alienates an understanding of slavery tied to the development of capitalism, and with it any impulse to overcome the problematic severing of racial domination and class subordination. To bridge this analytical and political divide, we might instead examine how the production of racial stigma that arises in support of chattel slavery has helped to foster the material, ideological, and affective infrastructures of appropriation and dispossession that have been indispensable to the rise of capitalism over a much longer period.

A key origin of race concepts was the differential ethical and material valuation of human subjects in slavery. Slave status was explicitly linked to race, gender, and sex within the planation household, upheld by private violence, and formally backed by state power. Wage labor (and even indentured servitude), by contrast, was increasingly nationalized and linked to a realm of public, social standing and limited state protection. As Jennifer Morgan and other historians have argued, the main legal innovation of chattel slavery in seventeenth-century North America was the assignment of hereditary force, by which captive Africans could only ever give birth to future slaves.[9] The unpaid labor of slaves (like that of all workers) rested on another crucial layer of unpaid work: social and biological reproduction conducted by women. The process of conception and reproduction under slavery, however, was violently coerced and attached to the creation of a new species of human capital, "sustained," in the words of Frederick Douglass, "by the auctioneer's block."[10] This biocapitalist innovation was in turn married to the slaveholder's power over life and death, expanding the ambit and varieties of corporeal violence that could be visited upon the bodies of slaves, up to and including homicide.[11]

The rise of the commodity form, as Marx tells us, advanced broader ideas about universal exchangeability, formal equality, and general abstraction from the particular properties of persons and things. The legal and government procedures and material processes that produced these effects, however, operated in a world of human beings who were themselves commodities (as well as instruments of credit and capital investment), and on the basis of communally articulated differences and divisions that were in turn recast under forms of abstract thinking, most notably racial science, whose lineage contaminated the development of the human sciences more generally. In this view, racial subordination might be thought of as something that materialized with the production and governance of normative class differentiation. It represents a kind of superordinate class inequality that has been structured into (certain variants of) capitalist social formation through an association of whiteness with property, citizenship, wages, and credit, along with the renewal of surplus or superexploited subjectivities and collectivities at the openly coercive, lawless, and law-defining edge of capitalist accumulation by dispossession.[12]

This is not a definitive assertion about the capitalist "origins" of race and racism. Rather, it is a suggestion that we should view racial differentiation as intrinsic to productive processes of capitalist value creation and financial

From War Capitalism to Race War

speculation. It changes an idealized game of merit and chance into a stacked deck: racially disparate fates have been manifested as devalued land, degraded labor, permanent indebtedness, and disposability. There has been no period in which racial domination has not been woven into the management of capitalist society; and yet, with important exceptions, thinkers in the Marxist tradition have largely failed to give sustained, sympathetic attention to this issue. It is the constitution and the exploitation of an objective order of market dependency, not direct racial violence and domination, that is thought to be continuously (re)productive of capitalist social and economic relations. But if land, labor, and money are fictitious commodities that make up the foundations of capitalism,[13] they also constitute what Patrick Wolfe has called the "elementary structures" of race.[14] This insight complicates tendencies within both the liberal and the Marxist intellectual traditions to think of race in terms of ascriptive fixity and thus to align racial differentiation with static notions of precapitalist particularity.[15] It highlights the modern, uniquely fabricated quality of racial distinctions as a domain for the elaboration of institutionalized coercion and related capacities for surplus extraction that persistently shadow normative processes of value formation in capitalist society.[16]

Specialization in violence was integral to early capitalism. Beckert names this "war capitalism": a form of commercial privateering backed but unimpeded by sovereign power and most fully realized in slavery, settler colonialism, and imperialism. Following Cedric Robinson, we might refer to this instead as *racial capitalism*, recognizing with Beckert that although it preceded industrialization, its technical, intellectual, and economic legacies were key to capitalism's expansion. Understanding racial differentiation as a directly violent yet also flexible and fungible mode of ascription might be more directly related to the conscription, criminalization, and disposability of poor, idle, or surplus labor—the historical process of forcibly divorcing "the producers from the means of production" that for Marx is capitalism's precondition. The creation of a pool of free wage laborers that derived from a process of "bloody legislation against the expropriated"—turning feudal peasants into beggars and vagabonds "whipped, branded, [and] tortured by laws grotesquely terrible, into the discipline necessary for the wage system"—closely parallels slavery in forcibly removing producers of value from their prior webs of social relations. "The starting point of the development that gave rise both to the wage-laborer and the capitalist," Marx writes, "was the enslavement of the worker. The advance made consisted in a change in the form of . . . servitude."[17]

As capitalism becomes what Marx calls "a never-ending circle," this dynamic changes in important ways. Capital now requires that labor both appear and disappear. What Marx calls "the tendency of capital to simultaneously increase the laboring population as well as to reduce constantly its necessary part (constantly to posit a part of it as reserve)" acquires a more or less automatic, even natural character.[18] "The disposable industrial reserve army," he writes, in another oblique reference to chattel slavery, "belongs to capital just as absolutely as if the latter had bred it at its own costs." While the initial barrier to forming a pool of wage laborer "could only be swept away by violent means," the mechanism for creating labor surplus develops into what Marx terms an "economic law," one that divides labor into "overwork" and "enforced idleness" as "a means of enriching individual capitalists." This process internalizes competition and insecurity among workers and in doing so "completes the despotism of capital." Marx goes on to detail various forms taken by the "relative surplus population . . . the floating, the latent and the stagnant, or lowest strata," which are composed of "vagabonds, criminals and prostitutes . . . the actual lumpenproletariat . . . who succumb to their incapacity for adaptation."[19] In these passages, Marx recognizes capitalism's active production of the working class as contingent and heterogeneous. He also reserves some of his most scathing and scornful prose for these degraded, unwaged laborers—those who are marked for premature death yet disrupt pretensions toward class simplification or unitary proletarian consciousness.[20]

As Marx writes, mature capitalism exists when "the silent compulsion of economic relations sets the seal on the domination of the capitalist over the worker." At this point, "direct force, extra-economic force is still of course used, but only in exceptional cases."[21] In this moment, the proximity of wage labor to the violent conditions that produced its dependency gives way to a working class divided into those whose productive capacities have been harnessed by the industrial machine and those whom Marx describes as "sharply differentiated from the industrial proletariat . . . a recruiting ground for thieves and criminals of all kinds."[22] This image of working-class differentiation cuts against the grain of Marx's radical recuperation of the abject term *proletariat* —literally, those left without reserves—to represent collective struggle. It also coincides with his periodic recourse to a version of progressive historicism that appears to be wedded to capitalism's civilizing potential, and which sacrifices his own prior discovery of the heterogeneity of forms of labor and its political meaning. The state-sanctioned force and violence originally required to create wage labor, moreover, does not disappear: it is retained in the forms of hierarchy and competition between workers, in the social requirements of policing unwaged labor that has migrated to poverty and the informal economy, and in imperial and nationalist interpellations of the urban and metropolitan working classes.

Inattention to these political effects, which frame but appear no longer to define relations of production, has led to confusions among Marxists between forms of domination and stages of development in which the unevenness of unpaid, disposable and surplus labor is opposed to the orderly fluctuations of waged and reserved labor. The exceptional cases in which direct force is used precisely include colonial spaces where slavery and other forms of coerced labor took root and where, Marx writes, "artificial means," including "police methods," are required "to set on the right road that law of supply and demand which works automatically everywhere else."[23] Marx's considerations on colonialism and slavery as matrices of "so-called primitive accumulation" here highlight the value and the limitation of his oeuvre for thinking about the development of racial ascription or the continuing salience of race as a relationship anchored in violence, dominion, and dependency. Marx skewers the bourgeois fairytale of a virtuous phase of so-called original accumulation achieved through the thrift and ingenuity of a "frugal elite," which condemned the unfortunate majority to a situation in which they would be forced (in Marx's words) "to sell . . . their own skins." In oft-quoted lines from *Capital*, Marx emphasizes the murderous origins of capitalism in a determinate history of Europe's armed commercial expansion, colonialism, racial slavery, and genocide: "The discovery of gold and silver in America, the extirpation, enslavement, and entombment in mines of the indigenous population of that continent, the beginnings of the conquest and plunder of India, and the conversion of Africa into a preserve for the commercial hunting of black-skins are all things which characterize the dawn of the era of capitalist production. These idyllic proceedings are the chief moments of primitive accumulation."[24]

An enduring historical and theoretical challenge posed by this sketch is how to interpret the temporal and conceptual cleavages between this singular and inceptive moment—"the dawn of the era of capitalist production," reliant on force and violence—and the era of capitalist accumulation proper that "automatically" enshrines as its logic the "silent compulsion" of market discipline that dispenses with extraeconomic coercion. In this New World iteration, "primitive accumulation" is not yet capitalism: it is plunder. The relationship that it bears to the more fundamental process of divorcing the producer from the means of production remains unclear. Marx's analysis in some ways blurs the distinction, for example, in his parallel references to "commerce in skins." Yet New World primitive accumulation is an indictment of capitalism, not an explanation of its dynamics. Much like the nineteenth-century workers who spoke of wage slavery to distinguish themselves from rather than align themselves with racial slaves, moreover, Marx (who knew better) suggests that a focus on the direct coercion of the producers not only misidentifies the source of capital accumulation but also deflects the central challenge of anticapitalist politics by reinforcing the "illusion" of independence and freedom proffered by capitalism's more "developed system of exchange." He calls this the semblance of freedom that "seduces the democrats."[25]

This passage highlights Marx's tendency to characterize political rights and civic inclusion as illusions. Yet, ironically, Marx's effort to undermine what he calls the "rule of abstractions" depends on the opposition between ascribed status and abstract labor. In the second epigraph to this chapter, from the *Grundrisse*, Marx presents ascribed status as a kind of immobility or "imprisonment," in contrast to wage labor, in which "individuals seem independent." The specific terms of ascription—feudal, caste, estate, and blood, to which we might add *slave*—recapitulate oppositions that animate liberal social-contract theory more generally, counterposing plural forms of arbitrary power and forms of hierarchical, nonvoluntarist, social ordering with the universalization of ostensibly modern, mobile, and dynamic forms of contract and free exchange. Where the majority of liberal thinkers saw education as an engine of meritocratic distinction and class mobility, Marx's analysis moves in the opposite direction, emphasizing capitalism's leveling *indifference* to any prior social condition, status, or standing. It does so, however, in an effort to unmask this "seeming" or "apparent" freedom from direct coercion, manifest hierarchy, and civic privation and reveal it as the grounds of a more extensive, universalizing domination under the terms of capitalist *abstraction*, which he writes, constitutes the "general form" and "theoretical expression of those material relations which are lord and master."[26]

Here, Marx's analysis leads to an inattention, even indifference, to how capital actually establishes new lines of social and historical genesis based

on the differentiation between free labor and less-than-free labor. Specifically, it overlooks how racial, ethnic, and gender hierarchies in laboring
populations are retained as a mechanism of labor discipline and surplus
appropriation, and even as a measure of capitalism's progressivism, insofar
as it purports to render such distinctions anachronistic in the long run. Marx
contrasts not only the free worker and the slave, but also the different relationships that the English yeomanry and former slaves have to capitalism.
For the emancipated slave, Marx writes, "the capitalist relationship appears
to be an improvement in one's position on the social scale. . . . It is otherwise
when the independent peasant or artisan becomes a wage-laborer. What a
gulf there is between the proud yeomanry of England . . . and the English
agricultural laborer!" While the yeomanry may have fallen further from
their initial station, they recuperate pride in a different form. "The consciousness (or better: the idea) of free self-determination, of liberty, makes a
much better worker of the [free worker] than the [slave], as does, the related
feeling (sense) of responsibility. *He learns to control himself, in contrast to the
slave, who needs a master.*"[27] As Marx notes elsewhere, this explains why
emancipated slaves reverted to self-provisioning, regarding "loafing (indul-
gence and idleness) as the real luxury good. . . . Wealth confronts direct
forced labor not as capital, but rather as a relation of domination. . . . which
can never create general industriousness."[28]

This differentiation between slavery and capitalism widens the gulf
between slaves and workers. As Marx writes in an axiomatic statement,
"Capital ceases to be capital without free-wage labor . . . as its general creative basis."[29] In this view, slavery's inefficiencies, including inhibiting the
possibility of increasing labor productivity through continuous reductions
of socially necessary labor time, actively *impeded* the development of capitalism.[30] Curiously, Marx, who persistently compares capitalism with slavery in order to undermine what he calls "a liberalism so full of consideration
for 'capital,'"[31] here yields to his opponents' intellectual tendencies, in

which capitalist social relations are framed through what Jairus Banaji calls "a seductive dichotomy of 'free' and 'unfree' labor, as if these categories were really opposites."[32] Marx's remarks on the affect, cognition, and habit-formation of free workers and freed slaves reinforces distinctions between them, even linking them to prior conditions of servitude. While the English workers' loss of customary rights, and subsequent proximity to the engines of value creation and the dispositions formed therein, places them in the vanguard of class struggle, both slave and ex-slave remain passive figures (inextricably linked), unable to connect to history's forward movement.[33]

Marx of course notes: "In the United States of America, every independent workers' movement was paralyzed as long as slavery disfigured a part of the republic. Labor in a white skin cannot emancipate itself, where in the black it is branded."[34] Yet slave emancipation, for Marx, was a prelude to a unified working-class struggle toward the eight-hour day. It is difficult to imagine Marx having any insight into social dynamics and movements that proceeded directly from slavery. C. L. R. James famously observed of the Haitian slaves who revolted at the end of the eighteenth century that "they were closer to a modern proletariat than any other group of workers in existence at that time" and capable of enacting a "thoroughly prepared and organized mass movement."[35] Thinking about the other side, his friend Eric Williams warned that the "outworn interests [of slavery], whose bankruptcy smells to heaven in historical perspective, exercise an obstructionist and disruptive effect" into the future, based upon the "powerful services it had previously rendered and the entrenchment previously gained."[36]

In part the limitation derives from the fact that Marx remains—even in his critical stance toward it—indebted to a republican conception of freedom defined as political opposition to arbitrary power. This conception fails to fully apprehend what the grounding of freedom in chattel slavery and its violent modalities of household rule meant for the development of capitalist freedoms going forward. Marx holds onto a problematic distinction between precapitalist slavery, which has what he terms a "patriarchal character," and Atlantic slavery, which was "drawn into the world market dominated by the capitalist mode of production."[37] However, when he formulates an opposition between (an illusory) political freedom and (a metaphorical) economic slavery, Marx is thinking of the earlier form. The Marx-inspired critique of capitalism, like popular nineteenth-century republican critiques of wage slavery, thus unwittingly become what Mary Nyquist calls "an important conductor of racialization. . . . that severs or weakens the "free" citizen's affective ties with enslaved Africans" and others imagined to be lodged within dependent, privative, ascribed identities.[38] Put differently, although Marx wants to overturn the idea that capitalism does away with servitude, when he adopts a Eurocentric historicism, he participates in a broader discourse in which slavery comes to be discussed less in terms of its material relationship to capitalism than as a kind of negative politicization, a form of insult and humiliation, a lack of political standing and social honor. Capitalist indifference and Marxist indifference in this sense collude ideologically in consolidating work and citizenship in a technique of governance based upon distinct domains of political identity and hierarchies of concern: a division between the capitalist power and despotic power, the former a type of public power that deepens dependency and conceals that dependency (for the worker), and the latter a mode of privation that is anachronistic and unable to achieve public standing.

Marx describes both "direct private violence" and organized state violence as the "midwife" of a capitalist mode of production, whose development, maturity, and superior productivity are predicated on an ability to dispense with cruder means. Capitalism is still a violent system, but its violence is immanent within a labor relation that no longer depends on coercive force. Not only is direct coercion a fetter on productivity gains, but the absence of coercion, in both legal and ideological terms, is also one of the ideological bulwarks of capitalist domination.[39] Given the sexual and gendered cut of slavery and colonization, the metaphor of the "midwife"—someone whose reproductive labor is essential but temporary—retains a certain resonance for framing the relationship of slavery and capitalism. The Marxist view of capitalism as a progressive historical force and a superior mode of production and social reproduction tends to either obscure or freeze our vision of the gendered racial violence indispensable to its "birth" as something that is essentially static, nonhistorical, and nonreproductive —a finite historical event whose traces in the present are vestigial and anachronistic. Capitalism may "come into the world dripping from head to toe in blood," as Marx writes, but it manages to clean itself up. The true novelty of its forward march, particularly on the narrow terrain of the free labor contract, depends on an abstract, autonomous, and immanent reproductive capacity.

Marx is hesitant, even ambivalent, on this issue. The English economist Malachy Postlethwayt, whom Marx read, was perhaps the first to describe the "African trade" as a "prop and support" of British free trade. Marx takes up this figure in various forms: for example, when he writes that "the veiled slavery of the wageworkers in Europe needed, for its pedestal, slavery pure and simple in the new world."[40] Elsewhere Marx recognizes without illusions that the "business of slavery is conducted by capitalists," that slavery only "appears as an anomaly opposite the bourgeois system itself," and that through the cotton trade, "the civilized horrors of overwork [have been] grafted onto the barbaric horrors of slavery and serfdom."[41] Indeed, one of his clearest statements on slavery was penned two decades before he wrote *Capital* and evinces what might be considered a more clear-sighted abolitionism, one that sees capitalism and slavery as conjoined within a single, global space: "Direct slavery is just as much the pivot of bourgeois industry as machinery, credits, etc. Without slavery you have not cotton; without cotton you have not modern industry. It is slavery that has given the colonies their value; it is the colonies that have created world trade, and it is world trade that is the pre-condition of large-scale industry. Thus slavery is an economic category of the greatest importance."[42]

By these lights we might begin by rewriting Marx's axiomatic statement, "Capital ceases to be capital without wage labor . . . as its general creative basis," in the following way: *Capital ceases to be capital without the ongoing differentiation of free labor and slavery, waged labor and unpaid labor as its general creative basis.* This differentiation provides the indispensable material and ideological support for the development of capitalism. The distinction between freedom and slavery operates in the interests of capital. Only by understanding the indebtedness of freedom to slavery, and the entanglement and co-constitution of the two, can we attain a critical perspective adequate to a genuinely anticapitalist politics.

The moment when Marx refuses the historicist separation of capitalism and slavery sharpens the argument that capitalist development represents a more general and generalizing form of domination. It actually pulls our thinking toward rather than away from the legacy of slave capitalism and capitalist slavery, and toward enduring articulations of race and capital, the problematic that Cedric Robinson has termed "racial capitalism."[43] Temporal cleavage gives way to simultaneity, a rejection of what Marx calls the "logical formula" that would regard coexisting, mutually supportive elements as sequential.[44] Only later does Marx characterize this relationship in teleological terms, describing "the incompleteness" of the "development of capitalist production," which joins to "modern evils, . . . inherited evils, arising from the passive survival of archaic and outmoded modes of production with their accompanying train of anachronistic social and political relations."[45] But the marking of certain relations as passive or anachronistic remains problematic. What if this incompleteness is a permanent feature of capitalism? Moreover, what happens when those supposedly passive or archaic modalities most closely linked to direct coercion not only are retained within the labor process but also shape the formation of the state?

From War Capitalism to Race War

North American slavery was a self-perpetuating mode of social reproduction. Outgrowing the externalities of the Atlantic slave trade, it sustained itself by a reproductive capacity built on violent control over the wombs of slave women and by the seizure and murderous depopulation of aboriginal lands. Nor did slavery simply wither away: ending it required a war of cataclysmic proportions. What followed for the majority of freed blacks was an era still marked by direct violence and coercion of labor under varieties of penal enforcement. Freeing slaves enlarged the instrumental and popular political ambit of racism as a tool of labor discipline (divide and rule), as a means of introducing new forms of labor coercion (so-called coolie labor), and as a weapon of class struggle (in which access to wage labor and labor organization was defended as a white privilege), and as an argument that great nations held colonies overseas. It also inaugurated an era of state and private violence that seized control over black household formation, sexuality, and embodiment through lynching, racial terror, penal labor, and enforced segregation in the interests of preserving and reproducing a racial-capitalist political economy with global implications. As Du Bois memorably wrote in his magisterial *Black Reconstruction in America* (which adopted a Marxist idiom), the "echo of that philanthropy which had abolished the slave trade, was beginning a new industrial slavery of black and brown and yellow workers in Africa and Asia."[46]

If the system built on racialized chattel slavery is understood as a variant of capitalism, might we not make the stronger claim that the configuration of capitalism that develops from it in turn develops racism as a dimension of its general form? If this iteration of capitalism, as part of its logic, reproduces divisions between productive humanity and disposable humanity, might we not further recognize how this very division has been mediated by the shifting productions of race as a logic of depreciation linked to, first, proletarianization as a condition of "wageless life"—the norm of capitalism insofar as it produces radical market dependency and surplus labor— and, second, the regular application of force and violence against those parts deemed outside the civically ordered world?[47] Finally, to the extent to which direct compulsion and organized violence are retained within capitalist social formations, might their conceptual import lie less in their relationship to the exploitation of labor and the extraction of surplus value than in their contribution to the development of cutting-edge techniques of control, surveillance, and sanctioned killing within the governance of capitalist social relations, both in defense of private property and in the active management of zones of insecurity and existential threat?

Within the Marxist tradition, Rosa Luxemburg comes closest to grasping the fluid nature of coercion, noting that "the accumulation of capital, seen as a historical process, employs force as a permanent weapon, not only at its genesis, but further down to the present day." It is precisely the failure of capitalism's universalization, particularly its dependence upon "non-capitalist strata and social organization . . . existing *side by side*," she writes, that produces "peculiar combinations between the modern wage system and primitive authority" and enables "far more ruthless measures than could be tolerated under purely capitalist social conditions." She cites as an example "the first genuinely capitalist branch of production, the English cotton industry."[48] What still needs jettisoning are the lingering references to a "pure capitalism" and "primitive authority" that reinstall the very oppositions that she otherwise challenges. Luxemburg echoes Marx's comment that "war developed earlier than peace . . . in the interior of bourgeois society" and anticipates Foucault: "A battlefront runs through the whole of society, continuously and permanently." This points to the institutionalization of coercion (specifically militarization) within capitalism, not only in the retention of the option of "primitive accumulation" but also as the guarantor of labor discipline and the disposability of surplus populations at the shifting borders of capitalism's circulatory movement (that is, global expansion).[49]

Civil society, as both Foucault and Marx argue in different ways, is the exemplary conceptual object of capitalism as a realm of (economic) freedom that fundamentally modifies the terms of (political) authority. If Marx is concerned with demystifying this process by suggesting the subordination of sovereign political status to economic tyranny, Foucault at times emphasizes the real limitation that market freedom places on the political life of the state. "The condition of governing well," Foucault writes, "is that freedom, or certain forms of freedom, are really respected."[50] The idea of a totalizing police power gives way to a form of policing focused on the prevention of "disorders" and "disasters" and the management of their probabilities. At the same time, both Marx and Foucault turn away from and exceptionalize the phenomenon of the bloody, annihilationist violence that haunts the modern episteme. In an echo of Marx's account of the diminution of overt force, Foucault, for example, aligns Nazi genocide with the retention of an otherwise atavistic sovereign right to kill as an "eruption of racism" within a field of government normatively defined by imperatives of population management and biopolitical growth. Like Marx, he ultimately forecloses the question of how to account for the retention of this always-waning, quasi-hallucinatory genocidal force.[51]

What needs to be considered here is not only spectacular violence but also the repetitive, incremental, slow, or concealed violence of appropriation. If socially necessary labor time constitutes the meaning of value for capital, as Jason W. Moore writes, such value is embedded in a "web of life" that capital insistently appropriates as necessary for the exploitation of formally free wage labor. Marxist theory, which defines capitalism in terms of economic exploitation and the production of surplus value that structurally separates economic compulsion from direct domination, fails to recognize what may be an even greater novelty of capitalism: the consistent extraeconomic processes of appropriation by which capital is able to "identify, secure and channel unpaid work outside the commodity system into the circuit of capital." As Moore writes, citing a longstanding Marxist feminist claim, "The appropriation of accumulated unpaid work in human form," including the labors of biological and social reproduction, provides the real historical conditions for "socially necessary labor time." A "narrow sphere" of productive relations, in this view, depends upon a "more expansive sphere of appropriation," in which cheap human and extrahuman nature "are taken up by commodity production."[52]

Embodied in the figures of the slave, the migrant worker, the household worker, and the unemployed, among others, appropriation encompasses forms of both coercion and ethical and political devaluation that are inseparable from capitalist processes of valorization. Thus, rather than opposing notions of absolute sovereignty and its power over life and death with ideas of a biopolitically productive materialist history, we might instead recognize how the two have been braided together through the conquest and commodification of black bodies (as well as the conquest and commodification of indigenous lands) that for Marx constitutes the moment of "so-called primitive accumulation." We might extend this idea of appropriation to include the unpaid work of women the world over, the accumulated unpaid work represented by labor migration, and war capitalism's differentiation between the internally ordered, rule-bound spaces of production and market exchange and the exceptional zones of armed appropriation. The latter are domains not only for enacting "plunder"—that is, primitive accumulation (or accumulation by dispossession)—but also for developing cutting-edge procedures and commercially fungible police and military infrastructures: the slaver's double-entry account book, the colonial railroad, the border control zone, freeway removals, forward military bases, and supermax prisons. Such innovations have generally proceeded insofar as they are unfettered by legally protected human being, thus creating the material basis for advancing new prejudices built upon the old.[53]

Returning to the problem of slavery, we might recognize how the supposed diminution of extraeconomic coercion has as its counterpart the retention and elaboration of logics of racialization, defined first through the war-slavery doctrine (by Hugo Grotius, Thomas Hobbes, John Locke, and others) and later in terms of ideas of race war, at the site of capitalism's recurrent crises and never-completed universalization. Actual slavery, which Locke describes as the continuation of a precivil state of war that develops into a relationship between a lawful conqueror and a captive, is retained for conceptualizing freedom as the end of *political slavery* and arbitrary rule within Euro-American colonial contexts. Here, the slaveholder's power over life and death is transferred to the sovereign political subject, possessively invested in whiteness. Meanwhile, racialization as a normative logic begins to "generate heritable liberties along with heritable slavery," as servility and incapacity (conceived as either inherent to or derived from the condition of enslavement) are elaborated as explanations for subjects whose very existence counts not only as an aggression against freedom but also against life itself, and who therefore can be permanently sequestered, governed without rights, or killed with impunity.[54]

As a final illustration, I turn briefly to the archives of black radicalism, by way of the passages from Frederick Douglass presented as epigraphs to this chapter. In the first passage, published three years before the *Communist Manifesto,* Douglass marks a new production of race at the moment of a transition from one labor regime to another: from slavery to wage labor. In Douglass's account, black entry into an order of abstract equivalence defined by the wage relation is understood by whites as a threat to their own wage-earning capacity. This threat is in turn narrated as a loss of country—or sovereign capacity—which calls forth the fantasy of a war of extermination against the offending party. This moment in Douglass's text is interesting for the ways in which it illuminates race making as a social, political, and affective process that eventually constitutes race as an irreducibly warlike relationship. Black and white, slave and free already exist as distinctions. But, at first Douglass tells us, the presence of the "free colored" poses no special problem. What initiates the shift "all at once"?

We might initially read the passage as confirming the conventional wisdom of theorists of racially segmented labor markets. However, in emphasizing that "things seemed to be going very well," and noting white fears of potential black monopolization of the trade as mere "allegation," Douglass is in fact doing more than establishing antiblack racism as a historically given condition that automatically reproduces itself. What is it about the mere presence of a "black carpenter" that threatens a total loss of livelihood? Why is the sense of threat so readily amplified and transferred to the thresholds of political identity and national subjectivity ("niggers taking the country")? Finally, how is the affect (fear, anger) translated into a genocidal impulse ("we all ought to be killed")? Put simply, how does the conjunction of race and labor become a conjunction of race and war? I suggest that race war, far from being an afterthought, in fact controls and mediates the entire sequence of events that Douglass describes. Indeed, one of the most striking aspects of Douglass's *Narrative* is the ways in which he consistently describes slavery as something other than the theft of black labor, emphasizing instead its violent, totalizing claims on black life.

In explaining these events, Douglass intentionally highlights the double threat of wagelessness and political degradation that the considered presence of the "black carpenter" evokes. In turn, he depicts the production of race (in this case, whiteness) as a process of binding juridical status and despotic power—keeping the "country," "putting on airs," and arrogating expansive, extracivil rights to kill. He defines all of this, moreover, in terms of a transition from slavery to capitalism. Generic whiteness is revealed as a specific relationship to blackness in its relationship to capital, one that seeks to banish the specter of wageless life evoked by both the prior association of blacks with slavery and actual conditions of market dependency. It is worth recalling in this context Du Bois's famous description of whiteness in *Black Reconstruction* as "a *public* and psychological wage." The association of whiteness with wages through the monopolization of fields of employment has been widely discussed. Less fully examined has been how the elevation of whiteness to the threshold of nationality actively links freedom with the management of public authority, specific mechanisms of violence, and an operational notion of (racial) nemesis.

The third epigraph of the chapter, from Douglass's *Notebooks*, offers a final amplification of my (admittedly provisional) efforts here to rethink the relationship between race and capital. It is tempting, on initial reading, to interpret Douglass's words *against* the claims developed here. After all, by taking on the garb of the common laborer, Douglass seems precisely to affirm as directly *emancipatory* the movement from household slavery to wage labor. But Douglass is actually making a more specific claim about what the capitalist wage relation looks and feels like from the standpoint of slavery. The feeling of joy ("the emotion which swelled my heart") produced by recognition of self-possession ("my hands were my own"), and the possibility of accumulating "more of the precious coin" are in this view entirely contingent on the prior condition of enslavement ("one must have been in some sense a slave"). The fact that Douglass escaped wearing a disguise paid for by Anna Murray, a free black woman, with savings from her domestic labor further deepens the intersectionality and interdependency on which any so-called freedom depends.

In both Douglass and Marx, the critical sense of the violence of proletarianization and market dependency (in transitions to capitalism) is retained most directly in reference to slavery (and, for Douglass, in black life that emerges from it). In 1855, Douglass observed, "The slaveholders with a craftiness peculiar to themselves, by encouraging the enmity of the poor laboring white man against the blacks, succeed in making the said white man almost as much a slave as the black slave himself. . . . The white slave has taken from him by indirection, what the black slave has taken from him directly, and without ceremony." In 1870, Marx elaborated on the antagonism of English toward Irish workers as "artificial, kept alive and intensified by the press . . . much the same as that of the 'poor whites' to the Negroes in the former slave states of the USA."[55] As Du Bois would later argue, the "real modern labor problem" lies closer to the condition of racial dispossession than to the prospects of normative, wage-earning stability. Capitalist freedoms and the enjoyment of them (life, liberty, and the pursuit of happiness) in turn require us continuously to "put on airs" and to cultivate a generous rage against the prospect of a bare life.

Atlantic slavery was the cornerstone of capitalist exploitation, appropriation, and dispossession over several centuries. It also bequeathed an enduring devaluation of black life. The production of race and class has depended on managing valuations and devaluations of black social and biological reproduction in the interests of capital accumulation and its social reproduction. From medical experimentation to crime statistics, debt peonage, labor market exclusion, rent harvesting, heightened toxic exposure, infrastructure deprivation and spatial isolation, usurious credit terms and financial predation, the racial differentiation thought to be extrinsic to capitalism since the end of slavery has in fact been both directly productive of value and integral to the technical development of capitalism, where new specializations in violence are field tested free from ethical judgment, setting off new rounds in which peoples separated from land, resources, and social bonds can be consumed in the interests of capital accumulation.

Marx recognizes that capital is built not only on its contradiction with exploited labor but also in a contradictory relationship to life itself. Capital accumulation spurs population increase and also voraciously depletes living labor. The constant, violent dislocation of these two processes requires constant management in the form of police and military solutions—that is, directly coercive interventions. It spurs forms of moral, temporal, and spatial sequestration that become part of the framework of crisis management, through which the simultaneous production of growth and death can be viewed less as a contradiction than as a necessary dimension of historical

From War Capitalism to Race War

progress.[56] Racism's toxicity, in this view, is a by-product of capitalist abstraction and a material event. It is as much our inheritance as is the environmental degradation resulting from capitalism's appropriation of cheap nature. The relationship of capitalism and slavery is in this way far-reaching. By exposing both the heterogeneity and the proximity of violence and economy, it also reveals "the broken time of politics and strategy."[57] Rather than a disorientation, it is the starting point for any reconstruction of anticapitalist politics.

CHAPTER THREE

The Afterlife of Fascism

Here there can be no special pleading. Here are considerations of equity and rectitude and moral right rendered void and without warrant and here are the views of the litigants despised. Decisions of life and death, of what shall be and what shall not, beggar all questions of right. In elections of these magnitudes are all lesser ones subsumed.

> Cormac McCarthy, *Blood Meridian, or the Evening Redness in the West* (1985)

Our nation is still somewhat sad, but we're angry. There's a certain level of blood lust, but we won't let it drive our reaction. We're steady, clear-eyed and patient, but pretty soon we'll have to start displaying scalps.

> George W. Bush, October 6, 2001

In an influential essay that supported the 2003 U.S. invasion of Iraq, Michael Ignatieff defended the idea of a U.S. empire on the grounds that it was not "like those of times past, built on conquest and the white man's burden."[1] There is a long tradition of rejecting parallels between the United States and prior forms of empire, which are understood to be predicated on coercion and colonization. Starting with the Jeffersonian ideal of the United States as an "empire for liberty," political consent and self-government have been continuously reaffirmed as constant and timeless American political virtues. Following "Indian removal" and on the eve of the U.S. war with

Mexico, for example, the expansionist pundit John O'Sullivan claimed that "no instance of aggrandizement or lust for territory has stained our annals. No nation has been despoiled by us, no country laid desolate, no people overrun."[2] Half a century later, reflecting on a new period of overseas expansion and war, including long occupations of Haiti and the Philippines, President Woodrow Wilson remarked, "If we have been obliged by circumstances . . . to take territory . . . we have considered it our duty to administer that territory not for ourselves, but for . . . those to whom it does really belong." Announcing the introduction of U.S. ground forces into Vietnam fifty years later, Lyndon Johnson believed the proposition was self-evident: "We have no military, political, or territorial ambitions in the area."[3]

If there is one constant in the history of U.S. expansionism, it is this discourse of disavowal. The problem of reconciling free development and democratic consent with offensive war and long-term military occupation, however, was as knotty two centuries ago as it is now. A principal means of resolution under settler expansionism was to define the "people" who were being despoiled, overrun, or occupied as nonpersons or subpersons —racial or quasi-racial threats to be eradicated or quarantined—and to describe the process of settlement as the execution of a providential design operating, as President Andrew Jackson put it, "beyond the reach of human laws."[4] Under the influence of liberal progressivism and exigencies of overseas colonization, the harshest versions of white supremacy were recast in the language of racial uplift and "benevolent assimilation." Still, the unpredictable recalcitrance of the natives led at least one U.S. field commander to warn in 1899 that "it may be necessary to kill half the Filipinos in order that the remaining half of the population may be advanced to a higher place of life than their present semi-barbarous state affords."[5]

During the twentieth century it became the self-appointed task of U.S. state power to recast the classic trope of imperialist historicism—where colonized subjects were eternally consigned to history's waiting room—as a relationship between mature and emergent nationalisms.[6] Yet even if we repress the legacy of Vietnam and ignore the spate of Wild West clichés George W. Bush employed to announce America's new wars, the stories from Guantanamo Bay, Abu Ghraib, and Fallujah mock the U.S. fantasy of global rule without colonial violence and submission. In December 2003, just a few months after "liberating" the Iraqi people, it was deemed necessary to convert the Iraqi town of Abu Hishma into a strategic hamlet ringed with razor wire and checkpoints, where all residents who wanted to travel to and from their village had to produce identity cards (printed only in English). As the Fourth Infantry company commander, Captain Todd Brown, explained, "You've got to understand the Arab mind; the only thing they understand is force."[7]

In the haze of fluctuating and failed rationales for the Iraq War, it was easy to overlook or mitigate its casual racism. Such racism was not predicated on strict conceptions of biological difference: it could just as easily draw on intellectually respectable notions of cultural incommensurability. Supplementing a condescending tutelary discourse about the Iraqi capacity for freedom and democracy (personified by the "good Muslim") was an insistent, Orientalist suspicion of menace and disability (in the form of the "bad Muslim").[8] A range of publications, from Bernard Lewis's widely disseminated ideas about "Muslim rage" to Raphael Patai's cultural anthropology *The Arab Mind*—studied by neoconservative intellectuals and military planners for its insights into the particular receptivity and vulnerability of Arab men to disciplining force, shame, and sexual humiliation—bear out Étienne Balibar's assertion that "neo-racist ideologues are not mystical heredity theorists, but realist technicians of social psychology."[9]

From its inception, the Iraq War conflated ethnic and religious signifiers—"Arab" and "Muslim"—with a politico-military label that refuses to distinguish civilian populations from military targets: "terrorism."[10] This trope was advanced through insistent, albeit factually discredited, claims by U.S. officials of links between the former Iraqi regime and Al Qaeda, and the assertion by George W. Bush that "by fighting the terrorists over there," we were fore-stalling the day when we might have to fight them "at home." Thus the *New York Times* columnist Thomas Friedman remarkably described "the real reason" for the Iraq war in the following way: "After 9/11 America needed to hit someone in the Arab-Muslim world. Afghanistan wasn't enough because a terrorism bubble had built up over there—a bubble that posed a real threat to the open societies of the West. . . . The only way to puncture that bubble was for American soldiers, men and women, to go into the heart of the Arab-Muslim world, house to house, and make clear that we are ready to kill, and to die, to prevent our society from being undermined by this terrorism bubble."[11]

Insinuating an essential relation between the "Arab-Muslim world" and "terrorism" (or often just "terror") broadly legitimated an unlimited, unilat-eral extension of U.S. state violence otherwise not permissible within ratio-nal, evidentiary discourses about security and interests and in apparent contradiction with U.S. professions of democratic idealism. The implication was that those who rejected this path resisted the commonsense and gut instincts of masses of Americans. As Bush put it in his 2005 inaugural address, the response to 9/11 redefined the nation as "a single hand over a single heart."[12] Thus, while the sovereign violence of a democratic people was preceded and conditioned by a range of quasi-racist, Orientalist tropes and assumptions, it was the "acts and acting outs" that fabricated new racialized divisions, institutions, and collectivities. Most important, a racist logic of endless war has been manifested and codified in the production of a new lexicon of power and euphemism for its targets: "ghost detainees," "extraordinary rendition," "unlawful combatants," "enhanced interroga-tion," and, in a chilling new epithet coined by armed drone operators, "squirters" (referring to the image of bodies exploding on electronic screens). Such terms denote those who stand outside the protections of any law, who possess no rights that the U.S. sovereign is bound to respect, and who are thus bodies that can be tortured or killed with impunity.

We are left to wonder if somehow the fabrication of nemesis and the creation of a new field of violent state action were not a major part of the point and purpose of the inauguration of a new long war. How otherwise do we explain the fact that the Bush administration was creating rationales for torture and ways to immunize U.S. interrogators from potential war-crimes prosecutions before there was even anyone to torture? How should we understand the pattern whereby each official disavowal of torture was followed by a reaffirmation of the policy upending the Geneva Conventions to create categories of war prisoners without legal status, along with promotions for the legal architects of the policy? False information about Iraq's links to Al Qaeda—based on a single source obtained by the CIA through rendition and torture of the terrorist suspect Ibn Shayk al-Libi, captured in Afghanistan—subsequently cast a pall over the entire series of events that the 9/11 attacks and the U.S. military response to them set in motion. To this day, no one has been held accountable for the lies that led to almost a decade of war in Iraq. The political failure to close the prison camp at Guantanamo Bay, the most notorious symbol of rights violations, is another case in point: of the 780 detainees from forty different countries held there over the past decades (of whom 55 remain), only 3 have been convicted of crimes against the United States. Despite these figures and the absence of any evidence that the discovery of any of the thirty or more terror plots that have been foiled since then resulted from rendition or "enhanced interrogation," the debate about torture's efficacy continues, and President Trump has promised to ramp up the action at Guantanamo again.[13]

The exemption of the U.S. president and his proxies from international and domestic laws governing war crimes such as torture was less an expression of a specifically functional or instrumental rationality than a symbolic act aiming to expand the zone where power operates without rights, the main corollary of which is the constitution of new subjects without rights. One of President Bush's initial responses to torture allegations in June 2004 was particularly revealing: "Look, I'm going to say it one more time. Maybe I can be more clear. The instructions went out to our people to adhere to law. That ought to comfort you. We're a nation of law. We adhere to laws. We have laws on the books. You might look at these laws. And that might provide comfort to you."[14] What is remarkable about this statement is its suggestion that "laws on the books" are primarily meant to be a palliative to passive, rights-bearing subjects within the imperium, even as it posits the U.S. sovereign as someone who is clearly distinct from those laws, beneficently aloof, offering instruction, dispensing comfort, with no need of rights, counseling adherence to law but with an implied capacity to revoke, peel away, or suspend the law as well.[15]

Rights, in this view, are granted at the dispensation of the sovereign executive. The problem that emerged was that the right not to be tortured and the right not to be enslaved are internationally recognized as nonnegotiable human rights. In other words, there can be no legal right to torture or to enslave: torture and slavery are always and everywhere crimes. This helps to explain the tortured logic of the now-infamous torture memos. The legal architects of the policy parsed existing definitions of torture so finely that common standards, like the infliction of "severe mental pain and suffering," were reduced to "pain equivalent to . . . organ failure . . . or even death."[16] Drawing on legal efforts to limit the constitutional claims of equal protection and challenges to cruel and unusual punishment, the memos argued that establishing that torture had occurred would require evidence of the "subjective intent" to commit torture and a lack of "good faith belief" that a given action was *not* torture. Indeed, the memos went so far as to argue that "knowledge alone that a particular result is going to occur does not constitute specific intent," as if an interrogation could have other objectives.[17]

Torture, in other words, is in the eye of the torturers. According to this view, it is possible to torture and yet not be a torturer. This subjective redefinition of torture gives resonance to Susan Sontag's provocative and disturbing contention that the Abu Ghraib photographs of U.S. military prison guards abusing Iraqi prisoners "are us." Although they evoked disgust and outcry, the photographs also revealed the sovereign violence enacted upon Arab and Muslim "bare life" as the mirror of Americans' collective security (or insecurity) and enabled the disavowal of that violence as something that is "not us," something fundamentally un-American.[18] For subjects with rights, viewing the photographs with condemnation for the perpetrators and sympathy for the victims simultaneously reaffirmed the dehumanization of victims and the rightful humanity of those in whose name these crimes were perpetrated. Yet in the space carved out by the legal defense of torture, the photographs also demonstrated that anyone's rights could be revoked and anyone could be tortured. Viewing the photographs thus consecrated rights-bearing subjects as individuals who occupied spaces of protection (rather than right), subjects who were permitted to worry about their own feelings and discomfort, to gaze upon the world with contempt and pity and yet with tacit recognition of the potential consequences of their expulsion from safety.[19]

In the period after 9/11, many scholars turned to the work of the philosopher Giorgio Agamben, which elucidated the relationship between the production of humanity as "bare life" and the exercise of sovereign political power. Agamben, building on the work of Carl Schmitt, defines sovereignty as the power to suspend normal legality and identifies this with the power of decision over life itself. *Bare life* is life that is included in the law only through its exclusion—life "stripped of every right" and "exposed to an unconditional threat of death," insofar as killing it does not constitute homicide.[20] Agamben also affirms Foucault's observation that racism is an embedded feature of modern liberal-democratic governance—in Foucault's words, a "way of introducing a break into the domain of life that is under power's control: the break between what must live and what must die." Racism remains indispensable as a means of legitimating the "murderous function of the State" in a period in which government powers have been defined primarily in terms of normalizing and securing the general conditions of social and economic life. By introducing a "biological-type caesura within a population," racial targeting has enabled the reassertion of an older form of sovereignty, the sovereign right to kill, in a social and political field defined by overriding imperatives of conforming human equivalence and "bio-political" regulation ("the power to guarantee life").[21]

Agamben argues that bare life and sovereign power are central to the genealogy of Western politics, which takes the form of an enduring and dangerous linkage between biology and kinship, on the one hand, and political association and public standing, on the other. Nazi violence and the paroxysm of the death camps for him represent the negative apotheosis of this tendency, in which bare life without political standing was subject to wholesale elimination by a modern state. The camp, he writes, "was the most absolute bio-political space ever to have been realized, in which power confronts pure life (that is, life) without any mediation."[22] This analysis highlights the persistent threat of regression inherent in all nationalist politics. Among its deficiencies, the abstract fungibility of "bare life" and the fixation on the concentration camp as the first actualization of the extreme danger inherent in Western politics reflect a lack of sufficiently deep or broad historical reference. For example, how should we situate the emergence of the U.S. "war-prison" in light of Agamben's account?[23] When the Bush administration declared that it was using "the great liberating tradition of America" in the service of "the expansion of freedom in all the world," should we have been surprised that in the train of this "expansion" came the stripping away of the political constitution and social history of those subjected to its extreme police and military measures?[24]

Marketed and advanced on the grounds of "securing our freedoms," contemporary U.S. war making has been central to the renovation and reimagination of modes for containing alleged civil threat that find their legal and cultural origins in histories of racial slavery, settler colonialism, and fascism.[25] This is not to say either that the figures of historical racism exhaust all possible meanings of U.S. nationalism or that racial, colonial, or fascist genealogies are without their own breaks, contradictions, and structuring dilemmas. At the same time, the failure to interrogate and effectively confront the way that contemporary displays of U.S. state power both enjoin old and fabricate new murderous divisions within humanity has today placed the entire world in danger once again.

Why bundle fascism into this discussion? Is it politically responsible to invoke a threat of fascism in the United States today?[26] The specter of fascism undoubtedly haunts U.S. political culture. As the antithesis of U.S. liberal democracy, it has been repeatedly invoked since World War II to tell us why we fight and who we are not. Thus, it is predictable that after first calling the "war on terror" a crusade, George W. Bush would correct the apparent misstep by redefining it as a fight against a "new totalitarianism." The latter formulation was affirmed in commentaries by public intellectuals on "Islamo-fascism" as the new menace of open societies. The notion of an "axis of evil," and the injunction to confront rather than appease each and every "new Hitler," became the ready-to-wear axioms for the new generation of happy warriors prosecuting a new era of "good wars."[27]

Intentional violence and threats of harm against unarmed civilians must be condemned whenever they occur—on every side of a conflict. The effort to set the "global war on terror" in a teleological progression of post–World War II struggles against tyranny, however, conflated a range of actors, regions, and time scales. The older tradition of frontier and colonial wars similarly sought to distinguish between "savage atrocities" and "civilized atrocities." Writing a few years after the 1857 Sepoy Revolt, for example, the English liberal John Stuart Mill defended the suspension of "international morality" in wars of colonial intervention on the grounds that "barbarians" could "not be depended upon for observing any rules," or trusted to place their "will under the influence of distant motives." Defined by the lack of any discernible rationality or ethic of mutuality, barbarians (like "terrorists") thus represented an essentialized threat to civilization. This conception not only obscured the asymmetries of power that were the sources of war and conflict; it also depoliticized and dehistoricized the counterviolence of dominated peoples.[28]

Writing in the *American Journal of International Law,* Captain Elbridge Colby, a considered expert on U.S. military doctrine, advanced this argument with distinctive clarity in the late 1920s: "The real crux of the matter of warfare between civilized and uncivilized peoples almost invariably turns out to be a difference in fact as well as in law. In fact, among savages war includes everyone. There is no distinction between combatants and noncombatants."[29] Ranging widely across the terrain comprised by the question of "how to fight savage tribes," Colby had British imperial precedents foremost in his mind ("the red-coated army that has fought . . . in more corners of the globe with more uncivilized and savage peoples than any other military in modern times"), but significantly, he also cited the "sound forebodings of an American who knew the redskin as he was and as he waged war." "The fact," Colby concluded, "is that when a tribe on the war-path measures its victories by the number of houses burned and the number of foes, combatant or non-combatant, cut up, you must use a different method of warfare. When Oriental peoples are accustomed to pillaging and being pillaged, accustomed to torturing and flaying alive distinguished prisoners, you are dealing with opponents to whom the laws of war mean nothing, who, as General Hull said of the American Indians, respect no rights and know no wrong."[30]

In the last instance, Colby reckoned, an all-out approach was more humane, for "a concrete illustration of overwhelming strange and devastating force may break down resistance completely and make for an early peace." The superior military technologies and organizational capacities of the colonizing power thus constituted a measure of civilization that licensed an extreme and discretionary violence. What Colby had in mind, well before their application in Europe in World War II, were measures like the terror bombing of civilian population centers and the use of concentration camps to control or punish combatants and noncombatants alike: these were innovations from the U.S. Indian Wars, the Philippines counterinsurgency, the Boer War in southern Africa, and British, French, and German campaigns in southeast Asia and other parts of Africa.[31]

The slippage in Colby's discourse from the frontier wars to conflicts with "Oriental peoples" further reflects the evolution of U.S. expansionist thinking in the period after the U.S.-Philippine war and the formal closing of the frontier. It illuminates how U.S. war making overseas continued to draw on the symbolic and racial capital of frontier expansion and Indian wars (not least in Vietnam, where Eldridge Colby's son, William Colby, would preside over the deadly Phoenix pacification program from his CIA post in the late 1960s). More recently, John Lewis Gaddis argued that the George W. Bush administration's doctrines of "preventive war" had their origins on the U.S. frontier, where securing freedom required cleansing the borderlands of "native Americans, pirates, marauders," and other "nonstate actors," who threatened the security of a growing population that sought to inhabit an "empire based on mutual economic advantage."[32] The dystopian fabulist Robert Kaplan similarly enjoined today's war planners to "remember" the U.S.-Philippine war and occupation (1898–1946), "one of the most successful counterinsurgencies waged by a Western army in modern times. . . . Given the challenges ahead, our experience a century ago in the anarchic Philippines may be more relevant than our recent experience in Iraq."[33]

Defenders of preventive, civilizing wars, past and present, have justified them by invoking the specter of biopolitical hazards existing outside any ostensibly rational framework of conflict resolution or negotiation. They generally neglect to consider the contradiction between the purely volitional world, purged of coercive power relations that they champion, and their advocacy of opening new frontiers of violence in order to expand its boundaries. What Michael Rogin once referred to as the "proto-totalitarian" scene of westward expansion involved the unleashing of powerfully regressive impulses that had supposedly been mastered by rational men.[34] Such violence was invariably sustained by the fantasy of the Other as a regressive being, as demonstrated by a range of cultural and behavioral markers (technological inferiority, impulsiveness, inscrutability, childishness, rage) grouped under the phenotypical sign of race. Just as significant, a kind of legal, moral, and psychic prophylaxis was established between the utopian vision of America as empire of right, the exterminatory violence that instituted it, and the enslavement it accommodated.

If, as Agamben suggests, we take Nazism to be the twentieth-century apotheosis of the historical production of human beings as "bare life," then the lifting of the prohibition on celebrating "savage wars of peace" and the effective indifference to torture and indefinite detention among U.S. officials and notable public intellectuals suggests that the current moment marks not a fight against new fascisms, but the historical renovation of "the inner solidarity of democracy and totalitarianism."[35] Langston Hughes once described the casualties of U.S. expansion, slavery, and segregation as the victims of "our native fascisms"; as careful scholars affirmed, fascism was largely a deviation of democratic regimes.[36] Thus, while democratic liberalism continually reimagines fascism as its monstrous Other, fascism might be better understood as its doppelganger—an exclusionary will to power that has regularly reemerged, manifesting itself in zones of internal exclusion within liberal-democratic societies (plantations, reservations, ghettos, and prisons) and in sites where liberalism's expansionist impulse and universalizing force have been able to evade their own constitutional restraints (the frontier, the colony, the state of emergency, the occupation, and the counterinsurgency).

Half a century ago, Karl Polanyi and Hannah Arendt were among the first to plumb the depths of the connection between liberal democracy and fascism. A key insight of their work, lost in the anticommunist consensus of the West following World War II, is that fascism, and Nazism in particular, was the offspring and the symptom of a crisis of liberal empires and their ostensibly democratic regimes. The self-image of U.S. liberal democracy was created from partial truths derived from the military defeat of German, Italian, and Japanese fascism in World War II. As "totalitarianism" began to be defined as a Soviet and implicitly anti-Western phenomenon, the origins of fascism within the political culture of Western liberalism became increasingly obscured.[37]

Polanyi viewed the rise of fascism in the 1930s as the by-product of a history of state-enforced laissez-faire, the effort to subordinate all human societies to a self-regulating market. This project, he argued, induced untenable incongruities between local forms of political development, both within national economies and in the world economy. The liberal utopia of a society free from coercive power, under the aegis of market exchange, had produced an intensively administered, culturally stripped world whose apogee was colonial domination. In the pursuit of an ideal of freedom as self-regulation, English liberals instead promoted violent state intervention that disrupted customary relationships to land, labor, and community. The market-enforcing state in turn advanced a social vision in which "the biological nature of man" was understood as the "foundation of a society that was not of a political order."[38] Violent methods and extraeconomic coercion could be dispensed with and the rule of law established once the market was master, or once workers were, in Marx's famous quip, "rightless and free." "As long as property was safe," Polanyi summarized, "hunger would drive people to work."[39] Fascism essentially reversed this polarity, reclaiming the biological basis of the nation-state as a militarized organic community against the self-regulating market.

The Afterlife of Fascism

In a different but complementary investigation of the formation of modern political society, Arendt argued that the genealogy of Nazism lay in the history of colonial expansion, specifically the turn-of-the-century colonization and genocide in German South West Africa (today's Namibia), where Heinrich von Trietschke (1898) echoed Mill and Colby in proclaiming that "international law becomes phrases if its standards are also applied to barbaric peoples."[40] Not only was late nineteenth-century imperialism funded through "race thinking," but colonial expansion played a central role in nationalizing the European masses and subordinating them to elitist, militaristic, and adventurist forms of leadership. "Nothing was more characteristic of power politics in the imperialist era," Arendt argued, "than this shift from localized, limited, and therefore predictable goals of national interest to the limitless goals of power after power that could roam and lay waste the entire globe with no certain nationally and territorially prescribed purpose and hence with no predictable direction."[41]

When Arendt wrote these lines in her new preface to the 1967 edition of *The Origins of Totalitarianism*, she was at least in part referring to the United States, which, she argued, had taken up the mantle of imperialism "on an enormously enlarged scale." She feared where this might lead and put her hope "in the Constitutional restraints of the American republic and the technological restraints of the nuclear age." Arendt did not want the catastrophic consequences of what she called "the half-forgotten" legacy of imperialism to be obscured, as she believed it had led to the cataclysms of the two world wars. The irony, however, was that her own framework may have aided in the forgetting. As others took up the formal equation of Nazism and Stalinism ("racism and communism"), Soviet communism came to bear most of the weight of "totalitarian" efforts to fabricate real utopias through mass murder. In the end, Arendt fell short of offering a genealogy of Nazi imperialism within Western imperialisms: her formulation of the "totalitarian system" displaced one of her original purposes, which had been to locate

Nazism within "the subterranean stream of Western history" that had "come to the surface and usurped the dignity of our tradition."[42]

Despite important differences in emphasis, Polanyi and Arendt both believed that the "dignified tradition" of reformist liberalism (and democratic socialism), rooted in authentic structures of democratic participation, market regulation, civil liberties, and political representation, offered antidotes to fascist deviationism. Writing before the full onset of anticolonial movements for national liberation, both failed to address the deeper issues of the colonial structuring of global power relations and the enduring contradictions between the theoretical universalism of liberalism and the exclusionary history of liberal democracies founded in racial slavery, frontier violence, and colonial expansion. In regarding New Deal liberalism as the harbinger of a durable and stable global liberalism, Polanyi further underestimated the extent to which new ideologies and proponents of "market utopianism" cum "modernization" would promote the destruction of nonmarket forms of social and cultural protection, particularly in the third world in the guise of modernization.[43] Meanwhile, Arendt's faith in the authentic virtues of U.S. democratic-republicanism reified the relationship between achieved political rights and permanent membership in the nation-state, failing to take into account the racially exclusionary character of U.S. democracy that made provisional or contingent rights a lasting feature of social life.[44]

Against the important openings they offered, both thinkers paradoxically contributed to an ideology of a U.S.-led "break" from the logic of empire and, by extension, fascism after World War II. They underestimated specific political tendencies in the U.S. social formation that, from the early days of the cold war, chafed against the restraints on market activity that reformist liberalism imposed at home, demanded the "rollback" of communism abroad, and sought to marginalize and contain domestic struggles over political membership, race, gender, and rights. Against the grain of the official liberal consensus favoring multilateral institutions, global free trade, and the universalization of national sovereignty and human rights, these rightwing forces reflected the global development of what Noam Chomsky has called "sub-fascism under U.S. tutelage": the grim world of counterinsurgency, proxy wars, death squads, preventative subversion through covert action, and the unprecedented militarization of U.S. society in the shadow of the nuclear annihilation threat.[45]

The effort to contain the spread of communism everywhere that came to define U.S. cold war doctrine theoretically extended America's "manifest destiny" to the entire world. In this vision, the United States was the global agent of freedom and "every space could in principle be defined . . . as an arena not yet won where destiny would be fought out right now." This claim was based on the ruse that the United States faced a demonic adversary bent on expansion, whereas it was the United States that was seeking to establish a hegemonic influence, access to resources, and safeguards for capital.[46] With white supremacy ostensibly defeated and discredited, anticommunism emerged as a more flexible rubric for negotiating discrepancies between the imperative to expand the "free world" and biopolitical eligibility for now ostensibly universal rights to historical agency, self-determination, and protections of national sovereignty. Walt Rostow, national security adviser to both Kennedy and Johnson, once described communists as "scavengers of the modernization process": anyone under communism's sway was deemed constitutionally incapable of meaningful or legitimate self-development.[47] Less facile with these clever recoding strategies, Curtis LeMay of the U.S. Strategic Air Command's promised to bomb the Vietnamese "back to the Stone Age," presumably the true material index of their inner constitution; and William Westmoreland, commander of U.S. forces in Vietnam, announced that "the Oriental doesn't place the same high price on life as the Westerner." When considered in the context of the tons of incendiary bombs and herbicides that the United States dropped on Southeast Asia during a decade of war, such statements signaled that these untold millions, who had to be bombed in order to be saved, had once again been reconstituted as "bare life."[48]

The tenacity of the Vietnamese resistance, combined with the intensification of antiracist and antiwar struggles in the United States, advanced powerful reconsideration of the violence and disavowal at the heart of U.S. imperial culture. The early 1970s marked the culmination of a reformist liberal trend, encapsulated in the slogan "civil rights and human rights," which inspired significant new congressional and public initiatives to monitor the use of covert and overt U.S. military and police power.[49] Most important, this was the apogee of political contention over the scope of rights and membership both domestically and globally. It was a moment when new political subjects were being created through the progressive politicization of the meaning and scope of rights discourse, which at its most expansive and visionary meant overcoming the gap between varieties of less-than-human status and the universalizing claims advanced in the vocabulary of freedom, democracy, and national sovereignty.

There is no gainsaying the political limitations of the so-called rights revolutions: how civil rights struggles were incorporated into new logics of bureaucratic and administrative control and depoliticized, how national sovereignty in the developing world instituted a range of new statist corruptions and murderous exclusions, or how the cant of human rights became a cover for a wide range of global power differentials, abuses, and interventions. Yet the grim present demands that we take careful inventory of the ground that has been lost over the past thirty years, particularly in the United States. An important benchmark for such consideration, as Colin Dayan suggests, might be the Supreme Court decision in *Furman v. Georgia* (1972), which abolished capital punishment in the United States. Furman marked the fullest elaboration of the legal precedent set by *Trop v. Dulles* (1958), the idea that "cruel and unusual punishment" was determined by "evolving standards of decency that mark the progress of a maturing society." Most important, it insisted that what was at stake in Eighth Amendment protection was not only pain thresholds but the irrevocable "human status" of the prisoner.[50]

Furman and the cases that immediately followed it also marked the first time in U.S. history that the U.S. Supreme Court openly disclaimed the legacy of slavery that had been retained in postslavery legal decisions and practices surrounding incarceration, or the idea that prisoners were "civilly dead" and thus "slaves of the state." Nested in the Thirteenth Amendment, which abolished slavery, was an exception for "punishment of crime." Crime and punishment in turn were central to the reinstitution of quasi-forced labor and political disfranchisement of free blacks in the post-Emancipation South.[51] The practices and institutions of the carceral state have long been central to the constitution of regimes of nonpersonhood that overlap with and potentially supersede regimes of racial exclusion, and this fact takes on particular significance in the post–civil rights era. For at the very moment when color-blind jurisprudence began to demand the elimination of racial references in law and institutional practice, crime and punishment, particularly under the auspices of the "war on drugs," began to fashion the prison as the preeminent U.S. racialized space.

In the 1970s, black men in the United States without a high school diploma had a 15 percent chance of being incarcerated in their lifetime; today that probability is closer to 70 percent. More than two million African Americans and over six million people in total cannot vote because of felony disfranchisement laws. Eleven states, mostly in the old Confederacy, disenfranchise more than 10 percent of their black population on these grounds. Black people constitute approximately 13 percent of the U.S. population, yet 40 percent of the inmates on death row and almost 40 percent of the overall domestic prison population are black.[52] Beginning in the 1980s, the Supreme Court, under Chief Justice William Rehnquist, started to systematically narrow the scope of rights claims advanced under both the Eighth and the Fourteenth Amendments. The technical basis of most of these decisions rested on requiring the less powerful or aggrieved parties to demonstrate the subjective intent and deliberation of the specific individuals who punish or who racially and sexually discriminate. The underlying judicial philosophy is often called "original intent" or "strict constructionism." Championed by organizations of right-wing jurists like the Federalist Society, this doctrine regards the admission or accrual of new categories of rights and new rights-bearing subjects not found in the Constitution to be the illegitimate usurpation of sovereignty by "activist judges." Further, it seeks to narrow the scope of the Equal Protection Clause of the Fourteenth Amendment by making rights dependent on the will of political majorities in individual states—ostensibly the only real basis of popular sovereignty. In this way, rights won for labor, disabled peoples, racial, religious and sexual minorities, women, and prisoners, whether codified in federal law or by judicial precedent, become politically revocable rights ("the rights of those who don't have rights").[53]

Given its roots in efforts to curtail domestic civil rights protection, we might consider whether the historical precedent for the legal defense of today's war-prison is racial slavery. Not only was slavery the means by which the United States covertly admitted into its political system and juridical discourse an institution that was both morally and legally abhorrent, even by the standards of the time, but it also marked the beginning of the enactment of laws of exception specifically designed to maintain and regulate a separate sphere of existence in which "the meaning of human" could be "held in suspension." Quoting from late eighteenth-century British West Indian statutes, Dayan identifies the uncanny logic by which slavery and freedom yielded their own distinctively dualistic system of justice: "The leading principle on which the government is supported is fear: or a sense of that absolute coercive necessity which, leaving no choice of action, supersedes all questions of right."[54] David Bromwich amplifies the point: "The object of torture is a slave. . . . To suppose that slavery is a matter of ownership is a half-truth that misses the political basis of the oppression. The evil consists in the ability to dominate other persons without check . . . armed with the assurance of impunity."[55]

The evolution of "standards of decency" that abolished slavery have been compared to the rejection of torture. Instead, we have witnessed a broader retrogression. The United States now incarcerates fully one-quarter of all the world's prisoners—well over 2 million persons. In the "global war on terror," as in the "war on drugs" that preceded and paved the way for it, crime and war blur together. Escalated by President Ronald Reagan, the so-called drug war conjured the demon of a singular, racialized threat to the U.S. body politic and began to habituate U.S. publics to the idea of a permanent and growing domestic prison complex. It introduced the widespread use of extralegal tactics like rendition through the kidnapping of foreign drug dealers and the outsourcing of their interrogation to torture-friendly countries. Under President Bill Clinton, it brought the broad expansion of domestic police powers through the Violent Crime and Law Enforcement Act (1994) and the Antiterrorism and Effective Death Penalty Act (1996), both precursors to the USA Patriot Act (2001). Finally, it began to create (just in time for the demise of the Soviet Union) the infrastructure of America's own gulag archipelago, which now extends from Camp Delta, in Guantanamo Bay, Cuba, to Camp Justice on the British island of Diego Garcia, domestic "supermax" penitentiaries like Pelican Bay in California, and unidentified "black sites" in the United States and around the world.

Some neoconservative intellectuals and their neoliberal brethren project that the "global war on terror" will last for forty years—as long as the cold war. Under its regime, the world is neither strictly a site of strategic territorial expansion by rival powers nor the object of a struggle for hegemony (though both of these principles and their associated tactics remain latent). Rather, today's U.S. war planners and their intellectual supporters view the entire world as an "open frontier." U.S. state power is uniquely charged with ordering this frontier to secure rational individualism and capitalist exchange.[56] The prison is the perfect foil for the kind of order that utopian neoliberalism seeks: a depoliticized order from which political conflict is forever banished by the threat of absolute constraint. This helps to explain why the concept of criminality and a science of policing loom so large in its field of vision and strategic action. The criminal, the barbarian, and the terrorist represent actors who lack self-control, who are incapable of inhabiting liberal subjectivity, and who therefore must be controlled through illiberal means (either extermination or the deprivation of their freedom).

In 1967, Richard M. Nixon announced that "our judges have gone too far in weakening the peace forces as against the criminal forces." Around the same moment, the so-called father of neoconservatism, Irving Kristol, described himself as "a liberal who had been mugged by reality."[57] The image of a mugging invoked the specter of black street crime, the alleged softness of liberal universalism, and rage that in the wake of the Vietnam War, the United States had lost its moral claim to be the world's exemplary nation-state and world-ordering power by catering to antiwar moralists and criminals. Thus began a long and arduous process of intellectually renovating American liberalism by attempting to break free from normative and legal restraints on U.S. power and to renaturalize exclusions from the national political community. Indeed, these efforts have been central to the steady consolidation of right-wing political power since the early 1980s. The rights of individuals and categories of persons are increasingly regarded as revocable by the sovereign power, and democracy is reimagined as an identity of "those who command and those who obey" under the aegis of market and nation.

The Afterlife of Fascism

The formulation of command and obedience is that of the political philosopher Carl Schmitt, whose Weimar-era critiques of liberal parliamentarianism have an uncanny resonance with U.S. right-wing jurisprudence, contempt for international law, and efforts to collapse executive and juridical authority in the name of the "global war on terror." In Schmitt's famous definition, the "sovereign is he who decides the exception" to established rules and social norms on the basis of an identification of "extreme peril" or "danger to the existence of the state." The state of emergency and the sovereign exception show up the inadequacy of modern liberalism's attempt to "repress the question of sovereignty" through the separation of powers, rational deliberation, individual rights protection, and public debate. Schmitt insists that this view does not require an imposition of dictatorship, since "the masses are won over through a propaganda apparatus whose maximum effect relies on an appeal to immediate interests and passions." Thus, he concludes, "in a democracy . . . those who command and those who obey are identical."[58]

Schmitt's identification of democratic unanimity and sovereign power is premised on the idea that the sovereign exception highlights the contradiction between the overinclusiveness of liberal notions of human equality and the forms of exclusion required by mass democracy. "Democracy," Schmitt writes darkly, "requires . . . first homogeneity, and second—if the need arises—the elimination or eradication of heterogeneity." Democracy is foremost an "equality of equals": it is the "risk of inequality" that gives meaning and substance to equality. Moreover, those who are governed without rights ("let them be called barbarians, uncivilized, atheists, aristocrats, even slaves") can be either inside or outside the nation-state. Most significantly, Schmitt points to the imperial-colonial scene of modern nationhood, rejecting as sheer pretense the idea of "a democracy of mankind." "Does the British empire rest on universal and equal voting rights for all its inhabitants?" he asks contemptuously. "It could not survive for a week on this foundation."[59]

Schmitt was prescient in predicting that states of emergency would force liberal democracy to "decide between its elements." Advancing a sharp critique of the universalizing claims of liberalism, he envisioned a divided space where the rule of law and right enjoyed by "civilized" peoples was predicated on a contiguous or adjacent space of state violence, exemplified by colonial history. In 1941, in his role as a Nazi jurist, Schmitt cited the international legal precedent for Nazi expansionism (*Lebensraum*) or the acquisition of "vital space": "The non-European space was without masters, uncivilized or semi-civilized, a territory for colonization and the object of conquest by European powers which thereby became empires thanks to their colonies overseas. So far, the colonies have been the spatial element upon which European law is founded." Adolf Hitler was blunter: "What India was for England, the Eastern territories will be for us. . . . The Eastern space must be ruled in perpetuity by the Germans. . . . The natives will have to be shot. . . . Our sole duty is to Germanize the country by the immigration of Germans, regarding the natives as redskins."[60]

Next to murderous anti-Semitism, the Nazis' ethnic claims to territorial space epitomize one of the horrors of fascist extremism, even as its colonial genealogy has been largely repressed. The question is whether we have really left behind the racialized concepts of national personhood and biopolitical killing that link the regimes of settler colonialism and National Socialism. In his acclaimed book, Gaddis claims that "we were all irradiated . . . that morning of September 11, 2001, in such a way as to shift our psychological makeup—the DNA in our minds—with consequences for years to come."[61] Framing 9/11 as a quasi-biological transformation of the American populace, he conjures a significant biopolitical "memory" for current war policy, namely the ethnic cleansing of the U.S. borderlands. In a globalizing, borderless world, Gaddis avers, tactics similar to those used on an expanding frontier may be required to police threats from new "nonstate actors" and the "failed states" that "breed" them.[62]

Such is the open defense of preventive war—valorized by colonial precedent yet tempered by pieties about the (provisional) humanity of those willing to accept U.S. tutelage in self-government. In this formulation, today's terrorist, like Mill's or Schmitt's barbarian, is not necessarily produced through an avowed commitment to a racial ideology. Rather, the barbarian and terrorist are specters haunting the liberal-democratic imagination: they represent what we are not, what we cannot trust, what lies beyond the domain of our politics, and therefore what we must subjugate, even if we must ourselves become barbarians or terrorists for a time in order to do so. Finally, it is the concrete acts of subjugation—and not their doctrinal coherence—that constitute the barbarian as a real, material being, perhaps precisely someone lacking constituent power in relation to liberal discipline and normalization. The production of barbarians and terrorists in turn tautologically justifies the initial policy—a tendency that has become more visible over the years, as postinvasion Iraq has become a field for multiplying "barbarisms" and "terrorisms" on all sides of the conflict.[63]

How long the long war will last is something that we may not know for years. In any case, we live in perilous times. To paraphrase Paul Gilroy, today the promise of liberal modernity is in question, and fascism is merely on hold.[64] Three sets of political strategies and tactics—the racial-carceral state, the bionatalist state, and the imperial warfare state—seem to have entered into heightened levels of coordination and symbiosis under neoliberal market rule. Seizing on the 9/11 emergency as its "moment of opportunity," the Bush regime rejected the constraints of "reality-based" policy assessment, arguing that a preponderance of will and force allowed it to fabricate reality according to providential design.[65] Such delusional self-belief, as Arendt warned, is the truest measure of the totalitarian cast of mind. At the same time, the notion that outrages such as sanctioned torture, wars of aggression represented as self-defense, indefinite incarceration, administrative massacres, kidnappings, and disappearances, mass deportations, denial of due process, secret prisons, and messianic fusions of propaganda, politics, and religion are exceptional to U.S. liberal democracy obscures our history. For a nation whose vaunted freedom was secured at the point where mass human bondage met genocidal expansion, what we are experiencing today is like a series of afterimages—the past-present that is these United States.

CHAPTER FOUR

Racial Formation and Permanent War

We are a nation of war—I mean a nation of law.

> Chris Wallace, Fox News Anchor, interviewing former New York mayor Rudolph Guiliani, November 16, 2009

A sovereign people are an armed people.

> Tea Party slogan, 2010

In their important book *Racial Formation in the United States from the 1960s to the 1980s,* Michael Omi and Howard Winant offer what might be described as a first draft of the racial politics of the post–civil rights era. Omi and Winant define "race" as "an unstable and decentered complex of social meanings" that is at once foundational to, and also made and remade in, the course of political struggles.[1] This way of describing race marked a salutary theoretical development that expressly worked against an incipient neoconservative discourse of "color-blindness" that sought, with increasing success, to undermine normative, legal, and political claims about racial inequality in the United States, in the wake of civil rights and formal equality, by erasing positivist racial classification from law and social policy. Omi and Winant acknowledge a naturalistic reference to differentiated human embodiment as the ideological kernel of race (a notion preserved by color-blind orthodoxy). They suggest, however, that when viewed in their formation, conceptions of racial difference go beyond references to phenotype and gross morphology and come already embedded in broader struggles over political power, social reproduction, and governance. Understood this way, race is a historically given and politically reconstituted field of projected meaning and investment integral to the aggregation of socially significant identities—a form of collective imagination and a way of imagining collectivity that is secondarily codified in legal and biological (and other) terms. Such a perspective has presented a strategic and theoretical challenge to all static, particularistic, and essentialist framings of racial identity and conflict, insisting upon both the universal effects of racial division across the social field and also upon the increasingly flexible and recombinant dynamics of U.S. racial orders.

More specifically, this was a comprehensive attempt to apply a new set of analytical rubrics to the dimensions of change and relative permanence in the ordering of racial hierarchy and domination in the context of the tremendous victories, decline, and political reversals of the black freedom movement in the United States. It was also an effort—perhaps more implicit than explicit—to provide intellectual resources for reconstructing an *integrated* and *majoritarian*, and yet also expressly *transformational*, antiracist politics. This effort was opposed to a host of contending visions from the Left that that either heralded a return to the putative fundamentals of class division from the armchairs of defeated social democracy or abandoned the field of social politics altogether, regrouping within the niche markets of multiculturalism or the shrinking silos of "identity politics." Written against these currents, and at the height of Reagan's America, *Racial Formation* was a brave and ambitious book. It sought to teach us how to talk about race in a period that was "all about race"—that is, one marked by a redeployment of the most vicious and invidious forms of pseudopositivist racial description (and prescription), as in Charles Murray's *Losing Ground* (1984) and Laurence

Mead's *Beyond Entitlement* (1985)—and yet one that asserted the normative value of color-blindness, in which nothing is about race.[2] Indeed, the steady bifurcation of reality and reference, in which an invidious racialism could masquerade as neutral empiricism while racial justice claims could be dismissed as without basis or foundation, represented a novel condition, one that continues to characterize the present.

Like a number of other texts and approaches, *Racial Formation* was situated within and sought to theorize broad transitions in the use and importance of racial ordering in the United States at the time of a decisive unwinding of institutional supports and policy orientations of welfare-state liberalism. This meant looking backward to what Omi and Winant described as the "great transformation," from the end of World War II through the 1960s, in which white supremacy was normatively discredited, and an inclusive, modestly ameliorative form of racial liberalism gained intellectual ascendancy. As numerous scholars have argued, this transition coincided with and was an analogue to the United States' emergence as the world's leading capitalist nation-state, a role defined by an unprecedented commitment to "securing" multilateral commodity production and exchange across the planet— by force, if necessary.[3] The overcoming of historic racial exclusion was widely described as a frame for legitimating U.S. claims to global leadership. To claim to be fighting "communist slavery" was not easily reconciled with continuing state-sanctioned discrimination against the descendants of U.S. slaves. From the 1950s, when the U.S. State Department intervened in support of school integration (on precisely these grounds) to the contemporary period, in which policy makers and pundits claimed that the 2003 invasion of Iraq was acceptable to the world because it was based on the demonstrated U.S. achievement of democracy for all (rather than on the assumption of "the white man's burden"), assertions of the nation's normative commitment to racial equality have become a banal truth, a staple of consensus ideology and official public discourse.

Within the normalizing frame of racial liberalism in the late 1960s, how-ever, a conflict raged across U.S. civil society about the speed and scope of reform. At one end of the political spectrum, a heterogeneous black-freedom movement coalesced around a critique of the limits of racial liberalism, despite debilitating internal differences over tactics and strategy. To this group, the formal achievements of civil and political rights for black people were merely an initial stage in a longer social and political struggle aimed at dislodging possessive investments in white privilege that structured (and distorted) both public attitudes and political economy in U.S. society. At the other end of the spectrum, a similarly heterogeneous politics of white self-interest regrouped around discourses and strategies ranging from states' rights, victims' rights, meritocratic individualism, and legal formalism to selective withdrawal from or privatization of public domains and (for the least advantaged) vigorous and at times violent defense of occupational sinecures and neighborhood boundaries. The great irony, of course, is that blacks would later be blamed for upsetting the applecart of racial liberalism, even as racial liberalism increasingly provided cover for reinforcing the rot-ten defenses of racial privilege and articulating new ones.

We have not yet fully assessed the broad reconstitution of racialized dis-parity in the ensuing period, when racial matters increasingly became a ref-erent and code for right-wing politics and social policy. Ronald Reagan's election was an inflection point: the self-proclaimed advocate of states' rights confidently launched his presidential campaign in Philadelphia, Mis-sissippi, the site of the notorious murders of the civil rights activists James Chaney, Michael Schwerner, and Andrew Goodman. At the same time, racial liberalism remained a basis for campaigns for the equalization of distribu-tion and recognition along racial lines, with notable successes, particularly in the media, professional sports, entertainment, and educational sectors. Jesse Jackson's Rainbow Coalition and Harold Washington's Chicago mayor-alty campaign, moreover, demonstrated the potential of black-led, multiracial coalition politics. On college campuses, the movement for South African divestment again called attention to racial exclusion and domination and showed how it could be reactivated as a public concern, with the capacity to galvanize social-justice activism. Growing attention to the "intersectional" and intraracial politics of gender and sexuality, particularly in law and social policy, augured new and expansive articulations of queer, feminist, and antiracist perspectives. Meanwhile, across the color line, the emerging histories of Asian and Latino/a presence in the United States complemented and at times contended with the monopolization of racial concerns by black/white paradigms.

Racial Formation was written against a backdrop of a more or less even contest, marked by both gains and reversals. Arguably, however, this view concealed a deeper process of bifurcation and fragmentation that had begun to reshape progressive racial politics. The neoliberal restructuring project that arose in response to the global economic downturn of the 1970s, and which became associated with the triumph of the governments of Reagan and Margaret Thatcher in the 1980s, marked the consolidation of an increasingly repressive, upwardly redistributionist tendency in governments of developed nations, one that sought to increase corporate profitability through a ruthless imposition of market discipline. This trend was most marked in the United Kingdom and the United States, where the purified liberalism of the "Washington Consensus" resonated with longstanding cultural predilections and corporate constituencies. These were, not coincidentally, also places where public fears grounded in race, crime, and national security became the means for "shifting the very character of hegemony": rather than seeking a new, expanded consensus that encouraged wider political participation, the government and elites sought a state of "managed dissensus" in which coercive projects—policing, punishment, and confinement—served as both key social-policy instruments and legitimating frameworks for securing popular consent, on a narrower basis if necessary.[4]

Put differently, this period saw the introduction of a racialized law-and-order project as the opening gambit in a broader reorientation of the very forms and dispositions of governance—what Stuart Hall and his collaborators describe in their landmark text *Policing the Crisis* (1978) as the emergence of an "exceptional state." Lyndon Johnson's vaunted "war on poverty," ostensibly aimed at maximizing welfare-state inclusion for the black poor through federally directed intervention, was gradually undercut by political attacks from racially motivated state and local officials and starved of resources by the escalation of the Vietnam War. What followed was a dramatic period of expansion of federal crime control, beginning with the passage of the 1968 Omnibus Crime Control and Safe Streets Act. In contrast to the war on poverty, law-and-order funding defaulted to conservative and Southern preferences for "block grants" that reinforced state and local police autonomy. In short, it revived rather than reformed the old federalist distributions of racialized policing. [5] This was followed by a longer period in which policing infrastructures and practices in the United States were augmented, militarized, and gradually released from legal strictures on the basis of a host of implicit and explicit fabrications of irredeemable black pathology, from wild youth to gangbangers, drug lords, and "street terrorists."

Indeed, this period represented another sort of inflection point with the rolling back of legal protections for the rights and bodily integrity of the accused and incarcerated, which had achieved its maximum extension in a series of landmark Supreme Court decisions in the 1960s and early 1970s.[6] In many ways Britain led these developments, as its new emergency powers for the preventive detention of potential domestic terrorists established an administrative regime of "anticipatory policing" increasingly freed from political oversight and judicial review.[7] From the "war on drugs" to today's "global war on terror," the new dispensation in Anglo-American liberalism has been characterized by a gradual merging of the discourses of crime and war: criminalization of threats to the social order has been accompanied by a consistent militarization of policing strategies and tactics, even as military action has increasingly been justified for the policing of foreign states recast as failed or criminal regimes.

The social engineering of the Reagan-Thatcher era operated on the premise that the silent (national) majority would be spared the unforgiving cuts of austerity, criminalization, and disposability. Thatcher's famous statement that "there is no such thing as society, only individuals and families," rested on the fantasy of "Little Britain" as a self-regulating moral and political domain—that is, it imagined prior racial and sexual divisions in a population whose presumptive political membership was naturalistically defined rather than the disorderly product of migration. Similarly, the Reagan era's ritualistic and violent gutting of public services drew on an implicit distinction between a virtuous, hard-working citizenry, in unquestioned possession of a sovereign right to have rights, and those whose rights were the product of elite condescension, minoritarian maneuvering, special interests, and activist jurists and therefore (at least potentially) politically revocable. Those seeking the regeneration of white identity politics sought new ways to exclude, or limit inclusion of, those for whom legal barriers and exclusionary stigmas had been reduced. The legal arena became a domain of especially fierce, racially inflected contestation with a series of orchestrated public attacks on affirmative action, bilingual education, the use of public services by illegal immigrants, and the use of data from racial classification to redress past inequality. The gradual triumph of color-blind jurisprudence in the ensuing decades ensured that claims for redress under the terms of antidiscrimination laws would be subject to the strictest scrutiny, even as assessment of the wide-ranging, disparate impacts of collective forms of racial inequality were rendered invisible or inaccessible under the minimalist, individualist, and reversible criteria of juridical formalism.[8]

Although the hard-edged racial themes of the Reagan restoration may have been a necessary condition for the rightward political realignment and electoral successes of the Republican Party during the 1980s and early 1990s, they proved insufficient to the more ambitious goal of permanently shifting the modalities of governance. Moderate racial inclusiveness, "diversity," and "tolerance" retained their ideological appeal, even in a public discourse that largely disavowed and disowned the historical depth and scope of the white supremacist distortion of social relations. While ballot initiatives and public legal challenges to affirmative action and antipoverty programs remained fertile arenas for advancing a politics of white self-interest, particularly at the state and local levels, popular Great Society expansions of welfare-state provision, like Medicaid and Head Start early childhood education, remained in force (though Medicaid is now in the crosshairs of the right-wing Congress and president). In retrospect, Lee Atwater's infamous, politically devastating Willie Horton television campaign ad, suggesting that George H. W. Bush's Democratic opponent, Michael Dukakis, would unleash black rapists and murderers on an unsuspecting public with his soft approach to crime, seems crude and caricatured in its overt appeals to racial fear. It may now be difficult to recall how figures like Rudolph Guiliani rose to prominence by leading a police riot on the steps of City Hall while promising to put "white guys back in charge" of New York City (although the rise of Trump shows that this mentality was hardly repressed). Significant national opposition to the establishment of a holiday to commemorate the life of Martin Luther King Jr. now seems like the action of a shrinking rear guard. Indeed, the leader of the first Congressional Republican majority in four decades, Newt Gingrich, publicly conceded that the one great success of modern liberalism had been its support for racial equality. However, disingenuous we might judge such pronouncements, particularly in light of the increasing tendency to encode racist appeals in color-blind discourse and nonracial language, it seems clear that antiblack racism had diminishing political returns, even if the pacification and subjugation of the disproportionately black urban poor proceeded apace.

The point here is not to endorse the thesis of a declining significance of race, nor to suggest that antiblack racism does not retain an everyday significance and latent force; rather, it is once again to demonstrate the growing complexity of and sharp bifurcations in racial meanings.[9] Elite recognition of the need to adjust the balance between consensus and coercion began precisely when formal democracy and legal inclusion for blacks had been stretched to their maximum point in the welfare-state framework. Predictably, as that framework was dismantled, blacks—the perennial canaries in the coal mine—were the first to suffer the consequences.[10] Less obvious or foreseeable was the extent to which this process would far exceed prophecies of "benign neglect" and extend to ambitiously coercive institutional forms, including the most extensive period of prison construction in human history in the last two decades of the twentieth century. It is arguable, moreover, that social analysis and political organization have substantially lagged behind these developments. Adolph Reed argues that the very normalization of racial liberalism had the effect of fundamentally narrowing the frame of social-justice politics, if not distorting it entirely, as if demonstration of racial inclusion and "diversity" could mark a just and conclusive settlement of social affairs even as neoliberal restructuring led to the most (racially) marked casualties of American society being economically abandoned, rendered disposable, and warehoused in prison.[11] In other words, not only have racial exclusion and racial inclusion paradoxically risen in tandem, but so have colorblindness and multiculturalism, which arguably stabilized as nonantagonistic (if contradictory) poles of contemporary (racial) commonsense. The two sides tend to contend with each other from a similar standpoint, one that accepts a shrunken conception of polity, public, and personhood underneath which the lines of race and class have grown both deeper and more obscure.

Indeed, the neo-Gramscian notion of a "racial war of position" advanced in *Racial Formation*, a contest that unfolds on the terrain of civil society and constitutes the domain of "normal" politics, ideology, and group identity, may proceed alongside and partially obscure social and institutional processes that have gradually and surreptitiously reattached racial meanings to state capacities to violently exclude categories of persons as "exceptional' security threats—that is to say, the reconstitution of a racialized relation as a zone of violence and insecurity that warrants active state augmentation and intervention. "Conventional wisdom holds that the United States faced an actual crime problem in the 1960s that was infused with racial politics," writes Naomi Murakawa. The fact is that the "U.S. did not confront a crime problem that was then racialized; it confronted a race problem that was then criminalized."[12] Put another way, the end of the 1960s marked the reactivation of an old reciprocity between acts of "legitimate" state violence and the "inhuman" worlds that become their object and rationale. In this mode of thought and social policy, violent state action and biopolitical security take precedence over any understanding of politics rooted in consensual democratic action—even if democratic consent is sought to ratify these agendas. Moreover, in this view, any visible manifestation of violence deemed illegitimate—regardless of its reality, source, or etiology—becomes prima facie evidence for the necessity of preemptive violence on the part of state powers, or powers that act in the name of the state. In this way, violence becomes the figure and ground, the consequence and cause, of a categorically new social relation. That is to say, even though such violence may be mapped along the lines of existing social cleavages and (racial) differentiations, it also produces differentiating effects at the point of its application.

This may offer one approach to the vexing question of how racial differentiation persists and reconstitutes itself across profound changes in and challenges to socio-legal, spatial, and racial orders (from plantation slavery to segregation and civil rights).[13] More specifically, it can begin to explain the apparent contradiction between the simultaneous normalization of racial liberalism and intensification of racially inscribed domination. If racism is defined, following Ruth Wilson Gilmore, as state-sanctioned production of group-differentiated vulnerability to premature death, then acts of state violence take precedence over ideological discourses as differentiating practices.[14] In other words, to answer the question, "What is racism?," one needs to begin not with the presumption of existing groups that are the victims of sanctioned harm, but with an account of the formation and institutionalization of structures and situations of protection and vulnerability for which post-hoc description of the characteristics of dishonored groups serve as a form of rationalization or justification. Retrospective rationalizations become central to reinforcing and reproducing disparate vulnerability, which is why ideological forms of racism need to be combated on their own terms. The social experience of stigma also often becomes part of the formation of cultures of resistance, group identification, and linked fates among oppressed peoples. In ideological terms, racism is knowable as a narrative structure of positions and habits of perception that corresponds with, and responds to, an *existing* regime of racial categorization and differentiation.[15]

The important question remains, however, of how new racial orders are constituted. Forms of past racial ordering are only partially predictive of racial (or nonracial) futures, particularly given the extent to which racial meaning precipitates political struggles and persists through periods of vast social and economic change. Social differentiations that come to be known as racial continue to be produced *in advance* of stable orders of racial reference and in contexts in which fields of racial reference are actively destabilized.

This kind of understanding seems particularly important today, when the historic forms of racist attribution and commonsense have been widely challenged, if not wholly discredited, and when the reproduction of racial disparity proceeds through a powerful discourse of disavowal. If racial liberalism has tended to reduce racial meaning to problems of individual perception and prejudice, the critical social constructionist view has a tendency to hypostatize race as "merely" ideological—that is, the more or less coherent expression of contending collective mentalities or group identities. As already suggested, the notion of race as a "decentered complex of social meaning" advanced by *Racial Formation* marks an important advance on this view. Not only does *Racial Formation* expressly resist efforts to cast race as "epiphenomenal," but it attempts to think through "racialization" as an active social process—"the extension of racial meaning to a previously unclassified relationship, social practice or group."[16]

At the same time, the identification of race as primarily a question of social meaning—even when that meaning has been understood to be productive of inequality in wealth, employment, housing, law enforcement, and other domains—continues to operate within a methodological discourse that imagines race as something that can ultimately be precipitated *out of* social relations, rather than as something that is constantly made and remade *as* a social relation. In other words, the problem is still how to specify what makes a certain social relation "racial," which generally means identifying the resurfacing of established forms of racial discourse or ideology to describe, interpret, or justify that social relation. This is why so much intellectual and political debate continues to turn on the positivist validity of racial classification, the question of discriminatory intent, or degrees of inclusion and exclusion, while failing to even recognize, let alone explain, the extraordinary resiliency of institutionalized racial disparity and domination—in the absence of either extensive legal support or a strong ideological justification.

Ironically, critical discourse about race today is most likely to task itself with identifying a situation as "racial" in the face of public absence of such recognition. In addition to its obvious intellectual and political weaknesses, the claim that race (still) matters, or that a particular institution or situation is "racist," however, rarely captures the paradoxical durability and novelty of contemporary racial conditions, which now include the delegitimation of formal racial categories and ideologies by antiracist struggles. The political decomposition of white supremacy has turned antiracists into detectives in search of the traces of racialized power. At the same time, it has imposed unprecedented ideological burdens upon putatively racist social movements and racially invidious policy prescriptions, forcing them to defend their nonracist bona fides even as they attempt to reconstitute a political constituency along racial lines. We are likely to misconstrue this situation entirely, however, if we imagine that ideological racism has ever been fully disarticulated from the complex forms of identification and modalities of political action in which it is embedded. Racist adherence would not be effective, nor would it infuse collectivities, were it not also a theory of political action and a persuasive account of the bases of social reproduction—including questions of labor, gender, sexuality and, above all, nationality. At the same time, locating the specifically racial component within contemporary political struggles is increasingly difficult, perhaps even impossible.

Indeed, the political complexity and contradictions of racial history in the United States have arguably never been as clearly on display as they are today. A highly visible coterie of black people, for example, have become rich, powerful players in the media, sports, entertainment, and military industries, even as a massive prison complex locks up one in nine black men between ages 20 and 34 and strips one in seven of the right to vote on the grounds of felon-disfranchisement statutes.[17] Three decades of more or less continuous immigration and household formation by peoples from Latin America and Asia now augur a remarkable demographic shift in the United States, even as police and military powers to confine, detain, deport, and kill predominantly Latino/a "illegal" immigrants and predominantly South Asian and Muslim "enemy combatants" have been expanded. The United States has had its first popularly elected black president, yet even his birthright was challenged by individuals and groups who also declared a desire to reinterpret the Fourteenth

Amendment and establish new prerequisites for "birthright" citizenship (*jus soli*) that would exclude "illegal" immigrants and their "anchor babies."

One would be hard pressed to support the claim that the field of contemporary U.S. politics is not thoroughly racialized. As suggested by *Racial Formation*, moreover, racial meanings continue to inform and to be transformed by political struggle. It is more difficult, however, to explain how extremely violent and unequal social relations—including those that may map onto existing racial cleavages—can now be immediately produced and publicly sanctioned without explicit reference to race. The categories of convicted felon, enemy combatant, and illegal immigrant each enact a violent and exclusive social relation through a process of criminalization without a racial prerequisite. They raise the question of whether all social relationships constituted through forms of extreme state violence should be considered "racial" or "racist"– which is to say they broach the central and unresolved question of how we can know something is "racial" or "racist" and why we might want to retain "race" as a category of analysis even when its epistemological grounds are shaky and its ontological basis largely refuted. The partial answer is that race talk (and especially critical discourse about race) provides the vocabulary that allows us to record and index the recurrent institutionalization and the unfinished contest over the uniquely violent foundations of Western modernity in slavery and freedom, colonization and self-government, in a period when those foundations have been obscured by platitudes about global markets and reconstituted by practices of permanent war.[18]

To take account of contemporary conditions, however, it is also necessary to challenge the implicit or explicit nationalist horizons that still tend to define the posing of racial questions and challenges—that is, a tendency to frame race as a question *for* the nation, rather than a question *of* the nation. From the standpoint of racial liberalism, for example, race and nation (and this goes back as far back as Ernest Renan's famous disquisition on the question) are antagonistic constructs of social and political identity.[19] Racial liberalism often retains the traces of a primordialist or naturalist conception of racial difference, but it invariably consigns it to the past and argues for the relativization, if not wholesale erasure, of racial particularity with respect to universal citizenship and socially consequential forms of national political identity and equality. Where racial liberalism posits nationalism as a species of universalism that progressively triumphs over forms of racial particularity, the agonistic notion of the nation as a racial formation, and the state as a racial state, tends to see racism as an ever-active, more or less permanent ideological constellation internal to the nation-state. Even in this conception, however, the nation-state continues to be imagined as the political horizon of ultimate *deracialization*. That is, projects of racial egalitarianism remain linked to the nation-form as both a pragmatic political reality and as an order of social mediation that is at least in some incipient sense nonracial or racially neutral.

But what if we think of race less as a meaning complex that is a given, anchored in a set of biological or ethnic classifications of specific population groups within a particular nation-state, and more as an epistemic field that has been extended and filled according to specific historical imperatives of national sovereignty? This is Western modernity's preeminent governing rubric. Such a perspective, I would suggest, can enable a fuller appreciation of both the empty foundationalism and the ceaseless reinvention that characterize the operation of race in modernity—what the poet Leroi Jones famously describes (in a famous disquisition on black music) as "the changing same."[20] Of foremost importance to reproducing race is a distinction between sovereign and nonsovereign space and the concomitant development of legal and ethical doctrines of sovereignty as conferring the right to use legitimate violence (up to and including the right to kill) in the colonial confrontation.[21] Racial classification emerged in this context as a flexible rubric for collectively marking and also individualizing a kind of "anticivilizational chaos" or excess, categorically opposed to sovereignty as a civil domain and protector of life.[22] Phenotype was one element among many in colonial racial classifications, which encompassed a wide range of markers of social, spatial, and embodied difference, including language, geography, behavior, culture, technology, religion, sound, and sexuality.[23]

For the last half century, U.S. global power has sought to cleanse sovereignty of its colonial-racial taint. Thus, as Nazi Germany and, to a lesser extent, imperial Japan came to be seen as the apotheosis of murderous, racist states, and violent processes of decolonization proceeded fitfully, the colonial contexts for the production of modern sovereignty were gradually erased. Ironically, the global visibility of U.S. racial dramas played an important role in this process. Despite the transnational contexts shaping the U.S. federal government's disavowals of white supremacy after World War II, black struggles were portrayed as a domestic, national concern, without any particular relationship to decolonization elsewhere in the world. Over time, in other words, a U.S. "exceptionalist" account of race carefully excised its colonial genesis. This erasure was implicitly recognized by astute commentators like Gunnar Myrdal and diplomats like Ralph Bunche, who understood that racial reform in the United States was essential to modeling a form of power capable of winning the allegiance of the emerging and soon-to-be-sovereign darker nations. The toxic brew of white supremacist intransigence and anticommunist militarism poisoned the reservoirs of respect and good feeling that anticolonial nationalists, from West Africa to Southeast Asia, including Ho Chi Minh, may have held for the United States in 1945. Meanwhile, radical black-freedom activists in the United States challenged the state's efforts to domesticate their struggles and separate them from opposition to imperial foreign policy and colonial war, emphasizing instead the "special type" or "internal" form of colonization they suffered.[24]

Comparative colonial accounts of black suffering have fallen on hard times since the late 1960s and early 1970s, even as transnational and diasporic accounts of black cultural and intellectual production have achieved

scholarly respectability and recognition as well as a degree of popular resonance. In the consensus view of civil rights history in the United States,
racial reform, democratic expansion, and national inclusion are the main
currents of the U.S.-led phase of global history. This view gained force during the second half of the twentieth century and up to the present day, particularly given the partial successes of the civil rights movement (up to and
including the election of Barack Obama). The severing of the link between
race and colonialism was part and parcel of the reification of race as a phenomenon primarily understood in terms of domestic law and positive science, which once again produced a situation in which a narrow (nationalist)
politics of racial classification and identification submerged more expansive
arguments about the relationship between race, ethics, political economy,
and foreign policy. As Barnor Hesse writes, this development not only pro-
foundly reduced the scope and significance of race, but it also began to
obscure its "prolonged historical invention and enactment" as a complex,
persistent marker of inferior social status, civil incapacity, and civil
threat.[25]

With the dominant narrative of civil rights success at the center, the
public understanding of U.S. racial politics foregrounds processes of citizen
deliberation, legal reform, and inclusive nation building. In recent years, a
host of bizarre and troubling formulations have been built upon this ideological edifice, from Michael Ignatieff's assertion that the 2003 US invasion
of Iraq was acceptable to the world because it was not built upon "the white
man's burden" to Secretary of State Condoleeza Rice's claim that the African
American civil rights movement helped the U.S. to "find its voice" as an
armed champion of democracy overseas. A *New York Times* article by Adam
Liptak purporting to explain the exceptionally high incarceration rates in
the United States today was especially revealing on this score: "Many specialists dismissed race as an important distinguishing factor in the American prison rate. It is true that blacks are much more likely to be imprisoned

than other groups in the United States, but that is not a particularly distinctive phenomenon. Minorities in Canada, Britain and Australia are also disproportionately represented in those nations' prisons, and the ratios are similar to or larger than those in the United States."[26]

Where Ignatieff and Rice linked civil rights successes to an exceptional overcoming of the ordering mechanism of race in the United States, Liptak effectively short-circuited any lingering negative racial exceptionalism through a comparative gesture, one that renaturalized racial disparities at a global scale. A demonstrated, invidious racial disparity in all the leading national formations of white settler colonialism supposedly illustrates the normalcy and race neutrality of *all of them*. While this may represent a particularly glaring kind of sophistry, it illuminates how race persists as empirical description and effect in observations about everyday life, even as it is disqualified a priori as a source of social action and power that might require adjudication. In a deeper sense, however, the quoted passage suggests quite precisely what may be the necessary parameters of our inquiry today—that is, not only how racial formation is irreducible to any specific national social formation, but also how it has been elaborated, assembled, and operationalized in relation to institutionalized, yet ideologically flexible zones of state-sanctioned violence and exclusion around the world.

When we contemplate the *longue durée* of modern social formations, including the United States, we might consider how sovereign violence, rather than political struggle, or legal and scientific codification "overdetermines" the field of racial meanings and effects. This effect is what W. E. B. Du Bois may have had in mind when he described the globally dominant racist formation of white supremacy of his day as "a kind of public and psychological wage."[27] Commentators on the association between whiteness and wages have tended to focus on the racial monopolization of fields of employment and the production of differentials within laboring populations that cut across socioeconomic class. As important, however, are the terms *public* and *psychological,* for they highlight the transfer of whiteness to the domain of nationality as an imagined community or public, or the constitution of race as a relation that links "democratic participation with the management of public authority and its specific mechanisms of violence."[28] In his classic argument about the origins of race in colonial Virginia, for example, Edmund Morgan showed how carefully elaborated gradations in modes of punishment were among the keys to the elaboration of distinctions between African slaves and European indentured servants: black bodies were whipped naked, whites could remain clothed.[29] Although Morgan was interested in illuminating the power of law to codify or ratify a racial project, this example contains a deeper meaning. The long eighteenth-century expansion of rights to political participation for whites in the United States was articulated as an increasingly privileged relationship to the modalities of official violence and its legal narration: what defined the race relation was the fact that blacks and Indians could be killed with impunity.

The prospect of state violence, even war, has never been far from the figuration or the conceptualization of race as form of social relation. Beyond the obvious pecuniary and erotic interests that weighed on his tortured conscience, for example, Thomas Jefferson believed that racial slavery had implanted a security threat at the heart of the U.S. republic. Blacks needed either to be quarantined or to be placed beyond the reach of admixture. If not, the "deep-rooted prejudices entertained by the whites: ten thousand recollections, by the blacks, of the injuries they have sustained" would eventually lead to a war of "extermination of one of the other race."[30] Jefferson explicitly imagines race war as civil war. The result of a traumatic and recurring state of injury, it produces a divided collective experience that can be neither forgiven nor forgotten, and which thus remains outside the domain of the regulated space of collective organization, rational action, and conflicts of interest. Blackness, in this context, is knowable only as threat, what Jefferson elsewhere described as that "immovable veil" that obscures what can only be a murderous wish or intention. The affinities of blackness with a discourse of crime are already emergent here. The great irony, as Jefferson implicitly recognized, is that it was the crimes committed by whites that constituted the real historical basis for the threat, which was in turn displaced onto and into black bodies.

It is the potential for black equality—one might say *black sovereignty* or *self-possession*—that activates the fantasy of race war. Race war, moreover, needs to be distinguished from "normal" war—that is, war fought under terms of mutual recognition between equal sovereigns. In race war and colonial war, there can only be one sovereign, and the opponent is not recognized as a political rival but rather viewed as an unjust enemy or a criminal. In *Settler Sovereignty*, Lisa Ford elaborates how this process began in the mid-nineteenth century. The early U.S. republic largely tolerated plural forms of sovereignty under rubrics of warfare and treaty agreements that regulated conduct among different indigenous "tribes" and the U.S. federal state, all of which were considered to be sovereign. By the 1830s, however, settler sovereignty had decisively expanded its purview, precisely by describing indigenous violence (and counterviolence) as a type of crime and in turn creating new legal narratives for settler violence. According to Ford, the shift from a discourse of war to a discourse of crime is central to the substantive erasure of native sovereignty.[31]

Interestingly, this period gave rise to a fairly wide-ranging conversation on how to mark the boundaries of war, a conversation in which we can observe how violence against colonial and racial subjects—that is, subjects deemed to be constitutively lacking sovereignty—is quite precisely unbracketed or suspended. War in racial and colonial situations, rather than marking a breach of normal politics—and "the continuation of politics by other means," as Clausewitz famously defined it—becomes the primary means of mediating and structuring social relations with those classified as potentially criminal or unjust enemies. In an early iteration of this logic, for example, Kant's *Metaphysics* (1797), after having laid out interdictions against war (including a ban on wars of extermination and subjugation), asserts, quite stunningly, and contrary to what Kant has just been arguing, that "the rights of a state against an unjust enemy are unlimited in quantity or degree." The "unjust enemy" is "someone whose publicly expressed will, whether expressed in word or in deed, displays a maxim that would make peace among nations impossible and would lead to a perpetual state of nature if it were made into a general rule."[32]

If U.S. settler sovereignty begins and ends with Indians, it lingers in complex ways on blacks and blackness. In contrast to the threat of otherness on the frontier, which was largely eliminated, blackness, cultivated and reproduced under the auspices of the slave regime, remained a permanent threat, one that required investing every white person with the right to kill. Here once again we see a blurring of a military and police relation: citizen militias and slave patrols were functional equivalents, the routes they charted along the plantation hinterlands aptly called "the beat."[33] The incipient race war, moreover, did manifest as a civil war—the greatest industrialized mass slaughter in modern history up to that time. After the war, blackness was legally suspended in freedom, much as it had been suspended in slavery, posing an enduring crisis for democratic sovereignty—even as it gradually also became a means to consider how to fundamentally expand the domain of democratic politics. The Reconstruction and post-Reconstruction era in the South was marked by the articulation of legal and extralegal violence by police and white vigilantes that focused on disrupting, if not destroying, black social relations at the point of social reproduction, and by the constitution of politics along paramilitary lines.[34]

It is arguable that civil war never really ended for blacks in the South: both legal and extralegal violence became norms of black life. As one U.S. senator put it, "The black man does not incite antagonism because he is black, but because he is a citizen."[35] The signal innovation in racial science following the Reconstruction was the development of racial crime statistics. As Khalil Gibran Muhammad shows, criminality rapidly became the key measure for adjudicating the fitness of black people for modern life, and black criminality became the most durable and "widely accepted basis for justifying prejudicial thinking, discriminatory treatment and the acceptance of racial violence as an instrument of public safety."[36] The Thirteenth Amendment had already shown the way forward, abolishing slavery except as punishment for crime. The period that the black historian Rayford Logan called the nadir was marked by a legal and quasi-legal regime of white terror in which thousands of black people were lynched and tens of thousands murdered in prison and on convict-lease plantations.[37] The resolution of formal black freedom—the granting of civil and political rights—was explicitly calibrated to the augmentation of police power. As the opinion in *Plessy v. Ferguson* reads when nationalizing antimiscegenation statutes, "Laws forbidding intermarriage of the two races may be said in a technical sense to interfere with the freedom of contract," but such regulation "has been universally recognized as within the police power of the state."[38]

The police powers delineated here are biopowers in the Foucauldian sense, but biopowers that are quite distinctly articulated to juridical rights as the exception that proves the rule : they invest the police with a formless authority precisely correlated to zones of rightlessness and statelessness elaborated through colonial and racial violence. In other words, this is neither a strictly formal nor a functionalist aspect of modern sovereignty: rather it is the application of the founding logic of sovereignty to justify expansions of the police power. John Burgess put it in the following revealing formulation in 1893: "The police power is the Dark Continent of our jurisprudence."[39] According to Brian Wagner, from the standpoint of power, what constitutes blackness is its rearticulation to the conditions of statelessness. Statelessness, or nonsovereign existence, might further be characterized as a condition of social dissolution that is understood as *anathema* to social reproduction. The modern police power is precisely correlated to "the Dark Continent" as the domain in which social and political life is always already suspended.

Although the modern police power was articulated to a politics of white supremacy, its prerogatives were defined not as a defense of racial particularity but as a defense of the constituent power of democratic (national) sovereignty. Put another way, we might say that racial distinctions have been made and remade as differentiations of zones of protection from and vulnerability to sovereign violence. Sovereignty, in turn, is simultaneously the object of popular-democratic claims and a form of institutionalized (or state) authority. Racist and antiracist politics have unfolded quite precisely within this space, yet it has hardly been an even contest. Drawing upon a liberal-democratic tradition, antiracist movements of the twentieth century tended to appeal to institutionalized (state) authority for recognition and protection of individual rights within a civil domain understood as a negotiated plurality. By contrast, racist and exclusionary movements have consistently based themselves upon an understanding of the homogeneous basis of sovereignty ("the rights of those that have rights") and in turn seek an identity or reciprocity with institutionalized (or constituted) power. For most of U.S. history, such reciprocity has been easily achieved, as institutionalizations of the military-police function have been articulated and enacted in relation to figures of nemesis both familiar and newly fashioned, exotic regimes and repertoires of difference close at hand.

What may be exceptional, or at least notable, about the United States is the depth, duration, and significance of its struggle and debate about racial exclusion. When we recognize the extent to which sovereign violence constitutes law, we can also recognize how questions of racial difference and their attendant conflicts have been swiftly envisioned as a threat to the survival of the state. Speaking at the height of the civil rights movement and in opposition to impending civil rights legislation, Barry Goldwater declared,

"Security from domestic violence, no less than from foreign aggression, is the most elementary and fundamental purpose of any government."[40] Goldwater was drawing on a nascent discourse that pitted the "rights" of citizens against the chaos, disorder, and incipient criminality of racial protest politics. Conservatives who followed in his wake increasingly understood that one did not need to uphold statutory racial discrimination but merely to draw compelling distinctions between law-abiding citizens and those who threatened their security. Race made all the difference to producing a compelling distinction. But the very category of *illegal* or *criminal*, particularly as it became part of the logic of an administrative apparatus, could increasingly do the work of racial sorting without explicitly maintaining the forms of racial codification that had been central to its origination.

In 1994, the passage of the largest crime bill in U.S. history established the preliminary legal and institutional architecture of the massively expanded national security state, something that grew paradoxically and in spite of the end of the cold war that had supplied the entire rationale for its initial growth.[41] Statutory provisions for the "rendition" of foreign drug traffickers and for the suspension of ancient strictures on the internal use of military resources and personnel accelerated the dissolution of moral and conceptual boundaries between practices of domestic policing and public safety and external military aggression, with effects on both sides. The self-styled global strategist and futurologist Robert Kaplan (reputedly Bill Clinton's favorite public intellectual) captured the zeitgeist in his widely read essay "The Coming Anarchy." Writing in the wake of the Los Angeles riots of 1992, Kaplan diagnosed a fundamental weakening of the U.S. nation-state as an engine of homogenization and conflict stabilization, ascribing the failures of both (yet again) to the pathologies of black urban dwellers, who, unlike the Jews and Irish before them, preferred the hostilities and illusory gratifications of "negritude" to the virtuous trials of assimilation. Kaplan further suggested that the dangers of the inner (racial) fragmentation of the nation-space were magnified by a global situation in which a contagion of state failures, particularly in Africa (where else?), had the potential to inflame conflicts along racial and civilizational lines. He observed (following the urban military theorist Martin Van Creveld) that fighting crime and waging war were gradually becoming indistinguishable and that "national defense" was no longer defined by unitary territorial logic but rather by multiscalar tactics and strategies of pacification and control.[42]

Kaplan's fixation on the disruptive and dangerous presence of black ontology at the internal borders of the United States is telling, as is his sense that the disruption of national homogeneity constitutes a threat to sovereignty that is functionally equivalent to an undeclared (race) war. It is important, in making this point, to observe with Fred Moten "the paraontological distinction between blackness and black people" if we are to grasp the ever-fungible articulations and rearticulations of race and sovereignty.[43] If blackness has been the principal figure and ground for defining and enacting a racialized *inhumanity*, particularly in U.S. history, it has also proved to be analogically flexible and part of a heterogeneous repertoire of racializing motifs that have informed the creation of a military-police apparatus at home and abroad. It was the triggering events of 9/11, moreover, that gave new energy to morbid visions of racial-civilizational decline, providing both retrospective and prospective logics for the substitution of warfare for welfare as the guarantor of social security. This shift has been echoed in shrinking kingdoms of privileged prosperity across the Western world. Where the pioneering Islamophobe Bernard Lewis explicitly linked terrorism and migration as the twin threats to European civilization, in analyzing the response to the 9/11 attacks John Lewis Gaddis reached deep into the American past, justifying new Bush administration doctrines of preemptive war on the grounds of an older sovereign right, the new nation's right to protect its open frontier against the depredations of "native Americans, pirates, and other marauders."[44]

If *Racial Formation* correctly diagnosed the ways in which racial invest-ments and referents were increasingly embedded within (if not constitutive of) broadly "hegemonic" political struggles and policy debates, it did not (and perhaps could not) foresee the extent to which race would continue operate as a means of wholesale, violent political and civil exclusion for large segments of the population, not only in the United States but wherever peo-ple were exposed to sovereign violence (much of which, incidentally, can be traced back to the spread of U.S. models and practices of policing, security, and war). The laudable goal of reanimating race as a vehicle of collective, egalitarian political aspiration faced a number of obstacles, ones for which extant languages and frames of civil-inclusionist, let alone nation-based, politics have proved inadequate. Indeed, the recent turn in intellectual dis-course to a largely *antipolitical* rubric comprising terms like *state of exception*, *bare life, social death*, and even *race war* might be said to index this state of affairs: that is, such approaches attempt to formally diagnose the limit con-ditions of the (exceptional) state form that has emerged as the norm in recent decades, even as they express a certain pessimism or even impotence with respect to conjunctural possibilities and ameliorative strategies. Thinking at the limit seems to limit thinking (especially critical thinking) to the most austere conceptualizations of enduring, or entirely unchanging, modalities of racial dominance and state violence (without hegemony) over time.

This is a challenging, paradoxical situation. On the one hand, the con-temporary historical understanding, comparative elaboration, and theoreti-cal conceptualization of U.S. racial formation have achieved a level of com-plexity and comprehensiveness unimaginable two decades ago. Building at least in part on the innovations of *Racial Formation*, hundreds of monographs and research projects have outlined how racial dispositions and powers have been shaped in the interstices of ideological struggle and institutional change, within a dialectic of social movement actors and government agen-cies, and at the nexus of foreign and domestic policies throughout the colonial and settler-colonial world. On the other hand, the application of state violence in the production of forms of group-differentiated spatial confinement, bodily dispossession, denial of civic honor and recognition, and vulnerability to violence, injury, and ill health (up to and including premature death) now proceeds largely without the requirement of an explicit codification of, or reference to, existing forms of group differentiation. (This situation is ironically mirrored in certain critical tendencies toward formalist, ahistorical theorization that sometimes proceed by means of rubrics like *bare life*.) Whether this is termed *a new racism, color-blind racism,* or *racism without race*, it is a form of power that produces disparate effects without prior ideological rationalization or explicit group targeting: indeed, the express absence (or explicit disavowal) of particularistic or "racial" intent in part legitimates such violence.

In the United States, we might say that it is the concrete institutionalizations of the militarized, carceral, war-on-terror state, rather than the struggle against Jim Crow and white supremacy, that form the background to the contemporary theorization of race and the struggle against racial division. It might be objected that the popular election of Barack Obama, a black man, to the presidency fundamentally altered this picture. Obama's rise was scripted from a carefully selected combination of African American civil-rights narrative elements and postracial prescriptive postures, adherence to color-blind policies, and multicultural pabulum. Obama also consciously sought to dampen the civilizational-enemy rhetoric of the long war. The racial panics his election engendered among elements of the far right—from the Trump-led "birther" movement to the Tea Party rhetoric that cast Obama as a demonic figure, even a new Hitler—attests to the destabilization and consequent scrambling of right-wing racial codes. Racist depictions of Obama generally tended to present him not as a figure of black subhumanity and dishonored kinship but rather in the mode of Orientalism and anti-Semitism, in which the racial other is represented as an enemy within, an inscrutable misleader who possesses unnatural, even superhuman powers, a person backed by foreign moneyed cabals—not our degraded kin, but one whose very birthright is foreign and fraudulent.[45] In another sense, however, Obama's election merely reaffirmed the ideological baseline of multicultural postracialism, against which a resurgent white supremacy is likely to continue to contend only with difficulty, particularly in the face of unfavorable demographic trends.

Kaplan highlights a key aspect of the contemporary crisis, framing it in the terms of the nationalist-racial panic that has been rising across the Western world over several decades. This panic suggests that a "quotient of homogeneity," in the words of Gopal Balakrishnan, is required for the continued existence of the nation-state.[46] In the United States, this question has long been mediated by the application of the equally fungible and strategically indeterminate term *white*, which reflexively precedes the constitution of political identity that "founds" democratic sovereignty. Yet over many decades, the power of whiteness to do this work of national cohesion has been substantively, perhaps even fatally, diminished. The promise of Obama as he identified with the civil rights narrative was a form of national sovereignty no longer grounded in the history of white supremacy. Instead, in his embrace of a more progressive neoliberalism, Obama seemed to define the completion of the post-1960s passive revolution, in which the exceptional state, born of the accumulation crisis of the West in its incipient moment of globalization, was given a new legitimacy and lease on life. With his election, the historic irresolution of black liberation, against which color-blind discourse protested too much and multicultural discourse softened or acceded too readily, could be officially declared completed. Trump's electoral success signals that the center did not hold, and that the apparent truce, or at least stalemate, in the ongoing civil war may give way to something far worse in its next incarnation. The danger is that the terrorist franchising and attacks on soft targets in the West that have increased with the long war have become

Racial Formation and Permanent War

the perfect foil for strengthening the formidable machineries of surveillance, violence, and control assembled by the exceptional state in past decades. Terrorism by shadowy actors sows the public fear and enmity that the authoritarian and antipolitical security state thrives on as a pretext for war—not only in distant theaters but within our own society.

CHAPTER FIVE

The Present Crisis

> This war has to be fought with the scale and duration and savagery that is only true of civil wars. We are lucky in this country that our civil wars are fought at the ballot box, not on the battlefield; nonetheless it is a true civil war.
>
> Newt Gingrich, remarks at the Eleventh Annual Resource Bank Meeting (1988)

Donald Trump's election to the U.S. presidency produced shock and disbelief among liberals, progressives, and leftists around the world. Even many who recognize the flaws in the myth of America's democratic perfectibility and exceptionalism mourn its passing. That said, there is a tendency to read too much into the results of elections. They do not provide us with an objective diagnostic of a country's political condition: they are voter mobilization projects (conducted, in the main, by elites). The interpretation of the results, their meaning, and their so-called mandate retains a character of political positioning, even score settling. The desire to parse and explain the disastrous outcome of a Trump electoral victory and a Republican Party majority in both houses of Congress is understandable. But because much of the early analysis neglected a longer-term explanation of how we got here, it has only contributed to our collective disorientation. Written in the months following the election, this chapter attempts to take a longer view.

Many first assessments of Trump's electoral victory had an unseemly character of piling on. The most egregious examples were the gangland triumphalism of some Trump supporters, for whom victory licensed acts of bigotry, intimidation, and humiliation. Some centrist liberals, worried about a loss of proximity to power, similarly aimed their fire at more vulnerable groups, warning that it was the solicitude for so-called identity politics and sectional concerns of immigrants, racial minorities, women, and LGBT communities that caused Clinton's electoral defeat. The *New York Times* presented, in the guise of description, a depiction of terminal racial conflict in the language of eugenics, calling the result an electric response by white voters to "long-term demographic decay."[1]

We would do well to look beyond efforts to reduce complexity in the current political climate or to presume that demography is destiny, especially when such thinking betrays fear-induced submission to Trumpism itself, by naturalizing some idea of ineluctable or spontaneous racial animus. We did not suddenly awaken in a different country the day after the election. We would have had a very different conversation if fewer than one hundred thousand voters had swung the other way in the upper Midwest, the epicenter of an economic catastrophe whose roots go back to the 1970s and early 1980s. Hillary Clinton won the popular vote by a margin of 3 million popular votes (winning almost exactly the number of votes Obama gained in 2012, although in a larger electorate). How would we be interpreting her victory if she had mastered the baroque math of the Electoral College?

I do not suggest that we should not be alarmed. In retrospect, it is Trump's ascendancy with a Republican Party majority that should have worried us most. Long before Trump emerged, the GOP was the most politically entrenched, racially homogeneous far-Right political party in the Western world, one that mobilized and welded together social conservatism, a near-fanatical commitment to upward wealth redistribution, climate-change denial, the rejection of socially useful public spending, hostility to taxation in support of transfer payments to the poorest and most vulnerable, racially coded appeals to law and order, and anti-immigrant animus. Its ascent was aided by opposition to gains in formal equality, particularly the reproductive rights of women, the civil rights of racial and sexual minorities, and the ethno-racial diversification of U.S. public institutions and public culture—including schools and universities. Republican public policy was informed by moral panics about crime, drugs, and welfare, and legal resistance to moderate reforms such as affirmative action, antidiscrimination remedies, voting-rights protection and abortion rights. The last time the Republican Party controlled all three branches of government was in 2001, and we know what ensued then. Before that, the last occurrence of this special alignment was 1928, right before the Great Depression.

In the 1990s, Bill Clinton completed the redefinition of the Democratic Party by quietly taking over the Right's dog-whistle racism and policy preferences: dressing down the rapper Sister Souljah; presiding over the execution of the cognitively impaired black prisoner Ricky Ray Rector; withdrawing his nomination of Lani Guinier for assistant attorney general when Republicans derided her as a "quota queen"; agreeing (as he put it) "to end welfare as we know it"; and passing the most comprehensive and punitive crime bill in U.S. history, defined through the imagery of "superpredators," street terrorists," and criminal migrants.[2] The first Clinton strategy (in this as in other things) was to meet the Right halfway: to neutralize appeals to white identity politics with domestically focused promises of economic prosperity for all"; to take a hard-line stance on crime and welfare; to ratchet up the deportation of undocumented immigrants and to confine amelioration of racial inequality to a repertoire of sympathetic nods toward diversity and demonstrations of personal commitment to interracial comity.

The initial windfalls of so-called free trade, financial deregulation, and the accelerated globalization of manufacturing that pumped up U.S. financial and real-estate markets during these years appeared to vindicate an approach that softened overt racial antagonism and presented neoliberal policy on finance, trade, and workfare requirements in a progressive guise: In the face of right-wing intransigence, Toni Morrison even conferred upon Clinton the honorary title of "first black president."[3] The old Midwestern industrial belt and the social safety nets that prevented catastrophe for the urban and rural poor were not only weakened but also being recast as incubators of individual dependency and dereliction rather than seen as a needed response to social and market failures. Meanwhile, U.S. prisons and jails, many newly built, were filling to capacity. The culture wars, tawdry scandals, and military misadventures of this period, including the impeachment of a sitting president, were indicators of a social and political system hurtling toward crisis.

Writing in the late 1990s, the philosopher Richard Rorty offered a prediction that, immediately following the election of Trump, many commentators invoked as if stumbling upon a lost prophecy. Rorty, along with others, recognized that one economic consequence of the globalization of trade and industry was the substantial loss of well-paying manufacturing jobs for American workers with no more than a high school education. He warned that inattention to the declining fortunes of this group, particularly among professional, college-educated suburbanites, would lead to a reactionary working-class revolt and the election of a divisive and dictatorial "strongman" to America's highest office.[4] He largely ignored the fact that the most creative and ambitious movement organizing during this period brought together trade unionists and environmentalists in opposition to institutions like the World Trade Organization and the International Monetary Fund (culminating in the 1999 protest in Seattle) and sought to challenge forms of globalist governance on the grounds of their erosion of labor rights, living standards, democratic accountability, and environmental protection.

Rorty might also have emphasized the effects of a long period of right-wing antitax revolts, the NIMBY politics of small property holders, military and carceral spending, and punitive social budgeting. These policies and attitudes undermined support for redistributive public investments in infrastructure, job training, and higher education to address the generational crisis wrought by deindustrialization and global outsourcing. Instead, Rorty and other left-liberal critics of multiculturalism, like Arthur Schlesinger Jr. and Walter Benn Michaels, framed the conflict in cultural terms (while ironically also criticizing such framing): in their view, an emphasis on a politics of identity and difference, advanced by university-trained liberals and progressives, had led to the neglect of the material grievances of the white working class. "One thing that is very likely to happen," Rorty wrote, "is that the gains made in the past forty years by black and brown Americans, and by homosexuals, will be wiped out. Jocular contempt for women will come back into fashion. . . . All the resentment which badly educated Americans feel about having their manners dictated to them by college graduates will find an outlet."[5]

The last point is the one that jarred: it appeared to be an apt description of Trumpism. Yet the diagnosis actually redoubled a type of elite contempt by failing to mark the fact that the *contempt of elites,* rather than the spontaneous and disorganized social feeling of those at the lower (class) end of the social order, was the far more significant cause. From Kevin Phillips to Lee Atwater and now Steve Bannon, the steady rightward political movement in the United States in recent decades has been aided by the strategic limning of an inner societal war through coded appeals to a white constituency. Figures like the silent majority, the Reagan Democrat, or the forgotten, hardworking American have been used to represent those dispossessed as a consequence of elite solicitude for racial outsiders. This approach has nourished a potent imagery of (male) whites whose misfortunes are tied to the rise of Asian capital, the wave of Mexican migrants, or the perfidy of black criminals; it has long been the dark art of U.S. partisan and electoral politics.[6]

Ironically, it was George W. Bush who softened this approach, promoting a more racially and ethnically inclusive "compassionate conservatism," with support for broad-based immigration reform that offered a pathway to citizenship for a significant number of undocumented migrants. After winning the inconclusive, contentious election of 2000, however, the Bush administration was politically adrift until the 9/11 terrorist attack licensed a different organizing project and principle, one long planned by a group of administration insiders: large-scale war in the world's energy heartlands. What the war promised but failed to deliver was a "new American century," in which continued U.S. arrogation of "global leadership" and military supremacy would also offer enduring material advantages for the great majority within the North American redoubt.[7]

Of course, it was a grand illusion. First on the Bush agenda was withdrawal from the Kyoto climate-change accords, followed by tax cuts for the very wealthy, including an extension of provisions protecting vast family estates. It was followed by an expansion of prescription drug benefits that failed to curb exorbitant profitmaking by big pharmaceutical concerns. The wars in Afghanistan and Iraq consumed everything else, with runaway, off-the books spending enabled for warfare and its growing legions of private contractors. At the height of its war powers, the Bush administration claimed a hold on a new post-truth world that feels eerily familiar—one in which history is made by access to superior violence and projections of force, which create the facts that those of us in the "reality-based community" will be compelled to witness and "write about."[8]

A joke circulated in those days that the U.S. public was to the Bush administration as a wife to her cheating, abusive husband, who, when confronted with evidence of his misdeeds, asks, "So who are you going to believe, me or your own lying eyes?" Integral to this bad relationship was the administration's open sanctioning of torture, rendition, and offshore detention, trafficking in brown bodies that could be taken and broken outside any national or international norms and laws of war. Despite its multicultural personnel, quickly forgotten humility about nation building, and vacillation on the language of a civilizational struggle against Islam, the Bush adminis-tration quite clearly embraced what Hannah Arendt once termed the expan-sionist tradition of thought that "equates power with violence" and that conceives of power in the most stripped-down, biological terms.[9]

Soon after the events of 9/11, Bush did his best Gary Cooper, warning, "We're steady, clear-eyed, and patient, but pretty soon we are going to have to start displaying scalps." Like military conflicts that unfolded on the Great Plains, in the Philippines, and in Vietnam, the Afghanistan and Iraq inva-sions showed that the demotic idiom of American capitalism on its "disor-dered frontiers" is savage war and race war, along with the proliferation of subjects without rights. No less an authority than the historian John Lewis Gaddis (and he was not alone) affirmed these transitive properties, casually remarking that arrogation of a preemptive violence against "non-state actors" in the name of global security drew on the usable past that North American settlers claimed in their twilight battles against "Native Ameri-cans . . . and other marauders."[10]

The calamity of unending war, crises of legitimation related to false claims about weapons of mass destruction, the scandal of torture, fiscal policies rooted in tax breaks for wealthy individuals and corporate actors, and a banking crisis that drove the country close to economic collapse deliv-ered a seemingly fatal blow to long-held illusions about links between U.S. imperial power and broadly held domestic prosperity. At the same time, the fin-de-siècle claims about a victory of the Left in the culture wars, including Rorty's argument that the diminution of "socially accepted sadism" represented a thin reed of civility in the winds of the political and economic disasters to come, overstated the case: the disaster was presaged by efforts to sanction sadism at the pinnacle of U.S. policymaking and legal thought.

That we would have spent the following decade arguing about whether torture was efficacious and desirable (a view that we seem poised to readopt), that the United States would continue to lead the world in arresting and incarcerating citizens and deporting noncitizens, that we would be continuously at war and poised for more war, or that we would have done so little to reduce or mitigate our toxic contribution to the planet's ecological commons was, to put it kindly, unanticipated then, even as it tends to be forgotten now by those who view the election of Trump as unprecedented or as a departure from our political tradition. But in many ways Trump is the creature of the long war; and it now appears that he wants to bring the war home.

To understand the lacuna in our collective political imagination—which rendered it unthinkable until right after the 2016 election that avowed racists, white supremacists, evangelical home schoolers, and climate-change deniers might be installed to direct national security, oversee justice, administer public education, and safeguard the environment—we must consider something equally unpredictable in the cycle of political events: the election to the presidency of Barack Hussein Obama, viewed as a harbinger of political stability, a return to normative conceptions of political communication and truth-telling, multilateralism and a sense of sobriety about the limits of American military power. A little-known first-term senator, whose claims to lead rested on slender antiwar credentials and surplus charisma, Obama, too, found his path obstructed by Hillary Clinton, anointed by Democratic Party insiders as the heir apparent in the wake of the disasters of the George W. Bush administration. Significantly, Clinton offered a reprise of Rortyian wisdom, touting her support among "hard-working Americans, white Americans . . . who had not completed college" as a necessary bulwark of any successful electoral campaign in the face of Obama's outsider challenge. She was also a foreign-policy hawk. It didn't work then, either; Obama, it appeared, had broken the mold, marrying multiculturalism to an ersatz populism.[11]

As the effects of the collapse of the housing market and the crisis of big financial institutions became evident, Obama's opponent, John McCain, in a sotto voce reference to the old racial humbug, announced that real Americans were the makers and not the victims of history.[12] Yet, despite the revelation of Obama's former associations with Bill Ayers and Jeremiah Wright—one a 1960s counterculture bomb thrower and the other a stridently anti-imperialist black nationalist—McCain actually pulled back from emphasizing Obama's racial alterity and foreignness (the approach favoured by his running mate, Sarah Palin, who also warned of "Second Amendment remedies"). McCain even publicly upbraided a would-be voter who labeled Obama a Muslim terrorist.

In retrospect, McCain's belated act of restraint and civility foretold the resumption of the inner war and the breakdown of the racial truce that liberals and conservatives appeared to have quietly organized around the poles of color-blind jurisprudence and neoliberal multiculturalism during the Bush years, including a growing acceptance of diversification among upwardly mobile, college-educated elites, corporate-friendly trade and finance policies, mass incarceration, and external war. But it was the housing crisis and threat of systemic financial collapse in 2008 that augured the potentially far bigger upset of this neoliberal, neoconservative order. Beneath his campaign message of "hope and change," Obama sounded more adversarial, populist notes (especially in 2012, running against the venture capitalist and corporate raider Mitt Romney). It was mostly political theater, barely pink meat for the base.

Obama's talk of financial "fat cats" outraged Wall Street's lords; they served notice, even though they did not defect. Along with Obama's more strident Tea Party opponents, they deployed an inflammatory rhetoric of totalitarian domination by out-of-control big government. Venture capitalists, private equity managers, and CEOs compared Obama's corporate-tax proposals to Nazi persecution of the Jews.[13] (This too was mostly theater, and today the ironies abound, as the very bankers who were targeted by Trump's veiled anti-Semitic attack on "globalist finance" on the eve of the 2016 election seem assured that his government will be, in the words of Lloyd Blankfein, CEO of Goldman Sachs, "market- and asset-friendly"). The partisan war, however, was real. Led by the fire-breathing, right-wing Southern senator Jim DeMint from South Carolina, then heading the Heritage Foundation, Obama's opponents vowed to "break him." Although they failed to cut off the head in 2012, they started landing huge blows to the body. The massive Democratic political losses at the state and Congressional level, beginning in 2009, were the first signal that all was not well. Supported by pools of dark money unleashed by the Supreme Court's *Citizens United* decision, from 2010 onward the GOP gained some one thousand seats in state legislatures and total control of the state legislatures in twenty-five states.[14]

In his policy approach, Obama was far short of the socialist revolutionary demiurge he was made out to be. In fact, his tenure can now be properly seen for the vast laundering operation that it was. Even when he had the most political leverage and authority, Obama conceded early to budget-balancing monetarists and tribunes of moral hazard, coming out against calls for a larger fiscal stimulus and a forceful settlement with the banks that would have stopped the foreclosure juggernaut that ruined so many homeowners. Hope and change were rapidly transformed into incremental reformism, including a degree of restoration of regulatory control over runaway finance, labor-friendly board appointments that mildly redressed wildly imbalanced power relations between capital and labor, the prohibition of sex-based wage discrimination, and the administration's signature effort on health care—a Democratic policy priority since 1948, but one that succumbed to the logic of market dependency, thereby keeping costs high for those most in need and including punitive financial sanctions as the bulwark of social benefit.

The Obama balance sheet is decidedly mixed. Although he lowered the volume of tough terror talk and sought to end the mandatory sentencing provisions that put so many low-level drug buyers and sellers in prison, he strengthened the framework and security architecture of the long war, including renewing Bush's open-ended executive war powers, expanding mass surveillance and government data-mining operations, and adding a lethal new element: targeted assassination by drone anywhere in the world. Obama tied the hands of lingering Iran hawks with a slender thread of an agreement that may now be undone. He supported gay marriage and federal antidiscrimination protection for LGBT workers and retained and expanded support for women's reproductive choice under the provisions of the health care law, but these measures are certainly on Trump's chopping block. He reestablished the United States' commitment to address climate change with reentry into global climate accords, but now big energy is positioned to rule the table. Obama made diplomatic overtures to Cuba, but the American gulag in Guantanamo Bay (territory secured over a century ago by gunboat diplomacy) that Obama promised to dismantle is intact. Rendition and torture are back on the agenda. Obama offered support for undocumented children of migrants under the Deferred Action for Childhood Arrival program (DACA), but he strengthened immigration enforcement bureaucracies, quietly deporting 2.5 million; under Trump, raids, roundups, and expulsions on an even larger scale are in the offing.

Obama was, admittedly, a steady hand in a moment of crisis and economic turmoil: he did less harm than his predecessor (and likely his successor), but his administration settled nothing of political consequence. Most significantly, albeit intangibly, he habituated ordinary people once again to the idea of positive and responsive government. Perhaps his greatest strategic failure was his decision to continue operating within the terms of the neoliberal market-state consensus. A progressive neoliberal, Obama attempted to reduce social and political volatility and to moderately increase the public commitment to collective risk sharing. This approach prevailed in matters of public finance, public health, race relations, political partisanship, diplomacy, nuclear nonproliferation, environmental degradation, and immigration, and even the limitation of the use of military force (the expansion of drones notwithstanding).

Obama also eschewed partisan politics and party building. He seemed to believe that restoring transparent and competent government within strict neoliberal policy parameters was commensurate with the epochal demands of social renovation that his own unlikely emergence was supposed to signify. Before the 2016 election, in the Rust Belt—where *globalization* was practically a swear word, and a few hundred thousand former Obama voters were deciding whether to gamble on Trump—Obama pushed for the unpopular Trans-Pacific Partnership free-trade agreement. Immediately after the election, in an uncharacteristically fumbling address, he spoke of "the peaceful transition of power," describing the election as an "intramural scrimmage" among people who "want what's best for the country." The fearful undertones reverberated as Obama expressed hope that Trump would uphold values that were formerly understood to be banal and commonplace: "a respect for our institutions, our way of life, the rule of law, and each other." He emphasized that his own administration accomplished what was its "mission from day one": to make government "run better," to be "more responsive . . . efficient . . . and service friendly."[15] In retrospect, it should not be surprising that this unifying pabulum, repressive tolerance, and small-ball, progressive tinkering failed to hold back the forces of repressive desublimation and social decay that Trump represents. Risk and volatility are back, bigly; the wrecking crew is back in charge.

Trump constituted himself early on as Obama's negative mirror image. From the moment he burst on the scene as a public figure in the late 1980s, with a full-page ad in the *New York Times* calling for the execution of the (wrongly convicted) black youths known as the Central Park Five, Trump proved to be a skilful reader and manager of the undercurrent of racist fear and contempt in the United States, as well as more conscious forms of white supremacist commitment. His insistent, conspiratorial questioning of Obama's Hawaii-issued birth certificate melded attention to Obama's blackness with assumptions about his foreignness, allegations of his Muslim fealty, and antipathy to dominant idioms of American civic religiosity. This was the crucible for his brand of "alt-right," post-truth politicking, one that cleverly inverted attacks on various iterations of minority "identity politics" and "political correctness" into an idea that American greatness depends upon reviving the vigor of an aggrieved and demographically besieged white majority.

A narrative that portrayed Obama's cool rise through elite institutions and community organizing to a postracial presidency offered us the alternative, reassuring, and ameliorative story of post-civil rights progress. Our mistake was to believe it, in spite of evidence to the contrary. Built on the idea that diversification of the elite is one of the primary indexes of legitimate government, and that sensitivity to various kinds of narrowly and subjectively defined "privilege" is an adequate standard of social justice, it suggested that despite wars, mass deportation, economic stagnation, and rising income and wealth inequality, all was for the best in the best of all possible republics, and Obama was its living embodiment. As he put it in a soaring, idealistic speech celebrating his victory in 2008, "If there is anyone out there who doubts that America is a place where anything is possible, who still wonders if the dream of our founders is alive in our time, who still questions the power of our democracy, tonight is your answer."[16]

Rhetorically and intellectually, Obama affirmed the best of the American liberal reform tradition, from abolition to the New Deal to the civil rights movement. At times, he seemed to exemplify a latter-day progressive maxim that the legacy of struggles of the victims of U.S. history against racial exclusion, labor exploitation, and sexual and gender discrimination represent the core of "our better history." But these affirmations were less a spur to militant, collective action than an inheritance he sought to personally embody.

If he could be elected, then it must be ascendant. Those inside the liberal bubble presumed that Trump's buffoonery, overt racism, and crude sexism would render him easy to defeat. Given that the Republican Party already controlled Congress and a supermajority of state legislatures, however, the idea that Trump was a weak candidate beggars belief. The rising racial tensions signaled by a barrage of extrajudicial and police killings of African Americans suggested deep-seated racial conflicts that were unresponsive to, and perhaps even triggered by, Obama's rise.

How Trump captured the Republican Party deserves more scrutiny, but he did not need to invent the playbook. An unorthodox politician with great understanding of male dogging rituals, he outmanned his opponents at every turn. Though less wealthy than some, he ultimately gained the backing of oddball right-wing billionaires with obscure agendas, like Robert and Rebekah Mercer, who had previously backed Ted Cruz, another insurgent, far-right candidate. More substantively, Trump dared to venture beyond the neoliberal and imperial terrain, welding a populism that invoked an abandoned generation of virtuous heartland producers to a foreign policy that emphasized hitting hard and unilaterally, but only against clearly marked enemies. Perhaps most importantly, he enjoined a brutal, sadistic inversion of the inclusionary niceties of neoliberal diversity talk with a return to a casual banter of racial, gender, and sexual punishment: arrest for abortion, criminal prosecution for participating in Black Lives Matter, registration and surveillance for Muslims, torture for terrorists. Nothing could have been more shocking to the creative classes, grown accustomed to tinkering with microaggressions and safe spaces within shrinking kingdoms of high cultural and educational attainment.

In light of the history sketched here, it is wrong to see Trump as an exception. The sense of collective disorientation in the face of his rise comes from the fact that the election resulted in the broad discrediting of the many experts (who now see fit to pronounce on its meaning). More significantly,

Trump's campaign was a determined exercise in flouting civilities and norms of consensual politics. Every shock—the humiliation of his opponents, incitement to violence against protesters, calumny against migrants, belittling of disabled people, "pussy grabbing" with impunity, outright lying, promises to tear up international agreements, and the threat to reject the result of a "rigged election" if he lost—seemed to render him unfit for office, according to wizened commentators; and yet many (though not the majority) disagreed.

As we learn more about Trump's domination of the media—including the role of fake-news farms; the investments in microtargeting, psychological profiling, and social-media news filtering under the auspices of the right-wing data firm Cambridge Analytica; and his embrace of Twitter as a vehicle of bullying and disinformation—we can see how Trump has become both a symptom and an accelerator of the broad degradation of our information ecology (much of which, not incidentally, has been advanced by decades of corporate-sponsored lying about our degraded physical ecology). In response to his loss of the popular vote, Trump asserted that millions of illegal votes were cast for Hillary Clinton. Perhaps these statements were made in preparation for advancing voter-suppression legislation on the federal level, as Republican domination of state legislatures has already advanced it at the state level.[17] The fight for the vote and against the abuse of fact will be among the many important lines in the battle to restore a degree of honest public communication and democratic procedure. With the Voting Rights Act gutted by the U.S. Supreme Court and legislation pending in multiple states to make voting less accessible through identification requirements and reductions in polling places and hours, the prospect is not favorable.

A more tangible question is how Trump will govern. There is a possibility that he will attempt to triangulate to a certain extent: for example, exchanging funding for pet infrastructure projects for a new round of tax cuts for the wealthy, along with radical deregulation of finance and industry. Even before he took office, he claimed to have successfully bullied and cajoled one firm, Carrier, to partially forgo a planned closure of its U.S. manufacturing operation in his vice president's home state, Indiana. Undoubtedly Trump's populism, which promises the subjugation rather than the activation of organized labor (especially public employee unions), will gain a few more concessions from capital than any left-wing populist would. What is less clear is whether he will accede to extreme right-wing demands of Congressional Republicans, including gutting Medicaid, accelerating the looting of public education, and bringing the Federal Reserve to heel with tight monetary policy. Although the last would be anathema to his spending promises, his appointments in key arenas of domestic policy—such as appointing Betsy DeVos, the billionaire champion of private Christian schools, charter schools, home schooling (and apparently also an advocate of easing child-labor statutes), as education secretary; Mike Price, the leader of the anti-Obamacare forces, to lead the Department of Health and Human Services; and Scott Pruitt, former attorney general of Oklahoma, climate change denier, and oil and gas enthusiast, as head of the Environmental Protection Agency—suggest that we are facing an extreme right-wing devolution.

One thing seems certain at the time of writing, halfway through his first hundred days. First, Trump will make good on his promise to ratchet up the inner war. He has already done so with his signature appointments of Steve Bannon and Stephen Miller of the far right-wing Breitbart News as his chief strategist and national policy adviser. His first significant executive order, a chaotically implemented travel ban that targeted Muslims from seven countries, was a shot across the bows (temporarily stalled by the courts and spontaneous protest), a signal to his base and to his supporters in the enforcement bureaucracies of the Department of Homeland Security. Trump is likely to lean heavily on the hard, racially motivated Right when he fails to actually bring back manufacturing jobs (as he promised), let alone get the coal fires burning again in Cambria County. The position of attorney general, aptly titled since this is the general for the inner war, has long been the administrative appointment watched most closely by the extreme Right. In Jeff Sessions, Trump has chosen someone who has made no secret of his desire to reverse engineer the twentieth century, returning us to a time when "the blacks" (as Trump calls them) knew their place, women were subordinated to men, and immigrants were subject to severe restrictions defined by racial and national origin.

In a recent book, Pierre Dardot and Christian Laval describe neoliberalism as "the rationality of contemporary capitalism, a capitalism freed from its archaic references."[18] Part of the genius of the millennial iteration of neoliberalism was that it promoted upward economic distribution in the context of commitments to formal rights and nondiscrimination principles. The public commitment to racial, gender, and sexual equity and equality became an index of capitalism's progressivism in a period marked by the savage erosion of occupational stability, union membership, educational opportunity, and public health support for the vast majority of working people. Unfortunately, this conjunction resulted in a major category error by parts of the Left, which began to view issues of social justice as simple tools of neoliberalism itself, rather than public goods that might need to be defended on their own terms. Just as Trump's election reflects cracks in the neoliberal order, his administration is also likely to test the durability of formal equality as one of the institutions of our social formation and, along with it, basic conceptions of democratic rights.

During the campaign it appeared that corporate America would reject Trump because of his unpredictability, his bigotry, and the likelihood that he would use his position for naked self-enrichment—in a word, kleptocracy. Blankfein's prediction of a "market- and asset-friendly" environment indicates that tax cuts and financial deregulation may be enough to buy them off in the medium term. Trump's Goldman Sachs–friendly appointments include the hedge-fund billionaire Steve Mnuchin, who made his

The Present Crisis

money peddling subprime mortgages before the 2008 crash, as treasury secretary. In this way, Trump's ideology seems less a rejection of neoliberalism *tout court* than its acceleration toward what Sheldon Wolin somewhat awkwardly termed "inverted totalitarianism," a moment when the neoliberal market state merges with an increasingly politicized corporate realm alarmed about the terms of order and rule.[19]

The loyalties of the military-industrial complex are less certain. Elements of the FBI (the main agents of the inner war) apparently supported Trump, as demonstrated by FBI director James Comey's intervention shortly before the election, putting Clinton's e-mail controversy back in the spotlight. Those charged with the outer war, however, including the CIA and the bulk of the national security bureaucracy, rejected him in favour of Clinton. The outgoing CIA director, John Brennan, termed Trump's calls to undo the Iran deal "the height of folly" and, with others, has decried Russian interference in the election on Trump's behalf and at the behest of his surrogates.[20] It remains to be seen whether Trump, the big boss man, someone intolerant of plural centers of power, someone who kept Hitler's speeches at his bedside, and someone who admires a wide range of authoritarian rulers abroad, will effectively tame these guardians of the national security state. In only the first weeks, of his presidency, leaked surveillance detailing preelection meetings of his national security adviser, Mike Flynn, with Russia's U.S. ambassador led to Flynn's ouster. Trump's firing of Comey while he was leading a widening FBI probe into the Russian links created an early sense of crisis and siege within the administration. These internecine battles represent one of the most consequential vectors in the coming period of struggle.[21]

Trump has derided the outer wars, leading many to identify him, mistakenly, as an isolationist and someone who augurs a break with the broad trajectory of post-1945 U.S. foreign policy. Emerging from the global wreckage of World War II, the U.S. imperium undertook a sustained, and unprecedented effort to organize a consensual, rule-bound world order based on multilateral free trade, democracy, and respect for national sovereignty. Arguably one of the moral and systemic requirements of this liberal-internationalist order was removal of the "archaic" residues of slavery, colonialism, and conquest, and with them the specter of violent revolution. With the United States as its guarantor, anticommunism, inflected by partisan competition between liberal doctrines of containment and coexistence and right-wing visions of rollback and offensive war against communist regimes, provided a grammar and strategy for policing world order. Covert and overt U.S. military interventionism and a series of big "small wars" gave the lie to U.S. postimperial pretensions outside Europe and Japan. But the vision of a long peace and the constitution of a democratic security community in Europe and East Asia achieved a significant measure of success.

When the millennial narratives of benign globalization and Francis Fukuyama's declaration of the "end of history," under the aegis of liberal free trade and unfettered capital mobility, announced the successful extension of this project at a global scale, it was already unraveling. Announcing Trump's victory, his clever consigliere Bannon offered a different story from the one we have typically been told about American global power, foretelling a restoration of native "American capitalism" to its place in the sun. In the eyes of Bannon and Trump, the bill has come due for the global protection scheme that the U.S. has run for the past seventy years. "The globalists gutted the American working class and created a middle class in Asia," Bannon declared. "Like [Andrew] Jackson's populism, we are going to build an entirely new political movement . . . it's going to be as exciting as the 1930s, greater than the Reagan revolution—conservatives, plus populists, in an economic nationalist movement."[22]

Here, the language of economy in Trumpism is also quite definitively a language of racial and national enemies and competitors. It is also a language generously sprinkled with social Darwinism, more reminiscent of late-nineteenth-century paeans to Anglo-Saxon supremacy than of the rise of

European fascism. What Trump and Bannon envision and want to hasten, with the cooperation of the emergent far Right in Europe, is a revival of a far more exclusionary capitalist order across Europe and North America, one defined by a civic and religious distinctiveness that they imagine to have been diluted by globalism and the rise of China in particular (a nation with which Bannon once frighteningly predicted war within five years).

It seems likely that there will be new wars. Two of Trump's top appointees are Marine generals who have expressed bellicosity toward Iran. Trump is better understood as a right-wing militarist than as an isolationist.[23] Asserting hemispheric dominance, ensuring the internal subjugation of racial and foreign others, and finishing the long Asia war have together comprised the American far Right's understanding of the proper U.S. orientation to the world since 1950. "Remember Pearl Harbor!" brought them out of isolation and into World War II. "The loss of China" became their cold war rallying cry. They supported General Douglas MacArthur's brinksmanship in Korea (including the threat of a nuclear first strike). Their constant moral and political pressure spooked liberals into Vietnam; the failure there they branded a "stab in the back." On the brink of the Reagan era, they rallied against the loss of the Panama Canal and stoked military and political interventions in Central America. After 9/11 they talked about taking Iraq's oil, but they also said, "Real men go to Tehran." They came to view the most militant Israeli settlers as their kin. As Bannon put it, "You have expansionist Islam and you have expansionist China. Right? They are motivated. They're arrogant. They're on the march. And they think the Judeo–Christian West is on the retreat."[24] The central premises of this global vision are war, predation, and a racial and civilizational divide (one that also runs through the United States). Somewhere in hell, Carl Schmitt and Samuel Huntington are smiling.

The cultivation of U.S. vernacular racism and the explicit rejection of norms that have been hallmarks of Trump's campaign are not incidental.

They signal a conscious understanding of relationships between various dimensions of progressive, regulatory power that need to be overturned: the belief in a shared and vulnerable global ecology, the value of an egalitarian and inclusive social ethic, the need to limit the power and dispensations of capital and private property, and of course the rules restricting the use of military force and police power. Trump, Bannon, and Sessions seem to count on the idea that they have a national constituency, one based on what Mike Davis has called "geriatric white privilege," and that they can expand that constituency by signaling a commitment to a white, Christian, native-born identity politics—forcefully extended, through the familiar ambit of "law and order," in the domain of border control—and the rollback of sexual and reproductive rights. The major weakness of this kind of politics, of course, is that it works assiduously to narrow its own base. Despite its durability in U.S. political life, openly racist and nativist rule is highly unstable; it tends to operate against the terms of hegemonic order and must necessarily prioritize force over consent.[25]

This type of politics has invited a comparison to fascism. Much of the discussion of fascism in the United States centers on making or dismissing faulty Nazi analogies. If we want to develop an account of what Langston Hughes called "our native fascisms," however, we need to think about how the development of extreme right-wing politics in the U.S. has been routed through American ideas about sovereignty, expansion, race, region, religion, entrepreneurialism, and individualism, including hostility to bureaucracy, legal universalism, and centralized authority.[26] The construction of racist individualism and settler freedom that distinguished the Jacksonian democracy idealized by Bannon, for instance, encouraged a slackness of centralized government control tethered to a violence exercised at its borders and margins, something that seemed chaotic, unstable, and disordered from the controlling seat of power. Considered in these terms, the Trump administration hardly needs organized paramilitaries to do its bidding, given the normative, historical, and institutional ways in which police powers in the United States operate as delegated and sovereign prerogatives to master and control indigenous and exogenous others.

Facing such an adversary, nothing would be more mistaken than to narrow our sights or reduce our political ambitions. As suggested, there has long been a tendency among U.S. and Western leftists to believe that an emphasis on identity politics within liberalism—that is, sectional attention to "social justice" and to the range of social and individual, public and private forms of discrimination that tacitly support and actively enforce racial, gender, sexual, and able-bodied hierarchies—has reduced concern for economic inequality and thus eroded the necessary basis for broader solidarities on the Left.

This debate was reignited by the contest between Hillary Clinton and Bernie Sanders for the Democratic nomination, when Clinton and many of her supporters charged that personal "sexism" (of the "Bernie Bros") and inadequate attention to "racial justice" (and "intersectionality") were constitutive features of Sanders's program, his broad focus on economic fairness and shared wealth, and his criticisms of Clinton's cosiness with financial elites. Using social justice as a weapon against economic justice was a depressing new low in the Clintons' triangulation politics. It reminded us how attention to social domination and limitation of policy concern to those deemed to be most vulnerable to social harm are often defining features of progressive neoliberalism, which has abandoned a defense of universalist and broadly redistributive economic policies in favor of means-tested allocations, thus acceding to the attrition of the strongest and most politically popular aspects of the welfare state.

Unfortunately, many identified with the weakened U.S. Left take the bait, imagining that the language of the economy can somehow be disembedded from a wider range of unequal social relationships. The rise of Trump, let alone a cursory reading of U.S. history, should caution against an emphasis on an economic populism that is inattentive to its racist and sexist coordination and packaging. Any flickering hopes that Trump will not govern according to hard-edged racist and sexist presumptions should have been doused by his initial cabinet appointments and his first few months in office.

People are immensely susceptible to racially divisive, even starkly violent proposals that seem to make sense of their suffering. A Left that believes that this tendency can simply be short-circuited by some kind of neutral call to common economic interests makes a major error—as demonstrated by continued assaults on voting rights, promises of relaxed supervision of local police agents by Sessions' Department of Justice, and new temptations to racist trolling and gaslighting in public and online (by legions of "mini-Trumps").[27] A Left that cannot fight on multiple fronts, protecting those who remain most vulnerable to state-sanctioned and extrajudicial violence while also defending principles of economic fairness—including forms of income support, affordable housing, and the right to health care and education—is likely to remain fragmented, isolated, and ineffective.

Languages of race and languages of class intermingle and recombine in the United States and all the old imperial and settler polities. At the level of campaign rhetoric, Obama was actually quite good at pegging the egalitarian recognition of divided class interests to a defense of multicultural democracy. The opposite formula, in which class division is avowed only when its animus can be directed toward vulnerable and appropriable scapegoats and threats, is more common, and in the absence of a countervailing discourse, it is unsurprising that it has regained traction. We should not necessarily mourn the demise of the progressive neoliberalism that characterized the Obama years (and that Clinton promised to continue). It was never more than a holding pattern against a fuller apprehension of the crisis, an effort to buy some time. We were likely to reap the consequence of its failures, even if the crisis has come sooner than many of us expected.

Rather than a new departure, Trump's rise nonetheless may represent the last gasp of boomer conservatives (and boomer liberals) who have stripped the country down by upwardly redistributing its wealth, shredding its already flimsy webs of social protection, prosecuting unnecessary wars overseas, punishing and jailing the poor at home, and neglecting the ecology that sustains our common life. Despite the rightward electoral shifts in Midwestern states, the white working class did not elect Trump. Those who elected Trump were the legions of older, wealthier, suburban white voters who vote Republican in every election, viewing the GOP as the true guardians of their economic self-interest and accumulated insider advantages. Trump also attracted evangelical and right-to-life voters willing to look past his personal immorality. The younger and substantially poorer voters whom Obama galvanized in 2008 largely stayed home. Like the legacy of NAFTA in the Midwest, the memory of Bill and Hillary Clinton's support of welfare reform and mass incarceration likely helped to hold down the black vote as well. Obama galvanized his coalition by promising new directions: a fairer economy; a less punitive, more racially just society; and a less bellicose relationship to the world. Because of his own limitations and entrenched opposition from political forces he could neither tame nor defeat, he could not deliver on these promises. But they are still things that the majority of people want.

Only a committed and organized political opposition, however, will be able to realize this proposition. To create such an opposition in the coming period, it will be necessary to strengthen natural bases of support in liberal civic institutions, including progressive churches; to strengthen and scale up local labor and community networks to defend increasingly vulnerable populations; and to develop national and popular political organizations on the Left, both within and outside the Democratic Party. Opponents of the administration should not pay much attention to episodic efforts of Democrats to find common ground with Trump on particular issues (even if only on tactical grounds, to exploit internal contradictions within the ruling party). The broad focus should be how we can derail the project of Trump and the GOP and where we want to go. Developing coherent and persuasive answers that can orient a more just and egalitarian approach to politics will require more strongly partisan vision, organization, and planning than we have seen on the political Left in recent decades. No one can be sanguine about the soundness of the Democratic Party as a vehicle for advancing these purposes. But in light of Bernie Sanders' success across the plurality of voting blocs and particularly among younger voters, it still seems like the necessary vehicle for electoral politics. Developing stronger linkages to similar political movements at the international scale will also be crucial. There is every reason to believe that the wreckage from Trump's rule is going to be terrible, and we had better build something that can help us outlast it and move forward.

Overcoming old divisions and distrust on the Left that arise from different emphases on economic and social justice, and, more specifically, on class as opposed to race and gender politics, requires determined effort. One way to bridge these divides would be to cultivate a more politically generous understanding of how racist commitment is activated. As I have argued, racism and racial animus are not fixed characteristics of an already defined group of people but a situational dimension of our common political life that is repeatedly mobilized. So-called white people and white workers in particular can be won over to a nonracist politics centered on economic justice; but it is necessary to actively build the constituency for that politics. In this effort the composite imaginary known as the "white working class" is likely to fail us analytically and politically every single time it is used, for it tacitly presumes that individual investment in whiteness conditions class solidarity, which is precisely the problem to be overcome.

More Americans now identify as working class than at perhaps any time since the 1930s and 1940s. This represents an enormous potential constituency for an inclusive, antiracist politics and for radical defense of our increasingly fragile commons. The term *white working class* reifies the link between whiteness and the material interests of working and unemployed people. It makes less and less sense in the context of the most hopeful, vibrant movements of today: the multiracial fight for the $15 hourly minimum wage; the organization of legions of home workers and domestic caregivers, the least visible and most diverse sectors of the working class (mostly women); the battles to prevent the poisoning of vital resources at Standing Rock, across Indian lands, and in the national commons, where ancient struggles for decolonization continue; the demands to be protected from arbitrary force and premature death at the hands of police; and the creation of sanctuary for those facing summary deportation and destruction of their kinship and neighborhood ties.

We clearly face an uncertain period in which those most responsible for a dire array of contemporary social, political, economic, and ecological predicaments will hold big levers of power, at least in the short term. But they are also the ones who will be tasked with solving intractable problems. Their inevitable failures will be our opportunity; we cannot afford to let another serious crisis go to waste.

Epilogue

The Two Americas

There must be two Americas: one that sets the captive free, and one that takes a once-captive's freedom away from him and picks a quarrel with him with nothing to found it on; then kills him to get his land.

Mark Twain, "To the Person Sitting in Darkness," 1901

A racist society can't but fight a racist war—this is the bitter truth. The assumptions acted on at home are also acted on abroad.

James Baldwin, *Freedomways*, 1967

As Barack Obama stood on the stage at Grant Park in Chicago on election night in 2008, the surge of optimism at his victory yielded to a strange unease in the pit of my stomach. I realized what caused this sensation as I consciously registered his reflected image in the bulletproof glass that almost imperceptibly framed his face. Even as Obama's ascent announced a new founding and the vindication of old foundations, that ghostly image conjured a recurrent, traumatic history of unfulfilled promises, unredeemed struggles, and unaccounted losses.

Any victor that night would have been so protected. Nevertheless, black existence and aspirations toward inclusion and equality in the U.S. are readily associated with a history of legal and extralegal violence deployed to produce and preserve racial distance and disparity. However unseemly, the prospective parallels between Obama and Martin Luther King Jr. in the run-up to the election conjured the threat of premature death. In turn, Obama's ostensible fulfillment of King's dream arguably had less to do with substantive political connections between the two men than with the racial form and symbolism of one life and its associated promise to redress the violent and untimely end of another.

Racism and violence—we live in the eddies of their past and their *presence*. Since Obama's rise, we have been exorcising the ghosts and demons of a still-unfinished civil war. George Wallace and Martin Luther King Jr., Bill Ayres and Jeremiah Wright were figures of the past made present, a war in Iraq built on distortion and lies, a Gulf Coast storm that laid bare an era of malign neglect, and a politician of hope and change who promised reconciliation and redemption from still more ancient crimes of a democracy built on stolen lives and lands. Those events also led to the emergence of the Tea Party and Donald Trump, who resurrected the power of racial calumny and wrongful accusation, tugging on threads of nativist fear and stirring the resentments of the thwarted Confederacy.

In retrospect, we can observe how Obama's winning strategy was to accentuate the value of his campaign's egalitarian racial appeal through disciplined and calculated nonreference. Invisible protective glass was a particularly apt metaphor for the reigning orthodoxy of color-blindness and postracialism, whose architecture has become more durable and less assailable with successive U.S. Supreme Court decisions foreclosing future racial redress through school desegregation, affirmative action, and voting-rights safeguards: a state-sanctioned barrier, increasingly hard to perceive or identify, between those who are protected from racially differentiated vulnerability and those who continue to bear its marks and suffer its consequences.

Obama's call to "choose our better history" might also be read in this light. On the surface, it constituted a rejoinder to alternative formulations, such as John McCain's campaign appeal to Americans as the "makers" and not the "victims" of history. Although McCain eschewed the direct (even murderous) racist appeals of some of his supporters, he still tapped the exclusivist, supremacist kernel of the American political tradition: racial nationalism often embedded within civic appeals to American universalism. Make history, my friends, he seemed to say, or become its victims. How to know the difference? Real Americans understand that making history sometimes requires turning another people into victims.

The idea of our better history, by contrast, embraced what Frederick Douglass explicitly identified as "the standpoint of the victims of American history." This standpoint is no endpoint, for it is through the struggles of the trammeled and dispossessed—slaves, women, workers, the segregated, disfranchised, and stigmatized—that "our better history" presumably has been realized. In other words, even as Obama evoked timeless values and solid foundations, the conception of history he advanced was powerfully revisionist and *revisionary*. Thus, while it is accurate to say that he resisted the prophetic and agonistic tones of black radicalism, he seemed to have internalized one of its central claims: without struggle, there is no progress.

In his "more perfect union" speech, and his arguably riskier 2004 preface to *Dreams from My Father,* Obama approvingly quoted William Faulkner: "The past isn't past; it isn't even dead and buried."[1] Neat lines of tribe and geography, time and syntax no longer separate victims and makers of history. Indeed, one might say victims become (and are continuously becoming) makers through assertions of will and acts of remembrance and communication that transform old divisions and augur reconciliation, even as they may threaten new victimizations. Tying his own American heritage to Asia and Africa, Obama challenged a post-9/11 security regime that privileged force and violence and implicitly linked the sprawling domestic prison complex to a widening military footprint overseas. The sense that Obama came into the presidency with this kind of historical understanding, cosmopolitan sensibility, and racial literacy engendered hope both here and overseas that he planned to wind down, if not end, the wars.

The day after Obama's inauguration, a *New York Times* headline announced the new president's first order for air strikes by unmanned predator drones in South Waziristan. The queasy disquiet from election night returned. Why had these disparate events produced the same uncanny sensation? What linked them, I realized, was how they encapsulated the paradox of Obama's ascent. For as much as an Obama presidency was framed in the progressive lineage of the long, black-led struggle for democracy in America, it was also captive to the violently truncated history of this struggle that still shapes the present. In the years that followed, the names Trayvon Martin, Michael Brown, Rekia Boyd, Tanisha Anderson, Sandra Bland, Tamir Rice, Philando Castile, Walter Scott, Abdulrahman al-Awlaki, and countless other nameless lives that did not matter and that were extinguished in the name of America's collective security testify to this point.

At its most profound and far-reaching, the black freedom movement proposed a general social transformation of the United States, one rooted in opposition to what King in his final hour called America's interrelated flaws: "racism, extreme materialism, and militarism."[2] The conventionally bifurcated account of the movement we now inherit—with one part annexed to the teleology of liberal democracy and its clichés of progress, and the other told as a tale of inner-city decline and sectarian racialism—fails utterly to reckon with this aborted challenge and vision. A post-civil rights legacy that has sought to conscript racial progress in the service of state legitimacy and to assign social decay and pathology to isolated individuals and vulnerable communities once again renders imperceptible the technical and ethical infrastructure upon which U.S. imperial citizenship has long depended: the differential valuation of human populations through the development and deployment of an institutional capacity and public willingness to kill and quarantine (and leave to die) from a distance.

The essays in this book represent a series of meditations on these inter-relationships as they have unfolded in and through the afterlives of U.S. slavery, continental conquest, overseas expansion, and contention with fascism, with specific reference to the contemporary history of race and politics. At its core, my inquiry has sought to show how race making and war making constitute an enduring nexus of U.S. government power that unfolds both at home and abroad. Equally significant, I have sought to demonstrate how racial devaluation has been inextricable from the state management of capitalism's destructive creation and creative destruction, which increasingly place the planet itself at risk.[3]

Scorched by the images of domestic climate refugees after Hurricane Katrina, I described the moment when the Bush administration dispatched its highest-ranking black official, Condoleeza Rice, to the Gulf Coast, where she argued that the damage on view was a "vestige of the Old South" and that the civil rights movement had helped the United States to "find its voice" as a champion of democracy overseas. These were odd and unconvincing statements at a moment when New Orleans and its people could be mistaken for ruined places like Baghdad and Kabul, occupied by U.S. military forces. But we must acknowledge that much of Obama's seemingly reparative and restorative quality circled back to Rice's claim. For even as visible and indisputable signs of racial division and neglect can be used to discredit our governors, the promise of overcoming racial division and its associated ills has become a powerful justification of state violence at home and abroad.

A fundamental aspect of Obama's appeal was a promise to bridge the discord of populations divided by race and war. His hawkishness on Afghanistan could even be rationalized on these grounds as political cover for a more deeply held antiwar position. Obama promised that he would close Guantanamo and end torture, rendition, and rightlessness; he also announced that he would rethink and scale back the "war on terror," if not end it altogether. Indeed, among the slew of ethically correct positions that later gave way to "realism," the candidate Obama once condemned the air war in Afghanistan as immoral and politically self-defeating on account of the routine and entirely predictable "collateral damage" it yielded. His rapid and symbolically significant retreat from many, though not all, of these positions—beginning with the continued arrogation of unlimited executive war power and extending to the widening of surveillance and data mining and drone strikes—ineluctably tied his administration to the national security dispensation that began after 9/11.

Donald Trump, who led a consistent and consciously racist opposition to Obama's presidency, is now in ascendancy. With Trump, the violent contradictions of the inner and outer wars are laid bare. For unlike Obama, Trump based his appeal on the promise to intensify divisions along lines of race, nation, and religion. His additional vow to abandon climate-change mitigation denies the very problem of the imperiled ecology that humans share. Trump poses an old question: who is entitled to freedom and security—or, more precisely, to the freedom of an unlimited security and the security of an unlimited freedom? One of the hallmarks of liberal-democratic claims to superior civilization has been the commitment to mitigate boundless violence in the name of boundless freedom for everyone. Though the oppositions between Obama and McCain, or Obama and Bush, or Obama or Clinton and Trump, are convenient shorthand for all those characteristic efforts to distinguish good from bad U.S. nationalism (that is, the civic from the racial, the patriotic from the jingoistic, the democratic from the statist), Trump reminds us that one feature is constant: to make (American) history, one still needs the stomach to make victims.

Though framed by the dangers of these times, my arguments are not intended to minimize contradictions in U.S. political culture or the significance and consequence of political struggle and contest. A better history exists, and come what may, we must fight for it. One problem is that powerful, centralizing state institutions have long been structured as the result of a bipartisan consensus, especially regarding so-called national security. We must ask, in what ethical universe is it possible to justify the eminently foreseeable destruction of civilian noncombatants? Is this "realism" or a philosophical standpoint according to which some human lives are simply less valuable and therefore expendable? I would expect that Barack Hussein Obama, of Honolulu, Jakarta, Nairobi, and Chicago's South Side, would categorically reject such a standpoint. Yet Barack Hussein Obama, president of the United States, became part of the mechanism that adopted it.

After World War II, American universalism sought to tie the preponderant uses of U.S. military force to aspirations for economic growth that would transform and uplift the entire world. This is what Henry Stimson meant when he called for "leadership towards life." Perhaps never has a secular, materialist enterprise of growth, hinged to universalist rather than exclusionist or eliminationist principles, been so tightly interwoven with the development of a commensurate apparatus of death dealing and destruction. The violence that began, but did not end, with World War II gained a rationale of expansive purpose against an allegedly expansionist enemy bent on world domination. It arose, too, in the face of fears loosed by a total breach of the laws of war with respect to civilian populations, especially war from the sky—including the first and so far only military use of nuclear weapons by the United States itself. But it also developed in the context of the massive shift in the world's cultural and racial orders augured by the promised end of European, Japanese, and U.S. colonialism.

Shortly before he died, Robert McNamara, one key architect of the Vietnam War, described his own dire contribution to the history of America's outer war as being "part of the mechanism that recommends." He also belatedly acknowledged a deeply criminal complicity.[4] Yet somehow the liberal-democratic belief that our forms of killing are not murder, and that force can be applied with thoughtful, prophylactic discretion, refuses to die. From the early twentieth century, air war and bombing from on high were a fundamental requisite of modern colonial power. After World War II, this simultaneously protective and destructive capacity enabled a double spatial and ethical displacement, according to which liberal-democratic society separated the boundless violence it enacted from the boundless freedom it claimed to uphold. A conservative balance sheet assessment estimates that eight million people were killed in U.S. or U.S.-sponsored wars after World War II, most of them fought in parts of the world once colonized or controlled by European powers. While it would be an error (one that redoubles American hubris) to imagine the United States as the source of all the world's conflict, trouble, or evil, the era of U.S. global power retained an integral relationship to violent historical legacies and practices of imperialism and colonialism that, in part because of the unique resiliency of its own settler-colonial heritage, was never adequately interrogated or used to properly revise U.S. self-conceptions.

We are now confronted by a world that has been steadily shrinking in several respects. Since the 1970s, in the United States, and in a context of low rates of economic growth, a great share of national income and wealth has gone to the top 1 percent of the population. It is finally dawning on us that living standards for the majority have been falling, and for many, life expectancy has been declining as well—a shocking revelation for Americans who were promised that global power meant unlimited growth. The international distribution of wealth accumulation has moderately increased without fundamentally transforming the lives of billions of poor people. The catastrophic environmental costs of capitalism have become self-evident, if still widely ignored. This is what the American age has wrought. At the same time, the world has grown smaller and closer in ways that present opportunities to think and act cooperatively. At his best, Obama gestured toward such opportunities and with them a soft landing for the U.S. empire. With Trump, the simultaneous recognition and denial that we have entered an age of economic contraction and a confrontation of fundamental environmental limits has enjoined a return to philosophies of force: the brutal adjudication of winners and losers through the old idioms of racist and economic predation.

At the end of his life and at the height of opposition to the Vietnam War, Martin Luther King Jr. argued against the idea that the achievement of civil rights had inaugurated an era of normal politics for the racially excluded in the United States, just as he challenged the belief that the *pax Americana* had delivered a just and legitimate developmental framework for previously colonized peoples. King took the risk of condemning the war: "I knew that I could never again raise my voice against the violence of the oppressed in the ghettos," he declared, "without having first spoken clearly to the greatest purveyor of violence in the world today—my own government." Through neglect of this legacy—the urgent challenge of just and sustainable development abroad and at home—the Obama presidency, and the hopeful alternatives it recommended to forty years of rightward drift of U.S. social, economic, and foreign policy, came to little. Rather, to use King's words, for many it added "cynicism to the process of death." To genuinely break this destructive spiral, a more insurgent and less teleological conception of our better history is required: the moral arc of the universe may bend toward justice, but power concedes nothing without a demand.[5]

King's commitment to nonviolence led him to recognize the intertwining of a history of racial self-definition (i.e., white supremacy) and militarization in defining the United States as a political community. Taking this stand did not necessarily make King a communist (as the FBI director J. Edgar Hoover asserted), but it did align him with a black radical intellectual tradition that conceptualized the global production of racialized disparity in terms of African slavery, colonial rule, class apartheid, and imperial statecraft. This approach refused to permit incremental racial integration within the United States to serve as a rationalization for policies that continued to thwart economic justice and just security for the world's peoples. It presciently warned, moreover, of persistent, spiraling, and unpredictable violence as long as material deprivation and assaults on human dignity consigned the world's poor and powerless to sociocultural and spatial zones where the fraying fabric of the social contract received the unforgiving cut of racialized governance.

As Taylor Branch writes, "American public discourse broadly denied King the standing to be heard on Vietnam."[6] Although the era brought profound social change, the failure to meet the challenges King posed continues to constellate the present. In martyrdom, King became a celebrated figure in a nation-state that ostentatiously declared an end to its historic devaluation of black life and again trumpeted its benign uses of military power. Progress in black civic inclusion and political representation—culminating in the historic election of Obama to the presidency—in turn inspired a hope that we were entering a new era of racial comity as well as a new era of U.S. foreign policy.

In the shadows, however, wars on drugs and terror, waged disproportionately against black and brown populations, expanded, filled U.S. prisons, and extended their global reach. The rioting and rebellions of the black urban poor across hundreds of U.S. cities following King's assassination demanded the largest domestic mobilization of federal troops since the Civil War. The disrepair of the racial strife of the early post–civil rights period— answered with Southern electoral strategy, antiurban public policy, law-and-order rhetoric, and street-level lockdowns—was the signal crisis, just as the failure to reckon the destructive consequences and acknowledge the criminal irresponsibility of U.S. intervention in Vietnam underwrote the ongoing, fatal belief in militarized solutions to foreign conflicts that gave rise to the latest, interminable war, now nearing the end of its second decade.

Those who hope to change the political course of the United States are heirs to this ambiguous and bifurcated political inheritance. The political and legal gains of the long civil rights era promoted greater racial tolerance and inclusiveness in U.S. society. Yet under the cover of such tolerance, it became increasingly difficult to connect the dots between the explicit exclusions and injustices of the past and the social structures and institutions of the present. The legal demise of white supremacy, and its seeming political and cultural decline, inspired new investments in the U.S. nation-state as a horizon of social equality and just distribution. At the same time, reassertions of U.S. militarism and police power—out of proportion to real threats and inflated to serve the designs of ambitious politicians and prosecutors, security professionals and arms merchants—have marginalized radical visions demanding that we cut the knot binding the public welfare to the warfare state.

In the wake of the cold war, 9/11 provided a new pretext for launching another era of long war. We live in its wastes. From 2015 to the time of this writing, a spike in international terrorist attacks, most of them sponsored or inspired by the Islamic State (ISIS), have killed more than 1,200 people around the world, most of them in Western Europe and the Middle East. That many of the leaders of ISIS began their careers in violence as Sunni insurgents against U.S. occupying forces, and spent time in U.S. detention facilities like Abu Ghraib and Camp Bucca in Iraq, is hardly ever remarked upon. The war that the United States allegedly launched to stop long-range terrorist networks spawned equally capable long-range terrorist networks. It is an evident failure, yet one that seems only to demand more war.[7]

Since 2015, U.S. police forces have killed well over two thousand criminal suspects. The numbers evoke the uncanny symmetry of a state of civil insecurity and a security state that is antagonistic to its own citizens at home. As Charles Tilley famously noted, the same acts of killing by terrorists and criminals on the one hand, and by soldiers and police on the other, are sharply distinguished only by "political judgment" that confers legitimacy on one while condemning the other as a moral abomination. Within this dichotomy, the capacity for political adjudication, recognition, and resolution is diminished in inverse proportion to the growth of an enmity structured around the idea of violent incommensurability between different types of people.

As I have argued throughout this book, this dynamic of fabricating difference through sanctioned violence has been the primary ground of race making in modernity, one that democratic visions of political order have not solved. In a country where the greatest likelihood of homicide by a stranger is at the hands of the police who are supposed to protect and serve, and where undeclared war around the world rumbles on in the background, the struggle for a solution presses upon us. Race making derives from the suspension of consensual norms and the legal and extralegal confabulations that uphold this suspension. War making has long been one of its central modalities. Across cities, reservations, borders, and battle zones, the remainders and renewed operations of America's inner and outer wars continue to bedevil us: ending them and undoing their damage is an urgent social and political task.[8]

PREFACE

1. W. E. B. Du Bois, "Social Planning for the Negro, Past and Present," *Journal of Negro Education* 5, no. 1 (January 1936): 110–25; W. E. B. Du Bois, *Black Reconstruction in America, 1860–1880* (New York: Free Press, 1998), 644.

2. John Burgess, *Political Science and Comparative Constitutional Law* (New York: Baker and Taylor, 1890), 46.

3. Alan Taylor, *The Internal Enemy: Slavery and War in Virginia, 1772–1832* (New York: W. W. Norton, 2014); Howard McFarland, *Fairfield Journal of Maine* (1899), quoted in Secretary Root's Record: "Marked Severities' in Philippine Warfare: The First Reports of Cruelty," available at Humanities Web, www.humanitiesweb .org/human.php?s=s&p=l&a=c&ID=1104&o, accessed May 23, 2017; anonymous black soldier quoted in Paul Kramer, *The Blood of Government: Race, Empire, the United States and the Philippines* (Chapel Hill: University of North Carolina Press, 2006), 102.

4. W. E. B. Du Bois, *Darkwater: Voices from within the Veil* (New York: Harcourt Brace, 1920), 34; Ralph Ellison, *Invisible Man* (New York: Vintage, 1990), 16; James Baldwin, "A Report from Occupied Territory," *The Nation*, July 11, 1966.

5. For a strong version of these arguments, see Adolph Reed Jr. and Kenneth Warren, *Renewing Black Intellectual History: the Ideological and Material Foundations of African American Thought* (New York: Paradigm, 2010). For the bowdlerized

rendering, see Walter Benn Michaels, "Let Them Eat Diversity," *Jacobin*, January 1, 2011.

6. Sheldon Danzinger, Koji Chavez, and Erin Cumberworth, *Poverty during the Great Recession*, Russell Sage Foundation and Stanford Center on Poverty and Inequality, October 2012, web.stanford.edu/group/recessiontrends/cgi-bin/web/sites/all/themes/barron/pdf/Poverty_fact_sheet.pdf; Melvin Oliver and Thomas Shapiro, *Black Wealth, White Wealth: A New Perspective on Racial Inequality* (New York: Routledge, 2006); Sarah Childress, "How Much Did the Financial Crisis Cost?" *Frontline*, PBS, May 31, 2012, www.pbs.org/wgbh/frontline/article/how-much-did-the-financial-crisis-cost/; Rex Nutting, "How the Bubble Destroyed the Middle Class," Marketwatch, July 8, 2011, www.marketwatch.com/story/how-the-bubble-destroyed-the-middle-class-2011-07-08.

7. Sam Dillon, "Study Finds High Rate of Imprisonment among Dropouts," *New York Times*, October 8, 2009, www.nytimes.com/2009/10/09/education/09dropout.html. One in ten male high-school dropouts are in jail or juvenile detention on a given day; for black men, the figure is one in four. Among the most gripping statistics is the figure of 1.5 million black men between the ages of twenty-five and fifty-four who are missing from public life because of incarceration or premature death. Justin Wolfers, David Leonhardt, and Kevin Quealy, "1.5 Million Missing Black Men," *New York Times*, April 20, 2015, www.nytimes.com/interactive/2015/04/20/upshot/missing-black-men.html?_r=2.

8. American Immigration Council, "The Growth of the U.S. Deportation Machine," March 1, 2014, www.americanimmigrationcouncil.org/research/growth-us-deportation-machine.

9. In 2015 and 2016, police in the United States killed more than two thousand criminal suspects, almost half of them black or Latino/a. Both the scale of killing by police and its racial disparity are significant: a hallmark of racism, and a key to its power, is that it produces disparate effects that both serve and mask more broadly applicable coercive authority. "The Counted: People Killed by Police in the US," *Guardian*, www.theguardian.com/us-news/ng-interactive/2015/jun/01/the-counted-police-killings-us-database.

10. The idea of "linked fate" is drawn from the germinal work of Michael Dawson. See his *Black Visions: The Roots of Contemporary African American Political Ideologies* (Chicago: University of Chicago Press, 2003). This kind of approach

shows how injuries of class are shared across groups that are thought to be racially differentiated. Recognition of rising morbidity among poor whites and accompanying discourses about their moral fecklessness and mental inferiority attest to this fungible proximity of race and class in America's racial capitalism.

11. The pundit Robert D. Kaplan provides a telling example of this kind of argument: "Without Manifest Destiny, there could have been no victory in World War II. But because settling that continent involved slavery and genocide against the indigenous inhabitants, American history is morally unresolvable. Thus, the only way to ultimately overcome our sins is to do good in the world." Robert Kaplan, "Why Trump Can't Disengage America from the World," *New York Times*, January 6, 2017.

12. Work along these different lines that has most influenced me during the writing of this book includes Ruth Wilson Gilmore, *Golden Gulag: Prisons, Surplus, Crisis and Opposition in Globalizing California* (Berkeley: University of California Press, 2006); Elizabeth Kai Hinton, *From the War on Poverty to the War on Crime: The Making of Mass Incarceration in America* (Cambridge, MA: Harvard University Press, 2016); Naomi Murakawa, *The First Civil Right: How Liberals Built Prison America* (New York: Oxford University Press, 2014); Amy E. Lerman and Vesla M. Weaver, *Arresting Citizenship: The Democratic Consequences of American Crime Control* (Chicago: University of Chicago Press, 2014); Kelly Lytle Hernández, *Migra! A History of the U.S. Border Patrol* (Berkeley: University of California Press, 2010); Amy Kaplan and Donald E. Pease, ed., *Cultures of United States Imperialism* (Durham, NC: Duke University Press, 1999); Melani McAlister, *Epic Encounters: Culture, Media, and U.S. Interests in the Middle East since 1945* (Berkeley: University of California Press, 2003); Stuart Schrader, *Policing Revolution: Cold War Counterinsurgency at Home and Abroad* (Berkeley: University of California Press, forthcoming); Jodi A. Byrd, *The Transit of Empire: Indigenous Critiques of Colonialism* (Minneapolis: University of Minnesota Press, 2011); Aziz Rana, *The Two Faces of American Freedom* (Cambridge, MA: Harvard University Press, 2014); Glen Sean Coulthard, *Red Skin, White Masks: Rejecting the Colonial Politics of Recognition* (Minneapolis: University of Minnesota Press, 2014); Dylan Rodriguez, *Suspended Apocalypse: White Supremacy, Genocide, and the Filipino Condition* (Minneapolis: University of Minnesota Press, 2009); Alyosha Goldstein, ed., *Formations of United States Colonialism* (Durham, NC: Duke University Press, 1999); Manu Vimalassery, *Empire's Tracks:*

Plains Indians, Chinese Migrants, and the Transcontinental Railroad (Berkeley: University of California Press, forthcoming); Laleh Khalili, *Time in the Shadows: Confinement in Counterinsurgencies* (Stanford, CA: Stanford University Press, 2013); Patricia Owens, *Economy of Force: Counterinsurgency and the Historical Rise of the Social* (Cambridge: Cambridge University Press, 2015); Andrew Friedman, *Covert Capital: Landscapes of Denial and the Making of U.S. Empire in the Suburbs of Northern Virginia* (Berkeley: University of California Press, 2013); Robert Vitalis, *White World Order, Black Power Politics: The Birth of American International Relations* (Ithaca, NY: Cornell University Press, 2015); Sadiya Hartman, *Lose Your Mother: A Journey along the Atlantic Slave Route* (New York: Farrar, Straus and Giroux, 2007); Frank B. Wilderson, *Red, White, and Black: Cinema and the Structure of U.S. Antagonisms* (Durham, NC: Duke University Press, 2010); Jennifer Morgan, *Laboring Women: Gender and Reproduction in New World Slavery* (Philadelphia: University of Pennsylvania Press, 2004); Monica Kim, *Humanity Interrogated: The Global Crisis of Warfare in the Interrogation Rooms of the Korean War, 1940–1965* (Princeton, NJ: Princeton University Press, forthcoming).

INTRODUCTION

1. While the U.S. mortality rate has been low, with just over 5,000 killed in action in Afghanistan and Iraq as of 2014, the 2.7 million U.S. soldiers who served in these campaigns have returned to a diminished, battered economy. More than fifty thousand have suffered grievous injuries requiring the amputation of limbs and experienced mental and physical disorders, including post-traumatic stress and respiratory and cognitive impairment from exposure to toxic chemicals. Zoe Wool, *After War: The Weight of Life at Walter Reed* (Durham, NC: Duke University Press, 2015); Matthew S. Goldberg, "Updated Death and Injury Rates of U.S. Military Personnel During the Conflicts in Iraq and Afghanistan," Working Papers Series of the Congressional Budget Office, Washington, DC, December 2014, www.cbo.gov/sites/default/files/113th-congress-2013-2014/workingpaper/49837-Casualties_WorkingPaper-2014-08_1.pdf.

2. Catherine Herridge, "Top General: 50,000-Troop Coalition Needed in Order to Crush Isis," *Fox News*, April 13, 2016, www.foxnews.com/politics/2016/04/13/top-general-50000-troop-coalition-needed-in-order-to-crush-isis.html.

3. Adam Taylor, "These are America's 9 Longest Foreign Wars," *Washington Post,* May 29, 2014, www.washingtonpost.com/news/worldviews/wp/2014/05/29/these-are-americas-9-longest-foreign-wars/?utm_term=.6a6d9259f45e.

4. Donald Rumsfeld, in conversation with Jonathan Salant, "National Press Club Luncheon with Secretary of Defense Donald Rumsfeld," National Press Club, February 2, 2006, www.press.org/sites/default/files/020206_rumsfeld.pdf, accessed May 23, 2017.

5. Richard Falk, "The Abandonment of International Law After 9/11," presentation at the Congressional Black Caucus Annual Legislative Conference 2005, Washington, DC, September 2005, www.wagingpeace.org/the-abandonment-of-international-law-after-911/.

6. Built on flimsy and ambiguous evidence (repeatedly presented as definitive and even as "bulletproof"), assertions of Iraq's operational links to the Al Qaeda hijacking and terrorist attacks on September 11, 2001, were doubted at the time by senior intelligence analysts the world over and never proved. Despite scant evidence, it was also asserted that Iraq had resumed its discontinued biological and chemical weapons programs, and George W. Bush made the further outlandish claim that Iraq was "reconstituting its nuclear weapons program." Against a backdrop of links to shadowy terrorists who had already attacked the United States, national security adviser Condoleeza Rice hinted at the dangers of proceeding with caution: "We do not want the smoking gun to be a mushroom cloud." Operation Iraqi Freedom was launched by the U.S. unilaterally, with the support of the United Kingdom and a small "coalition of the willing," on the grounds that the Iraqi dictator, Saddam Hussein, had to be prevented from using so-called weapons of mass destruction, or WMDs. The specter of nuclear holocaust notwithstanding, the stated rationale for the war was settled on, as Paul Wolfowitz cannily observed, for "bureaucratic reasons." Paul Kerr, "Bush's Claims about Iraq's Nuclear Program," Arms Control Today, September 1, 2003, www.armscontrol.org/print/1361, accessed May 23, 2017; Wolf Blitzer, "Search for the Smoking Gun, January 10, 2003, CNN, www.cnn.com/2003/US/01/10/wbr.smoking.gun/; "Deputy Secretary Wolfowitz interview with Sam Tannenhaus, Vanity Fair," May 9, 2003, U.S. Department of Defense, News Transcript, http://archive.defense.gov/Transcripts/Transcript.aspx?TranscriptID=2594.

7. Henry L. Stimson, "The Challenge to Americans," *Foreign Affairs* 26 (October 1947): 5–14.

8. Alain Locke, "Color: The Unfinished Business of Democracy," *Survey Graphic*, November (1942): 455–59: see also Robert Vitalis, *White World Order, Black Power Politics: The Birth of American International Relations* (Ithaca, NY: Cornell University Press, 2015).

9. For an extended discussion of Myrdal, see Nikhil Pal Singh, *Black Is a Country: Race and the Unfinished Struggle for Democracy* (Cambridge, MA: Harvard University Press, 2005); Thomas Borstelman, *The Cold War and the Color Line: American Race Relations in the Global Arena* (Cambridge, MA: Harvard University Press, 2001), 76. Lodge served as U.S. ambassador to the Republic of Vietnam in the early 1960s. Paul Bedard, "Rare Letter: Nixon feared U.S. racism would help Soviets win Cold War," *Washington Examiner*, May 6, www.washingtonexaminer.com/rare-letter-nixon-feared-us-racism-would-help-soviets-win-cold-war/article/2622326_2017.

10. Fred Halliday, *The Making of the Second Cold War* (London: Verso, 1987).

11. Thomas Ferguson and Joel Rogers, *Right Turn: The Decline of the Democrats and the Future of American Politics* (New York : Hill and Wang, 1986).

12. Principal Deputy Undersecretary of Defense, "Memorandum for Secretaries of the Military Departments, Chairman of the Joint Chiefs of Staff, Under Secretary of Defense for Acquisition, Assistant Secretary of Defense for Program Analysis and Evaluation, Comptroller of the Department of Defense," February 18, 1992, available at the American Presidency Project, University of California, Santa Barbara, http://nsarchive.gwu.edu/nukevault/ebb245/doc03_extract_nytedit.pdf.

13. Richard Nixon, "Ninth Annual Message to Congress," January 22, 1970, www.presidency.ucsb.edu/ws/?pid=2921; "Haldeman Diary Shows Nixon was Wary of Blacks and Jews," *New York Times*, May 18, 1994, www.nytimes.com/1994/05/18/us/haldeman-diary-shows-nixon-was-wary-of-blacks-and-jews.html.

14. Jonathan Simon, *Governing through Crime: How the War on Crime Transformed American Democracy and Created a Culture of Fear* (New York: Oxford University Press, 2007; Elizabeth Kai Hinton, *From the War on Poverty to the War on Crime: The Making of Mass Incarceration in America* (Cambridge, MA: Harvard University Press, 2016).

15. The most analytically precise causal account to which this formulation is indebted is Ruth Wilson Gilmore, *Golden Gulag: Prisons, Surplus, Crisis and Opposition in Globalizing California* (Berkeley: University of California Press, 2006). A blistering and comprehensive overview is provided by Ta-Nehisi Coates, "The Black Family in the Age of Mass Incarceration," *The Atlantic*, October 2015.

16. Gilmore writes: "Racism is the state-sanctioned or extralegal production and exploitation of group-differentiated vulnerability to premature death," *Golden Gulag*, 16. See also Michelle Alexander, *The New Jim Crow: Mass Incarceration in the Age of Colorblindness* (New York: New Press, 2010); Loïc Wacquant, "Class, Race and Hyperincarceration in Revanchist America," *Daedalus* 139 (2010): 74–90.

17. Richard Nixon and his national security adviser, Henry Kissinger, viewed Chile as part of a sphere of U.S. control, an example of how the idea of hemispheric suzerainty remained operative. As Kissinger observed when approving the coup that deposed Allende: "I don't see why we need to stand by and watch a country go communist due to the irresponsibility of its people. The issues are much too important for the Chilean voters to be left to decide for themselves." Pierre Guerlain, "Hillary Clinton and the Kissinger Wing of the Democratic Party," *Huffington Post*, February 10, 2016, www.huffingtonpost.com/pierre-guerlain/hillary-clinton-and-the-k_b_9199554.html.

18. Michael Crozer, Samuel P. Huntington, and Joji Watanuki, *The Crisis of Democracy: Report on the Governability of Democracies to the Trilateral Commission* (New York: New York University Press, 1973).

19. Stuart Schrader provides the most comprehensive account available of the military revolution in policing in the United States during the 1960s. Stuart Schrader, *American Streets, Foreign Territory: How Counterinsurgent Police Waged War on Crime* (Berkeley: University of California Press, forthcoming); Paul Labarique, "The Manhattan Institute: The Neo-conservatives Lab," Voltaire Network, September 15, 2004, www.voltairenet.org/article30072.html, accessed May 23, 2017; Daryl Gates with Diane K. Shah, *Chief: My Life in the LAPD* (New York: Bantam Books, 1992), 120.

20. John Diamond, *The CIA and the Culture of Failure: US Intelligence from the End of the Cold War to the Invasion of Iraq* (Stanford, CA: Stanford University Press, 2008).

21. The shot across the bows was an article written by Daniel Patrick Moynihan that deplored the "tyranny of the UN's new majority." The article won Moynihan praise from Ford administration insiders like Donald Rumsfeld, followed by Moynihan's appointment as U.S. ambassador to the United Nations. It is a key document in the neoconservative foreign policy revolution. See Daniel P. Moynihan, "The United States in Opposition," *Commentary,* March 1975, www.commentarymagazine.com/articles/the-united-states-in-opposition/, accessed May 23, 2017.

22. Mahmood Mamdani, *Good Muslim, Bad Muslim: America, the Cold War, and the Roots of Terror* (New York: Pantheon Books, 2004).

23. "Chronology: Evolution of the Bush Doctrine," PBS *Frontline,* 2003, www.pbs.org/wgbh/pages/frontline/shows/iraq/etc/cron.html, accessed May 23, 2017.

24. Walter Isaacson, "Madeleine's War," *Time,* May 17, 1999, http://content.time.com/time/world/article/0,8599,2054293,00.html.

25. Nathan J. Robinson, "Bill Clinton's Act of Terrorism," *Jacobin,* October 12, 2016, www.jacobinmag.com/2016/10/bill-clinton-al-shifa-sudan-bombing-khartoum/, accessed May 23, 2017.

26. Michael Howard, *The Invention of Peace: Reflections on War and the International Order* (New Haven, CT: Yale University Press, 2000), 28, 29.

27. Mamdani, *Good Muslim, Bad Muslim.*

28. David E. Sanger, "In Reichstag, Bush Condemns Terror as the New Despotism," *New York Times,* May 24, 2002, www.nytimes.com/2002/05/24/world/in-reichstag-bush-condemns-terror-as-new despotism.html.

29. The theocratic, morally absolutist and the secular, culturally pluralist approaches are not diametrically opposed. Despite their differences, both work to depoliticize conflict defining the enemy as either immoral or criminal.

30. Talib Kweli, *The Beautiful Struggle* (Rawkus Records, 2004).

31. Michael Ignatieff, "The Burden," *New York Times Magazine,* January 5, 2003.

32. G. John Ikenberry, "Illusions of Empire: Defining the New American Order," *Foreign Affairs* 83 (March–April 2004): 144–54.

33. John Lewis Gaddis, *Surprise, Security, and the American Experience* (Cambridge, MA: Harvard University Press, 2004), 9.

34. Jay Garner, interviewed by reporters from the *National Journal* in 2004. This quote was reproduced in several publications, for example by Jim Lobe, "Chalabi, Garner Provide New Clues to War," Antiwar.com, February 21, 2004, www.antiwar.com/lobe/?articleid=2004, accessed May 23, 2017.

35. Robert Kaplan, "Supremacy by Stealth," *The Atlantic*, July-August, 2003. The most valuable account of counterinsurgency I have read is Laleh Khalili, *Time in the Shadows: Confinement in Counterinsurgencies* (Stanford, CA: Stanford University Press, 2013), 248.

36. Gaddis, *Surprise, Security*, 16; Robert D. Kaplan, *Imperial Grunts: On the Ground with the American Military, from Mongolia to the Philippines to Iraq and Beyond* (New York: Vintage Books, 2006), 4.

37. Bing West, *No True Glory: A Frontline Account of the Battle for Fallujah* (New York: Random House, 2006), 18.

38. Matthew Cole, "The Crimes of the Seal Team," *Intercept*, January 10, 2017, https://theintercept.com/2017/01/10/the-crimes-of-seal-team-6/, accessed May 23, 2017.

39. Amy Kaplan, "Where Is Guantanamo?" *American Quarterly* 57 (September 2005): 854.

40. Mohamedou Ould Slahi, *Guantanamo Diary* (Boston: Little Brown, 2015). In response to Slahi's rebuke, his American captor unflinchingly replied: "African tribes sold their people to us" (212).

41. Hazel Carby, "A Strange and Bitter Crop: The Spectacle of Torture," Open Democracy, October 11, 2004, www.opendemocracy.net/media-abu_ghraib/article_2149.jsp; Spencer Ackerman, "Guantanamo Torturer Led Brutal Chicago Regime of Shackling and Confession," *Guardian*, February 18, 2015, www.theguardian.com/us-news/2015/feb/18/guantanamo-torture-chicago-police-brutality.

42. Barack Obama, *Dreams from My Father* (New York: Crown, 2007), iv.

43. Barack Obama, inaugural address, January 21, 2009, https://obama whitehouse.archives.gov/blog/2009/01/21/president-barack-obamas-inaugural-address.

44. Steven R. Weisman, "Rice in Alabama Draws Parallels for Democracy Everywhere," *New York Times*, October 22, 2005, www.nytimes.com/2005/10/22/world/rice-in-alabama-draws-parallels-for-democracy-everywhere.html.

45. Mary Dudziak, *Cold War Civil Rights* (Princeton, NJ: Princeton University Press, 2002).

46. Hannah Arendt, *The Origins of Totalitarianism* (New York: Harcourt Brace, 1979), 138.

47. "Troops Told 'Shoot to Kill' in New Orleans," *ABC News Online*, September 2, 2005, www.abc.net.au/news/2005-09-02/troops-told-shoot-to-kill-in-new-orleans/2094678; Sabrina Shankman, Tom Jennings, Brendan McCarthy, Laura Maggi, and A. C. Thompson, "After Katrina, Cops Were Told They Could Shoot Looters," *San Francisco Bay View*, September, 5, 2010, http://sfbayview.com/2010/09/after-katrina-new-orleans-cops-were-told-they-could-shoot-looters/, accessed May 23, 2017. The black artist Kanye West discerned both the racial valence of looting and the links between the inner and outer war that were exposed in New Orleans: "I hate the way they portray us in the media. If you see a black family, it says, 'They're looting.' If you see a white family, it says, 'They are looking for food.' . . . We already realize a lot of the people who could help are at war right now, fighting another way, and they've . . . they've given them permission to go down and shoot us." Kanye West, interviewed by Mike Meyers, "A Concert for Hurricane Relief PSA—'George Bush Doesn't Care About Black People,'" *Genius*, September 2, 2005, https://genius.com/Kanye-west-a-concert-for-hurricane-relief-psa-george-bush-doesnt-care-about-black-people-annotated accessed May 23, 2017.

48. Ruth Wilson Gilmore, "Race, Prisons and War: Scenes from the Gilmore History of U.S. Violence," *Socialist Register* 45 (2009): 73–87; Jeremy Scahill and Daniella Crespo, "Blackwater Mercenaries Deploy in New Orleans," September 10, 2005, www.truth-out.org/archive/component/k2/item/57127:blackwater-mercenaries-deploy-in-new-orleans, accessed May 23, 2017; Klein, cited in Michael Eric Dyson, *Come Hell or High Water: Hurricane Katrina and the Color of Disaster* (Basic Books, 2007), 67. See also Jan Nederveen Pieterse, *Globalization or Empire?* (New York: Routledge, 2004).

49. Martin Luther King Jr., "Beyond Vietnam," speech given in New York City, April 4, 1967, http://kingencyclopedia.stanford.edu/encyclopedia/documentsentry/doc_beyond_vietnam/; Jack O'Dell, Climbin' Jacob's Ladder: the Black Freedom Movement Writings of Jack O'Dell, ed. Nikhil Pal Singh (Berkeley: University of California Press, 2010).

50. Nikhil Pal Singh, "Beyond the 'Empire of Jim Crow': Race and War in Contemporary U.S. Globalism," *Japanese Journal of American Studies* 20 (2009): 89–111.

51. Michel Foucault, *Society Must Be Defended: Lectures at the Collège de France, 1975–1976*, trans. David Macey (New York: Picador, 2003), 15–17.

52. Ibid., 15. Rather than tracking the concrete, historical, and group-differentiated permutations of modern racial orders, Foucault suggests that by the late nineteenth century, the waging of "race war" had been absorbed by state regimes of biopolitical regulation, through which a military or warlike relationship was transformed into a biological, or quasi-biological, one. At this point, he writes, "the enemies who have to be done away with are not adversaries in the political sense of the term; they are threats, either external or internal, to the population and for the population." Biopolitics, in his account, involves the management of social risks, birth and death, public health, criminality, and so forth in the interests of protecting life. Racism "breaks out" at the moment it becomes necessary for the state to kill in order to preserve life. Racism alone, Foucault writes, justifies the "murderous function of the State." It is

> the mechanism that allows bio-power to work. . . . What in fact is racism? It is primarily a way of introducing a break into the domain of life that is under power's control: the break between what must live and what must die. . . . It is in short a way of establishing a biological-type caesura within a population that appears to be a biological domain. . . . At the end of the nineteenth century, we have then a new racism modeled on war. It was, I think, required because a bio-power that wished to wage war had to articulate the will to destroy the adversary with the risk that it might kill those whose lives it had, by definition to protect, manage, and multiply. The same could be said of criminality . . . and the same applies to various anomalies. (Foucault, *Society Must Be Defended*, 255–58)

I am indebted to Leeroom Medevoi for this discussion. See his "Global Society Must Be Defended: Biopolitics without Boundaries," *Social Text* 25, no. 2 91 (2007): 53–79.

53. Thomas Jefferson, *Notes on the State of Virginia* (New York: Penguin, 1999), 100; President Jackson's message to Congress, "On Indian Removal," December 6, 1830; Records of the United States Senate, 1789–1990.

54. Senate Foreign Relations Committee, "1966 Fulbright Hearings, General Maxwell Taylor," C-Span, February 17, 1966, www.c-span.org/video/?404585-1 /1966-fulbright-vietnam-hearings-general-maxwell-taylor.

55. Jodi A. Byrd, *The Transit of Empire: Indigenous Critiques of Colonialism* (Minneapolis: University of Minnesota Press, 2011).

56. Paul Berman, "Donald Trump Is No Andrew Jackson, and Other Errors of Stephen Bannon," *Tablet*, December 12, 2016, www.tabletmag.com/jewish-news-and-politics/219613/donald-trump-andrew-jackson, accessed May 23, 2017; Michael Walzer, *Just and Unjust Wars: A Moral Argument with Historical Illustrations*, (New York: Basic, 2006), 85; Patrick Wolfe, *Traces of History: Elementary Structures of Race* (London: Verso, 2016).

57. Odd Arne Westad, *The Global Cold War: Third World Interventions and the Making of Our Times* (Cambridge: Cambridge University Press, 2005), 22.

58. John Grenier, *The First Way of War: American War Making on the Frontier* (Cambridge: Cambridge University Press, 2008), 225.

59. U.S. Declaration of Independence (1776); www.archives.gov/founding-docs/declaration-transcript.

60. Richard Tuck, *The Rights of War and Peace: Political Thought and the International Order from Grotius to Kant* (Oxford: Oxford University Press, 2001), 176.

61. Stephanie McCurry, *Masters of Small Worlds: Yeoman Households, Gender Relations, and the Political Culture of the Antebellum South Carolina Low Country* (New York: Oxford University Press, 1997).

62. The concept of the United States as an "empire state" is developed by Moon Kie Jung in *Beneath the Surface of White Supremacy: Denaturalizing U.S. Racism, Past and Present* (Stanford, CA: Stanford University Press, 2015).

63. Richard Hofstadter, "Reflections on Violence in the United States," in *American Violence: A Documentary History*, ed. Richard Hofstadter and Mike Wallace (New York: Alfred A. Knopf, 1970). An abridged version appears in the *Baffler*: http://thebaffler.com/ancestors/reflections-violence-united-states.

64. Hofstadter observes: "Since our violence did not typically begin with anyone's desire to subvert the state, it did not typically end by undermining the legitimacy of authority." Ibid.

65. Karen Fields and Barbara Jeanne Fields, Racecraft: The Soul of Inequality in America (New York: Verso, 2014).

66. "America's Deadly Drones Programme," *Reprieve*, www.reprieve.org.uk/case-study/drone-strikes/, accessed May 23, 2017; Marina Fang, "Nearly 90 Percent of People Killed in Recent Drone Strikes Were Not the Target," *Huffington*

Post, January 3, 2017, www.huffingtonpost.com/entry/civilian-deaths-drone-strikes_us_561fafe2e4b028dd7ea6c4ff, accessed May 23, 2017.

67. Mark Mazower, *Hitler's Empire: How the Nazis Ruled Europe* (New York: Penguin, 2008).

68. Deborah Rosen, *Border Law: The First Seminole War and American Nationhood* (Cambridge, MA: Harvard University Press, 2015).

69. James Q. Whitman, *Hitler's American Model: The United States and the Making of Nazi Race Law* (Princeton, NJ: Princeton University Press, 2017).

70. "Memorandum for William J. Haynes, General Counsel for the Department of Defense, re: Military Interrogation of Alien Unlawful Combatants Held outside the United States," March 14, 2003, available at American Civil Liberties Union, www.aclu.org/files/pdfs/safefree/yoo_army_torture_memo.pdf, accessed May 23, 2017; "Modoc War: Headquarters of the Department of the Columbia," Portland Oregon, September 10, 1873, *Congressional Series of the United States Public Documents*, 98; Jodi Byrd, *Transit of Empire: Indigenous Critiques of Colonialism* (Minneapolis: University of Minnesota Press, 2011), 227.

71. Michael Rogin, *Fathers and Children: Andrew Jackson and the Subjugation of the American Indian* (New York: Alfred A. Knopf, 1975), 312. Rogin called Jacksonian democracy the first majoritarian "Southern strategy" in U.S. politics, in that it sought to emphasize the interests that the South shared with the rest of the country and to minimize the divisiveness of slavery by maximizing the importance of expansionist claims against both decrepit European empires and racial enemies. Although the Jacksonian synthesis ultimately forestalled immediate conflict, it arguably deepened the unresolved conflict over the future of slavery; it also proposed regeneration through Western violence as an answer to intractable race and class conflicts of U.S. capitalist development.

72. David Lloyd and Patrick Wolfe, "Settler Colonial Logics and the Neoliberal Regime," *Settler Colonial Studies* 6 (2016): 109–18. See also Aziz Rana, *The Two Faces of American Freedom* (Cambridge, MA: Harvard University Press, 2014).

1. RACE, WAR, POLICE

1. W. E. B. Du Bois, *Dusk of Dawn* (New York: Oxford University Press, 2014).

2. Benjamin Franklin, "Observations Concerning the Increase of Mankind, the Peopling of Countries, etc., . . ." (1751), in *The Papers of Benjamin Franklin*, vol. 4, ed.

Leonard W. Labaree, Whitfield J. Bell, Helen C. Boatman, and Helene H. Fineman (New Haven, CT: Yale University Press, 1959), 225–34; Thomas Jefferson, *Notes on the State of Virginia* (New York: Penguin, 1999). See also David Waldstreicher, *Slavery's Constitution: From Revolution to Ratification* (New York: Hill and Wang, 2009), 26.

3. V. J. Kiernan, *America: The New Imperialism* (New York: Verso, 2005), 25.

4. Local assertions of settler sovereignty consistently blurred questions of authorized purchase, just war, and self-defense, and along with them, the "semblance of Native voluntarism" in the empire's expanding borderlands. Patrick Wolfe, *Traces of History: Elementary Structures of Race* (New York: Verso, 2016), 143.

5. Here and elsewhere I am indebted to Aziz Rana, whose important book defines the contours of what he calls "settler freedom": *The Two Faces of American Freedom* (Cambridge, MA: Harvard University Press, 2010).

6. Fred Moten and Stefano Harney, *The Undercommons: Fugitive Planning and Black Study* (New York: Minor Compositions, 2013), 57.

7. Cheryl Harris, "Whiteness as Property," in *Critical Race Theory: The Key Writings That Formed the Movement*, ed. Kimberlé Crenshaw, Neil Gotanda, Gary Peller, and Kendall Thomas (New York: New Press, 1995); George Lipsitz, *The Possessive Investment in Whiteness: How White People Profit from Identity Politics* (Philadelphia: Temple University Press, 2009).

8. Bryan Lyman, "A Permanent Wound: How the Slave Tax Warped Alabama Finances," *Montgomery Advisor*, February 5, 2017, www.montgomeryadvertiser.com/story/news/politics/southunionstreet/2017/02/05/permanent-wound-how-slave-tax-warped-alabama-finances/97447706/, accessed May 23, 2017.

9. Michel Foucault, *Security, Territory, and Population: Lectures at the Collège de France, 1977–78*, trans. G. Burchell (New York: Palgrave Macmillan, 2009), 4.

10. Matthew Frye Jacobson, *Whiteness of a Different Color: European Immigrants and the Alchemy of Race* (Cambridge, MA: Harvard University Press, 1999).

11. For an extended discussion, see Nikhil Pal Singh, *Black Is a Country: Race and the Unfinished Struggle for Democracy* (Cambridge, MA: Harvard University Press, 2005).

12. Thomas Jefferson, *The Writings of Thomas Jefferson* (New York: Heritage Press, 1967), 4:420.

13. Robert Parkinson, *Common Cause: Creating Race and Nation in the American Revolution* (Chapel Hill: University of North Carolina Press, 2016); Robert G. Par-

kinson, "Did a Fear of Slave Revolts Drive American Independence?" *New York Times*, July 4, 2016, www.nytimes.com/2016/07/04/opinion/did-a-fear-of-slave-revolts-drive-american-independence.html.

14. Thomas Paine, *Common Sense and the American Crisis* (New York: Penguin, 2012).

15. Samual Purviance, quoted in Adam Rothman, *Slave Country: American Expansion and the Origins of the Deep South* (Cambridge, MA: Harvard University Press, 2007), 17.

16. John Locke, *Second Treatise on Civil Government* (Indianpolis, IN: Hackett, 1980); Richard Tuck, *The Rights of War and Peace: Political Thought and the International Order from Grotius to Kant* (Oxford: Oxford University Press, 2001), 175.

17. Locke, *Second Treatise*, 11; Charles Mills, *The Racial Contract* (Ithaca, NY: Cornell University Press, 1997), 87.

18. Ellen Meiskins Wood, *The Empire of Capital* (London: Verso, 2005), 96.

19. Carl Schmitt, *The Nomos of the Earth in the International Law of the* Jus Publicum Europaeum (New York: Telos Press, 2006).

20. Tuck, *Rights of War*. See also Mary Nyquist, *Arbitrary Rule: Slavery, Tyranny, and the Power of Life and Death* (Chicago: University of Chicago Press, 2013).

21. Walter A. Hixon, *American Settler Colonialism: A History* (New York: Palgrave Macmillan, 2013), 39.

22. Locke, *Second Treatise*. As Marcus Dubber puts it, "The most clear-cut illustration of police power before the invention of American 'police power' . . . is provided by the governance of slaves." Markus Dirk Dubber, *The Police Power: Patriarchy and the Foundations of American Government* (New York: Columbia University Press, 2005), 61.

23. As Domenico Losurdo writes, liberalism "went hand in hand with the delimitation of a restricted sacred space: nurturing a proud, exclusivist self-consciousness, the community of the freemen inhabiting it was led to regard enslavement, or more or less explicit subjection, imposed on the great mass dispersed through the profane space, as legitimate. Sometimes they even arrived at decimation or annihilation." Domenico Losurdo, *Liberalism: A Counter-History*, trans. Gregory Elliot (London: Verso, 2014).

24. Andrew Dilts, *Punishment and Inclusion: Race, Membership, and the Limits of American Liberalism* (New York: Fordham University Press, 2014), 90. Even as the

enemy in a just war was marked as a kind of criminal, crimes against property made a person into a particular kind of enemy. The *criminalization* of the enemy (as Carl Schmitt astutely noted) became a hallmark of modernist appropriations of the just-war tradition, which in this way began to blur the lines between police and military action in spaces of colonial conflict or civil unrest: that is, zones where sovereignty was contested or in question.

25. Locke, *Second Treatise*, 45.

26. Richard Tuck summarizes Locke's political theory as one that "allows arbitrary powers of life and death to the masters of slaves taken in war; and which allows settlers to occupy the lands of native peoples without consulting their wishes in any way" (*Rights of War*, 177).

27. Peter Onuf, *Jefferson's Empire: The Language of American Nationhood* (Charlottesville: University of Virginia, 2000), 81–82.

28. Peter Onuf and Nicholas Onuf, *Federal Union, Modern World: The Law of Nations in an Age of Revolutions, 1776-1814* (Madison, WI: Madison House, 1997), 157.

29. Rana, *Two Faces of American Freedom* (Cambridge, MA: Harvard University Press, 2014); Lorenzo Veracini, *Settler Colonialism: A Theoretical Overview* (London: Palgrave Macmillan, 2010).

30. This discussion is indebted to Veracini, *Settler Colonialism*. See also Moon Kie Jung, *Beneath the Surface of White Supremacy: Denaturalizing U.S. Racisms Past and Present* (Stanford, CA: Stanford University Press, 2015), 62.

31. This was the Jeffersonian vision of individual U.S. states as little republics, whose claims to state and local sovereignty were not thought to contravene the larger claims of the federal union. "Imperialism and republicanism," as a recent work puts it, were in this way "inseparable twin influences in the creation and growth of political culture in the United States." Fred Anderson and Andrew Cayton, *The Dominion of War: Empire and Liberty in North America, 1500-2000* (New York: Viking, 2004), xxi. Settlers, in the terms of another recent theorist of settler colonialism viewed themselves in "isopolitical" terms: that is, they "imagined [themselves as] a single political community across several jurisdictions," local and translocal at the same time. Veracini, *Settler Colonialism;* see also Lorenzo Veracini, "Isopolitics, Deep Colonizing, Settler Colonialism," *Interventions* 13 (2011): 171–89.

32. Michael Hardt and Antonio Negri, *Multitude: War and Democracy in the Age of Empire* (New York: Penguin, 2005). The term *race management* is developed more explicitly in relation to the labor process in David Roediger and Betsy Esch, *The Production of Difference: Race and the Management of Labor in U.S. History* (New York: Oxford University Press, 2012).

33. Lisa Ford, *Settler Sovereignty: Jurisdiction and Indigenous People in America and Australia, 1788–1836* (Cambridge, MA: Harvard University Press, 2011).

34. Edmund Sears Morgan, *American Slavery, American Freedom: The Ordeal of Colonial Virginia* (New York: Norton, 2003 [1975]).

35. Georgia General Assembly, "A Compilation of the Patrol Laws of the State of Georgia in Conformity with a Resolution of the General Assembly" (Milledgeville, GA: S. & F. Grantland, 1818).

36. Sally Hadden, *Slave Patrols: Law and Violence in Virginia and the Carolinas* (Cambridge, MA: Harvard University Press, 2003), 85.

37. Leon Litwack, *North of Slavery: The Negro in the Free States, 1790–1860* (Chicago: University of Chicago Press, 1965), 58.

38. Saul Cornell and Eric Ruben, "The Slave-State Origins of Modern Gun Rights," *The Atlantic*, September 30, 2015.

39. Ulrich Bonnell Phillips, *American Negro Slavery: A Survey of the Supply, Employment and Control of Negro Labor as Determined by the Plantation Regime* (New York: D. Appleton and Company, 1918), 500.

40. Steven Kantrowitz, "Refuge for Fugitives," *Boston Review*, May 16, 2017, http://bostonreview.net/race/stephen-kantrowitz-refuge-fugitives, accessed May 27, 2017.

41. John William Burgess, *The Middle Period, 1817–1858* (New York: C. Scribner's Sons, 1897), 378.

42. Ernst Freund, *The Police Power: Public Policy and Constitutional Rights* (New York: Callaghan & Company, 1904), 3; John Burgess, *Political Science and Constitutional Law* (New York: HardPress, 2013 [1893]), 2:136.

43. Theodore Roosevelt, "Annual Message to Congress," December 6, 1904; see also Markus Dubber and Mariana Valverde, eds., *The New Police Science: The Police Power in Domestic and International Governance* (Stanford, CA: Stanford University Press, 2006), 190.

44. Khalil Gibran Muhammad, *The Condemnation of Blackness: Race, Crime, and the Making of Modern Urban America* (Cambridge, MA: Harvard University Press, 2011), 4.

45. Plessy v. Ferguson, 163 U.S. 537 (1896).

46. Alfred McCoy, *Policing America's Empire: The United States, the Philippines, and the Rise of the Surveillance State* (Madison: University of Wisconsin Press, 2009).

47. Paul Kramer, *The Blood of Government: Race, Empire, the United States, and the Philippines* (Chapel Hill: University of North Carolina Press, 2006), 138.

48. Alfred Thayer Mahan, "A Twentieth Century Outlook," *Harper's New Monthly Magazine*, September 1897, 527.

49. Marilyn Lake and Henry Reynolds, *Drawing the Global Color Line: White Men's Countries and the International Challenge of Racial Equality* (Cambridge: Cambridge University Press, 2008), 64.

50. Ibram Kendi, *Stamped from the Beginning: The Definitive History of Racist Ideas in America* (New York: Nation Books, 2016), 297.

51. Chae Chan Ping v. United States, 130 U.S. 581, 1889 (the Chinese Exclusion Case). See also Matthew Lindsay, "Immigration as Invasion: Sovereignty, Security and the Origins of Federal Immigration Power," *Harvard Civil Rights–Civil Liberties Law Review* 45 (Winter 2010): 1–56.

52. Mae Ngai, *Impossible Subjects: Illegal Aliens and the Making of Modern America* (Princeton, NJ: Princeton University Press, 2004), 11. Bruce Cumings, *Dominion from Sea to Sea: Pacific Ascendancy and American Power* (New Haven, CT: Yale University Press, 2009), 208.

53. Robert Vitalis, *White World Order, Black Power Politics: The Birth of American International Relations* (Ithaca, NY: Cornell University Press, 2015).

54. Quoted in Max Weber, *Essays in Sociology* (New York: Routledge, 2009), 71–72.

55. Kelly Lytle Hernández, *Migra! A History of the U.S. Border Patrol* (Berkeley: University of California Press, 2010), 117, 130.

56. Carl Schmitt, *Writings on War* (Malden, MA: Polity, 2011), 115.

57. Schmitt, Nomos *of the Earth*, 170.

58. Schmitt, *Writings on War*, quoted in Enzo Traverso, *The Origins of Nazi Violence*, trans. Janet Lloyd (New York: New Press, 2003), 63.

59. Schmitt, Nomos *of the Earth*, 321.

60. Quoted in Mark Mazower, *Hitler's Empire: Nazi Rule in Occupied Europe* (New York: Penguin Books, 2009), 4.

61. Charles F. Sloane, "Dogs in War, Police Work and on Patrol," *Journal of Criminal Law and Criminology* 46 (1955–56): 388. See also Tyler Wall, "For the Very Existence of Civilization": The Police Dog and Racial Terror," *American Quarterly* 68, no. 4 (December 2016): 861–82.

62. Sloane, "Dogs in War," 389, 388.

63. William F. Handy, Marilyn Harrington, and David J. Pittman, "The K-9 Corps: The Use of Dogs in Police Work," *Journal of Criminal Law and Criminology* 52 (1961): 336. The liberal-minded academics Handy and Pittman were at that time consultants to the St. Louis Metropolitan Police Department, and Pittman went on to serve as a consultant to Lyndon Johnson's Commission on Law Enforcement and the Administration of Justice in the compilation of the study *The Challenge of Crime in a Free Society* (Washington, DC: U.S. Government Printing Office, 1967).

64. Handy, Harrington, and Pittman, "The K-9 Corps," 337.

65. Frank Donner, *Protectors of Privilege: Red Squads and Police Repression in Urban America* (Berkeley: University of California Press), 305.

66. Philip Caputo, *Indian Country* (New York: Bantam Books, 1987).

67. With a contract for $25 million, this enterprise represented the first major U.S. commitment to what would later be termed "civic engagement" south of the 17th Parallel following the French defeat and the 1954 Geneva Conventions. Though a largely failed experiment (according to Sloane's own "end of tour" account), this early effort at overseas police "modernization" provided the template for many schemes to follow, including the notorious Phoenix program, overseen by Robert Komer, William Colby, and others and organized under the auspices of the Office of Police Assistance in the U.S. Agency for International Development, which spent over $300 million on police training in Vietnam between 1962 and 1975. "The greatest possible use is being made of South Viet-Nam as a laboratory for techniques and equipment related to the counterinsurgency program," Maxwell Taylor wrote to John F. Kennedy in 1962. See Jeffrey H. Michaels, "Managing Global Counterinsurgency: The Special Group (CI), 1962–1966," *Journal of Strategic Studies* 35 (2012).

68. In his "New Frontier" speech, delivered in Los Angeles in November, 1960, John F. Kennedy said: "I stand here tonight facing west on what was once the last frontier." He described the nation as poised once again "to conquer enemies that threatened from within and from without."

69. W. H. Parker, "The Police Role in Community Relations," *Journal of Criminal Law and Criminology* 47 (1956): 376–77.

70. William H. Parker, *Parker on Police* (Springfield, IL: Thomas, 1957), 60.

71. Parker, "Police Role in Community Relations," 376–77.

72. Parker, *Parker on Police*, 8.

73. Parker, "Police Role in Community Relations," 377.

74. In Parker's words, "One person threw a rock, and then, like monkeys in a zoo, others started throwing rocks." Quoted in Edward M. Davis, "Past Police Chiefs," *Los Angeles Times*, April 17, 1992, http://articles.latimes.com/1992–04–17 /news/mn-732_1_los-angeles-police. As evidence of the seriousness with which Parker's ideas were considered, the collection of his writings, *Parker on Police*, was edited by the legendary police scholar O. W. Wilson, dean of the School of Criminology at the University of California, Berkeley.

75. *To Secure These Rights: The Report of the President's Committee on Civil Rights* (1948), 20, Harry S. Truman Library and Museum, www.trumanlibrary.org /civilrights/srights1.htm, accessed May 27, 2017; Naomi Murakawa, *The First Civil Right: How Liberals Built Prison America* (Oxford: Oxford University Press, 2014).

76. Quoted in Robert M. Fogelson, *The Los Angeles Riots* (New York: Arno Press), 126.

77. "Troops Fight L.A. Rioters," *Chicago Tribune*, August 15, 1965. See also Tracy Tullis, "A Vietnam at Home: Policing the Ghettos in the Counterinsurgency Era," PhD diss., New York University, 1999.

78. Don Moser, "Their Mission: Defend, Befriend," *Life Magazine*, August 25, 1967, 25–31; W. W. Rostow to the President, July 28, 1967, "Riots (1)," Box 32, Office Files of Harry McPherson, LBJ Presidential Library, Austin, TX. Rostow is quoted in Tullis, "A Vietnam at Home," 24, and also in Stuart Schrader, "American Streets, Foreign Territory: How Counterinsurgent Police Waged a War on Crime," PhD diss., New York University, 2015, 32. I am especially indebted to Stuart for drawing my attention to the importance of this document.

79. Frank Armbruster, "A Military and Police Security Program for South Vietnam," in *Can We Win in Vietnam?* (London: Pall Mall Press), 255. Armbruster also reiterates the value of dogs here, describing them as "an old and proven method of tracking down criminals and looking for guerillas in the forest" (267).

80. Quoted in Jeremy Kuzmarov, *Modernizing Repression: Police Training and Nation-Building in the American Century* (Amherst: University of Massachusetts Press, 2012), 145. One of the biggest prison uprisings in U.S. military history occurred at the Long Binh stockade, the primary incarceration center in Vietnam (known as Camp LBJ), on August 28, 1968, when two hundred black military prisoners donned white kerchiefs and African-styled robes made from Army blankets and rioted, leaving one white inmate dead and destroying the stockade.

81. Jack O'Dell, "A Special Variety of Colonialism," *Freedomways* 7, no. 1 (Winter 1967): 7–15.

82. Martin Luther King, Jr. "The Other America," speech at Grosse Point High School, Michigan, March 14, 1967, www.gphistorical.org/mlk/mlkspeech/, accessed May 27, 2017.

83. Samuel F. Yette, *The Choice: The Issue of Black Survival in America* (Silver Spring, MD: Cottage Books, 1971), 22.

84. Charles Maechling Jr., "Camelot, Robert Kennedy, and Counter-insurgency: A Memoir," *Virginia Quarterly Review* 75, no. 3 (1999): 438–58. See also Marilyn B. Young, "'I Was Thinking, as I Often Do These Days, of War'": The United States in the 21st Century," *Diplomatic History* 36, no. 1 (2012): 1–15. The OIDP document is available at http://orchestratingpower.org/lib/COIN /Overseas%20Internal%20Defense%20Policy/OIDP.pdf, accessed May 23, 2017.

85. Thompson is referenced in Richard Critchfield, *The Long Charade: Political Subversion in the Vietnam War* (New York: Harcourt Brace and World, 1968), p. 163.

86. Office of Planning Policy and Research, *The Negro Family: The Case for National Action*, U.S. Department of Labor, March 1965, www.dol.gov/oasam /programs/history/webid-meynihan.htm,accessed May 23, 2017.

87. McGeorge Bundy, "The End of Either/Or," *Foreign Affairs* 45, no. 2 (1967): 194.

88. Quoted in Stephen T. Hosmer and Sibylle O. Crane, "Counterinsurgency: A Symposium, April 16–20, 1962" (Santa Monica, CA: Rand Corporation, 2006).

134. As Kitson noted of the gathering, "Although we came from such widely divergent backgrounds, it was as if we had all been brought up together from youth. We all spoke the same language. Probably all of us had worked out theories of counterinsurgency procedures at one time or another, which we thought were unique and original. But when we came to air them, all our ideas were essentially the same." He never paused to consider that the production of sameness might be a function of a fiercely exclusivist self-consciousness informed by a dramatically similar reading of the objects of counterinsurgency.

89. Arthur Schlesinger, *Robert F. Kennedy and His Times* (Boston: Houghton Mifflin, 1978), 189.

90. Edward C. Banfield, *The Unheavenly City Revisited* (Prospect Heights, IL: Waveland Press, 1990), 175.

91. Samuel Huntington, quoted in Stuart Schrader, "To Secure the Global Great Society: Participation in Classification," *Humanity: An International Journal of Human Rights, Humanitarianism, and Development* 7, no. 2 (Summer 2016): 225–53.

92. James Q. Wilson and Richard J. Herrstein, *Crime and Human Nature* (New York: Simon and Schuster, 1985); George R. Kelling and James Q. Wilson, "Broken Windows: The Police and Neighborhood Safety," *The Atlantic*, March 1982, www.theatlantic.com/magazine/archive/1982/03/broken-windows/304465; George Kelling, "Don't Blame My 'Broken Windows' Theory For Poor Policing," *Politico Magazine*, August 11, 2015, www.politico.com/magazine/story/2015/08/broken-windows-theory-poor-policing-ferguson-kelling-121268; Edward Banfield, quoted in Justin Peters, "Loose Cigarettes Today, Civil Unrest Tomorrow: The Racist, Classist Origins of Broken Windows Policing," *Slate*, December 5, 2014, www.slate.com/articles/news_and_politics/crime/2014/12/edward_banfield_the_racist_classist_origins_of_broken_windows_policing.html.

93. Adam Yarmolinsky, *The Military Establishment: Its Impacts on the American Establishment* (New York: Harper & Row, 1971), 193, 408.

94. John Conroy, "Tools of Torture," *Chicago Reader*, February 3, 2005, www.chicagoreader.com/chicago/tools-of-torture/Content?oid = 917876 qtd.

95. Darius Rejali, *Torture and Democracy* (Princeton, NJ: Princeton University Press, 2009), 582.

96. Daryl F. Gates, *Chief: My Life in the LAPD* (New York: Bantam, 1992), 109–10.

97. *Report on the NYPD'S Stop-and-Frisk Policy*, New York City Bar Association, May 2013, www2.nycbar.org/pdf/report/uploads/20072495-StopFriskReport.pdf, accessed May 23, 2017; Floyd et al. v. City of New York, August 12, 2013, USDJ opinion and Order 08 Civ. 1034 (SAS), 12–13, http://online.wsj.com/public/resources/documents/nystop0812.pdf.

98. Benjamin Franklin, "A Conversation between an Englishman, a Scotchman and an American on the Subject of Slavery," *London Public Advertiser,* January 30, 1770; available online at National Archives, Founders Online, https://founders.archives.gov/documents/Franklin/01-17-02-0019, accessed May 23, 2017.

99. James Foreman Jr., *Locking Up Our Own: Crime and Punishment in Black America* (New York: Farrar, Strauss and Giroux, 2017), quoted in Adam Schatz, "Out of Sight, Out of Mind," *London Review of Books,* May 4, 2017.

100. Department of Justice "Lawfulness of a Lethal Operation Directed against a US Citizen Who Is a Senior Operational Leader of Al-Qa'ida or an Associated Force," white paper, November 8, 2011, 9, available on the website of the Federation of American Scientists, http://fas.org/irp/eprint/doj-lethal.pdf.

101. Gwynn Guilford and Nikhil Sonnad, "What Steve Bannon Really Wants," *Quartz,* February 3, 2017, https://qz.com/898134/what-steve-bannon-really-wants/; Sarah Zhang, "Will the Alt-Right Promote a New Kind of Racist Genetics?" *The Atlantic,* December 19, 2016.

102. FBI Uniform Crime Reporting System, *Crime in the United States, 2015,* FBI: UCR, released fall 2016, https://ucr.fbi.gov/crime-in-the-u.s/2015/crime-in-the-u.s.-2015/persons-arrested/persons-arrested.

2. FROM WAR CAPITALISM TO RACE WAR

1. For an original and exemplary statement of this viewpoint, see Robert Brenner, "Agrarian Structure and Economic Development in Pre-industrial Europe," *Past and Present* 70 (February 1976): 30–75. Brenner sharpens the polemical stakes of this argument, taking on various modes of "dependency" and "world-systems theory" for "displac[ing] class relations from the center of economic development" and for failing to recognize "the productivity of labor as the essence and key of [capitalist] economic development." See Robert Brenner, "The Origins of Capitalist Development: A Critique of Neo-Smithian Marxism," *New Left Review* 104 (July-August 1977): 26–92.

2. Ellen Meiskins Wood, *The Origin of Capitalism: A Longer View* (London: Verso, 2002). Following Brenner, Wood writes, "The wealth amassed from [slavery and] colonial exploitation may have contributed substantially to further development, even if it was not the necessary precondition for the origin of capitalism. . . . If wealth from the colonies and the slave trade contributed to Britain's industrial revolution, it was because the British economy had already for a long time been structured by capitalist property relations" (149).

3. Stephanie Smallwood, *Saltwater Slavery: A Middle Passage from African to American Diaspora* (Cambridge, MA: Harvard University Press, 2007), 30. As much as any other contemporary thinker, Smallwood strives to link the logics of slavery as social death and as a novel form of commodification: "The Atlantic market for slaves changed what it meant to be a socially, politically or economically marginalized person. . . . Captivity . . . was not a temporary status . . . not [a situation] of extreme alienation within the community, but rather of absolute exclusion from any community," and the fashioning of "bodies animated only by others' calculated investment in their physical capacity" (35).

4. Sven Beckert, *The Empire of Cotton* (New York: Vintage, 2014), 92, 114. See also Eric Williams, *Capitalism and Slavery* (New York: Putnam, 1966 [1944]). Important contributors to the contemporary resurgence of Williams's argument include Walter Johnson, Edward Baptist, Stephanie Smallwood, and Julia Ott. Williams argued that slavery profits were central to the rise of industrial capitalism. This controversial thesis was subjected to death by a thousand historiographical cuts in the decades following its publication. Arguably the most disturbing aspect of Williams's argument was his fundamental challenge to those who emphasized slavery's vestigial character in order to moralize and legitimate subsequent capitalist development—in effect freeing capitalism from a debt to slavery. Writing when U.S.-led international capitalism sought to extract itself from the racial and imperial matrix in which it had developed, Williams provided an unsettling dose of skepticism: "This does not invalidate the arguments for democracy, for freedom now or for freedom after the war. But mutatis mutandis, the arguments have a familiar ring." "We have to be on our guard," Williams wrote, "not only against the old prejudices, but against the new which are being constantly created" (212). Frank Tannenbaum exemplified the kind of orthodoxy that Williams unsettled during the period of his writing: "The Negro race has

been given an additional large share of the face of the globe for its own. It received this territory as a kind of unplanned gift. . . . It is in its own nature, no different than the process which has occurred as a result of the allurement which led millions of Americans to labor in American mines, fields, and factories. . . . The result has been moral. It has proved a good thing for the Negroes in the long run. They have achieved a status, both spiritually and materially, in the new home to which they were brought as chattels." Frank Tannenbaum, "A Note on the Economic Interpretation of History," *Political Science Quarterly* 61 (1946): 248–49.

5. Dipesh Chakrabarty, "Universalism and Belonging in the Logic of Capitalism," *Public Culture* 12, no. 3 (2000): 653.

6. For a powerful contemporary theory that develops this view, see Jason Moore, *Capitalism in the Web of Life: Ecology and the Accumulation of Capital* (New York: Verso, 2015).

7. Karl Marx, *Capital, Volume I: The Process of Production of Capital* (New York: Vintage, 1967 [1867]), 925, 374–81, 225. Here are the respective quotations in full: "Whilst the cotton industry introduced child-slavery into England in the United States, it gave the impulse for the transformation of the earlier, more or less patriarchal slavery into a system of commercial exploitation. In fact the veiled slavery of the wage laborers in Europe needed the unqualified slavery of the New world as its pedestal" (925). "Capital therefore takes no account of the health and the length of the life of the worker, unless society forces it to do so. Its answer to the outcry about the physical and mental degradation, the premature death, the torture of over-work, is this: Should that pain trouble us, since it increases our profit (pleasure)?" (381). "If labor-power can be supplied from foreign preserves . . . the duration of [the worker's] life becomes a matter of less moment than its productiveness while it lasts. . . . It is accordingly a maxim of slave management in slave importing countries, that the most effective economy is that which takes out of the human chattel in the shortest space of time the utmost of exertion that it is capable of putting forth" (225).

8. Frank Wilderson, "Gramsci's Black Marx: Whither the Slave in Civil Society?" *Social Identities* 9, no. 3 (2003): 230. For a related argument more in keeping with my approach in this chapter, see Walter Johnson, "The Pedestal and the Veil: Rethinking the Capitalism/Slavery Question," *Journal of the Early Republic* 24, no. 2 (2004): 299–308.

9. Jennifer Morgan, "Archives and Histories of Racial Capitalism: An Afterword," *Social Text* 33, no. 4 125 (December 2015): 153–61, doi: 10.1215/01642472-3315862. See also Jennifer Morgan, "Partus Sequitur Ventrum: Slave Law and the History of Women in Slavery" (forthcoming).

10. Frederick Douglass, "Reception Speech at Finsbury Chapel, Moorfield, England, May 12, 1846," in *My Bondage and my Freedom* (New York: Miller, Orton and Mulligan, 1855), 412. "We have in the US slave-breeding states . . . where men, women and children are reared for the market, just as horses, sheep and swine are raised for the market. Slave-rearing is there looked upon as a legitimate trade; the law sanctions it, public opinion upholds it, the church does not condemn it. It goes on in all its bloody horrors, sustained by the auctioneer's block."

11. What Wilderson has termed "gratuitous violence" retained an instrumental value as exemplary violence, a deterrent to much-feared resistance and revolt. More recently, Edward Baptist has made a compelling case for the relationship between bodily torture and surplus extraction under slavery. Edward Baptist, *The Half that Has Never Been Told: Slavery and the Making of American Capitalism* (New York: Basic Books, 2015).

12. The notion of accumulation by dispossession is a contemporary reframing of Marx's so-called primitive accumulation. See Gillian Hart, "Denaturalizing Dispossession: Critical Ethnography in an Age of Resurgent Imperialism," *Antipode* 38, no. 5 (2006): 977–1004. Also see Michael Perleman, *The Invention of Capitalism and the Secret History of Primitive Accumulation* (Durham, NC: Duke University Press, 2000).

13. Karl Polanyi, *The Great Transformation: The Political and Economic Origins of Our Time* (Boston: Beacon Press, 2001 [1944]). By describing land, labor, and money as "fictitious commodities,"' Polanyi emphasizes the imposition of the logic of the self-regulating market and universal commodification as the defining features of capitalism. Further, he emphasizes how processes of commodification broadly encompass not only the domain of labor and its social and biological reproduction but also the ecological matrix of life itself, and the mediums and modes of exchange that constitute social horizons. The subjection of all three domains to the "market mechanism" threatens the very conditions of social existence, stripping human beings of "the protective covering of cultural institutions . . . defiling neighborhoods and landscapes," and subjecting pur-

chasing power to disastrous "shortages and surfeits of money" (76). This formulation challenges both liberal and Marxist tendencies to construct the economy as an analytically autonomous domain. At its best, the notion of fictitious commodification draws our attention to the state-enforced, noncontractual, and dominative bases of capital accumulation, as well as to dynamics of "social protection" or resistance that often draw upon nonmarket norms of land, labor, and money (including potentially reactionary ones). "Laissez-faire was planned, planning was not," Polanyi famously writes, and "the stark utopia" of the free market found the answer to its deepening crisis to be the fascist response. See also Fred Block, "Karl Polanyi and the Writing of "The Great Transformation,'" *Theory and Society* 32, no. 3 (2003): 275–306; Nancy Fraser, "Can Society Be Commodities All the Way Down? Polanyian Reflections on Capitalist Crisis," Fondation Maison des Sciences de L'homme, Working Paper no. 18, August 2012.

14. Patrick Wolfe, "Land, Labor and Difference: Elementary Structures of Race," *American Historical Review*, 106, no. 3 (2001): 866–905.

15. David Kazanjian, *The Colonizing Trick: National Culture and Imperial Citizenship in Early America* (Minneapolis: University of Minnesota Press, 2003).

16. The literature on varieties of capitalism not only emphasizes contingent, differing institutional arrangements compatible with actually existing capitalism but more strongly argues that there is no capitalist mode of production as such, only configurations or forms of capitalism "compatible with a variety of forms of labor exploitation." See Jairus Banaji, *Theory as History: Essays on Modes of Production and Exploitation* (London: Historical Materialism, 2010), 11.

17. Marx, *Capital, Volume I*, 875.

18. Karl Marx, *Grundrisse: Foundations of Political Economy* (London: Penguin, 1993 [1867]), 400.

19. Marx, *Capital, Volume I*, 784, 789, 793, 797.

20. The slave and the lumpenproletariat may resemble each other by, as it were, falling absolutely outside a relationship of capitalist exploitation. This insight, of course, has been a spur to thinkers like Frantz Fanon and George Jackson, though I do not pursue it here. I am indebted to Tavia Nyong'o for this insight. See also Peter Stallybrass, "Marx and Heterogeneity: Thinking the Lumpenproletariat," *Representations* 31 (1990): 81.

21. Marx, *Capital, Volume I*, 940, 899.

22. Karl Marx and Friedrich Engels, *Class Struggles in France, 1840–1850*, in *Collected Works*, 10 (London: Lawrence and Wishart, 1893), 62. Quoted in Stallybrass, "Marx and Heterogeneity," 84.

23. Marx, *Capital, Volume I*, 937. Marx writes: "In the old civilized countries the worker, although free, is by a law of nature dependent on the capitalist; in the colonies this dependence must be created by artificial means." He is not referring to slavery here, but he could be. The problem of the colonies is that there is too much freedom for workers to opt out and to become "independent landowners, if not competitors with their former masters in the labour market." Marx also hastens to add: "We are not concerned here with the condition of the colonies. The only thing that interests us is the secret discovered in the New World by the political economy of the Old World" (936, 940).

24. Ibid., 873, 915.

25. Marx, *Grundrisse*, 164.

26. Ibid.

27. Marx, *Capital, Volume I*, 1031, 1033 (italics in original).

28. Marx, *Grundrisse*, 326.

29. David Roediger, *The Wages of Whiteness: Race and the Making of the American Working Class* (New York: Verso, 2007).

30. Charles Post, *The American Road to Capitalism: Studies in Class Structure, Economic Development and Political Conflict, 1620–1877* (New York: Haymarket Books, 2012).

31. Marx, *Capital, Volume I*, 391.

32. Banaji, *Theory as History*, 13.

33. Marx, *Capital, Volume I*, 382. Just as the worker's idea and feeling of freedom have important material effects, so does the transformation of freedom into a kind of status distinction. "Capital . . . takes no account of the health and length of the life of the worker," Marx writes, "unless society forces it to do so." This is of course a reference to the English class struggle, mostly one-sided in Marx's view, in which the worker may succeed in securing limits on the working day but is "compelled by social conditions to sell the whole of his active life, his very capacity for labor. in return for the price of his customary means of subsistence, to sell his birthright for a mess of pottage."

34. Marx, *Capital, Volume I*, 414.

35. C. L. R. James, *The Black Jacobins: Toussaint L'Ouverture and the San Domingo Revolution* (New York: Vintage Books, 1989 [1938]), 86.

36. Williams, *Capitalism and Slavery*, 211.

37. Marx, *Capital, Volume I*, 345.

38. Mary Nyquist, *Arbitrary Rule: Slavery Tyranny and the Power of Life over Death* (Chicago: University of Chicago Press, 2013), 366.

39. Heidi Gerstenberger, "The Political Economic of Capitalist Labor," *Viewpoint Magazine*, September 2014, https://viewpointmag.com/2014/09/02/the-political-economy-of-capitalist-labor/.

40. Marx, *Capital, Volume I*, 925. Postlethwayt is quoted in David Waldstreicher, *Slavery's Constitution: From Revolution to Ratification* (New York: Hill and Wang, 2010), 27.

41. Kazanjian, *The Colonizing Trick*, 21; Marx, *Grundrisse*, 464.

42. Karl Marx, *The Poverty of Philosophy* (Moscow: Foreign Language Publishers, 1958 [1847]), 125. In a set of brilliant essays, Gopal Balakrishnan describes the Marx of this early period as an "abolitionist." He writes: "Only later would Marx come to see a contradiction between free wage labor and slavery. Now he assumed that American slavery was an integral part of the world system of bourgeois society . . . the Marx of this period was a ruthless abolitionist." Gopal Balakrishnan, "The Abolitionist—II," *New Left Review* 91 (January-February 2015): 69–100.

43. Cedric Robinson, *Black Marxism: The Making of the Black Radical Tradition* (London: Zed Press, 1983).

44. Marx, *Poverty of Philosophy*, 124.

45. Marx, *Capital, Volume I*, 91.

46. W. E. B. Du Bois, *Black Reconstruction in America, 1860-1880* (New York: Free Press, 1998), 632–34.

47. As Michael Denning writes, *proletariat* is not a synonym for wage labor "but for dispossession, expropriation and radical dependence on the market." Michael Denning, "Wageless Life," *New Left Review* 66 (November-December 2010): 81.

48. Rosa Luxemburg, *The Accumulation of Capital* (New York: Monthly Review Press, 1968 [1951]), 372 (italics in original).

49. Marx, *Grundrisse*, 109; Michel Foucault, *Society Must Be Defended: Lectures at the Collège de France, 1975-1976*, trans. David Macey (New York: Picador, 2003), 51.

50. Michel Foucault, *Security, Territory, Population: Lectures at the Collège de France, 1977-1978*, trans. Graham Burchell (New York: Picador, 2009), 353.

51. Foucault, *Society Must Be Defended*, 260. Although Foucault develops an idea of race war as integral to modern statecraft, his account is idiosyncratic and equivocating. In examining Nazi violence, he appears to validate an exceptionalism marked by temporal relegation: "Nazism alone took the play between the sovereign right to kill and the mechanisms of biopower to this paroxysmal point. But this play is in fact inscribed in the workings of all States. In all modern States, in all capitalist States? Perhaps not" (261).

52. Jason Moore, "Endless Accumulation, Endless (Unpaid) Work?" *Occupied Times*, April 29, 2015, https://theoccupiedtimes.org/?p=13766,accessed May 23, 2017.

53. Moore, *Capitalism in the Web of Life*, 70, 224. See also Smallwood, *Saltwater Slavery*, 35.

54. This discussion is heavily indebted to Nyquist, *Arbitrary Rule*, especially chapter 10 and the epilogue.

55. Frederick Douglass, *Autobiographies* (New York: Penguin, 1994), 330; Marx, letter to Siegfried Meyer,1870, quoted in David L. Wilson, "Marx on Immigration," *Monthly Review* 68, no. 9 (2017), https://monthlyreview.org/2017/02/01/marx-on-immigration/, accessed May 23, 2017.

56. Melinda Cooper, *Life as Surplus: Biotechnology and Capitalism in a Neoliberal Era* (Seattle: University of Washington Press, 2008), 60.

57. Daniel Bensaid, *Marx for Our Times: Adventures and Misadventures of a Critique* (New York: Verso, 2002), 23.

3. THE AFTERLIFE OF FASCISM

This chapter, first published in 2006, was written during the height of the Iraq torture scandal. It has been revised and updated for this volume.

1. Michael Ignatieff, "The Burden," *New York Times Magazine*, January 5, 2003, 41.

2. John O'Sullivan, quoted in Tomas Hietala, *Manifest Design: American Exceptionalism and Empire* (Ithaca, NY: Cornell University Press, 2003), 193.

3. Woodrow Wilson, quoted in Mary Renda, *Taking Haiti: Military Occupation and the Culture of U.S. Imperialism, 1915-1940* (Chapel Hill: University of North

Carolina Press, 2002); Lyndon B, Johnson, quoted in Marilyn Young, *The Vietnam Wars, 1945-1990* (New York: Harper Perennial, 1991), 119.

4. Andrew Jackson, quoted in Robert Remini, *Andrew Jackson and His Indian Wars* (New York: Viking, 2001), 123.

5. Quoted in Renato Redentor Constantino, "The Shocking (and Relevant) Truth about Our Occupation of the Philippines," *History News Network*, February 4, 2004, http://historynewsnetwork.org/article/3675, accessed May 23, 2017. See also Reynaldo Illeto, "The Philippine-American War: Friendship and Forgetting," in V*estiges of War: The Philippine-American War and the Aftermath of an Imperial Dream, 1899-1999*, ed. Angel Shaw and Lewis Francia (New York: New York University Press, 2002), 2–21.

6. The idea of the "waiting room of history" is from Dipesh Chakrabarty, *Provincializing Europe: Postcolonial Thought and Historical Difference* (Princeton, NJ: Princeton University Press, 2000).

7. Dexter Filkins, "Tough New Tactics by US Tighten Grip on Iraq Towns," *New York Times*, December 7, 2003.

8. Mahmood Mamdani, *Good Muslim, Bad Muslim: America, the Cold War, and the Roots of Terror* (New York: Pantheon Books, 2004).

9. Étienne Balibar, *Race, Nation, Class: Ambiguous Identities* (New York: Verso, 1991), 23. See also Seymour Hersh, "Chain of Command," *New Yorker*, May 17, 2004, 38–43; Emram Qureshi, "Misreading the Arab Mind," *Boston Globe*, May 30, 2004; Bernard Lewis, "The Roots of Muslim Rage," *Atlantic Monthly*, September 1990; Raphael Patai, *The Arab Mind* (New York: Hatherleigh Press, 2002).

10. This conflation has been three decades in the making. See Melani McAlister, *Epic Encounters: Culture, Media, and U.S. Interests in the Middle East, 1945-2000* (Berkeley: University of California Press, 2001).

11. Thomas Friedman, "Because We Could," *New York Times*, June 4, 2003.

12. George W. Bush, inaugural address, quoted in *New York Times*, January 6, 2005.

13. David Rose, "The Real Truth about Camp Delta" and "The Rule of Violence," *Observer*, October 3, 2004; James Meek, "The People That Law Forgot," *Guardian*, December 3, 2003; Jonathan Steele, "Bush Is Now Thinking of Building Jails Abroad to Hold Suspects for Life," *Guardian*, January 14, 2005.

14. Quoted in Tom Englehardt, "American Gothic: Self-Portrait with Shackles for the Year 2005," *TomDispatch*, www.tomdispatch.com/post/2102/, accessed February 12, 2005.

15. Ibid. Englehardt goes on to quote the relevant passages from the fifty-six-page memo titled "Detainee Interrogation in the Global War on Terrorism": "Congress lacks authority to set the terms and conditions under which the President may exercise his authority as Commander in Chief to control the conduct of operations in war. . . . Accordingly we would construe the law to avoid this difficulty and conclude that it doesn't apply to the President's detention and interrogation in the war on terror."

16. Lisa Hajjar, "Torture is a Crime—Always, Everywhere," paper presented at annual meeting of the American Studies Association, Atlanta, November 13, 2004. The Tom Englehardt quote is from "George Orwell, Meet Franz Kafka, Part 2," *TomDispatch*, June 15, 2004, http://www.tomdispatch.com/post/1494/, accessed May 23, 2017. Documented examples of U.S. torture practices in the so-called global war on terror include being chained in so-called stress positions; being left in extreme cold or heat; being deprived of sleep and subjected to bright lights and loud music; having fingernails torn out; being burned with lit cigarettes; partial strangulation; death threats; mock drowning or waterboarding; being hooded, beaten, and kicked; and being subjected to electric shocks and simulated acts of sexual assault and humiliation. Hajjar notes that despite U.S. officials' distaste for post–World War II international law, British and Israeli precedents for using torture in Northern Ireland and the occupied territories became useful in the absence of U.S. case law on the subject. Even here, officials cherry-picked supporting evidence, ignoring, for example, the fact that as early as 1977, Britain renounced as inhumane various torture techniques, including beatings, electric shocks, mock executions, and sexual abuse. See Lisa Hajjar, "In the Penal Colony," *The Nation*, February 7, 2005, 23–26.

17. Englehardt, "George Orwell, Meet Franz Kafka."

18. Susan Sontag, *Regarding the Pain of Others* (New York: Picador, 2003). It was the demand for so-called actionable intelligence on the growing insurgency in Iraq that led to the transfer of General Geoffrey Miller from Guantanamo to Abu Ghraib and the formal introduction of the aggressive torture regime into the Iraq war. See Hersh, "Chain of Command."

19. Sontag, *Regarding the Pain of Others*.

20. Giorgio Agamben, *Homo Sacer: Sovereign Power and Bare Life* (Stanford, CA: Stanford University Press, 1998), 183.

21. Michel Foucault, *Society Must Be Defended: Lectures at the Collège de France, 1975–76*, trans. David Macey (New York: Picador, 1997), 254.

22. Ewa Plonowska Ziarek, "Bare Life on Strike: Notes on the Biopolitics of Race and Gender," *South Atlantic Quarterly* 107, no. 1 (2008): 89–105, available online at http://springtheory.qwriting.qc.cuny.edu/files/2015/01/Ziarek.pdf, accessed May 23, 2017.

23. "War-prison" is Avery Gordon's term. Avery Gordon, "The U.S.-Abu Ghraib Continuum," paper presented at the Plenary Panel on Torture, Prisons, Militarism, and the Racial State at the annual meeting of the American Studies Association Annual Meeting, Atlanta, November 13, 2004.

24. These phrases are from George W. Bush's inaugural address, available at *CBS News*, January 20, 2005, www.cbsnews.com/news/george-w-bush-inaugural-address-2005/.

25. I am indebted here to Colin Dayan's brilliant essay "Cruel and Unusual: The End of the Eighth Amendment," *Boston Review*, October–November 2004, www.bostonreview.net/BR29.5/Dayan.html.

26. Following Senator Robert Byrd's courageous stand against the Iraq War, invoking Hermann Göring's famous declaration of how easy it was to manipulate the masses into supporting war, many other commentators noted the Bush administration's fascist tendencies. Sheldon Wolin, for example, described the Bush regime as a form of "inverted fascism." See Sheldon Wolin, "A Kind of Fascism Is Replacing Our Democracy," *Newsday*, July 18, 2003.

27. Paul Berman, *Terror and Liberalism* (New York: W. W. Norton, 2004); Tom Friedman, "Divided We Stand," *New York Times*, January 23, 2005; Michael Ignatieff, "Iraqis Fight a Lonely Battle for Democracy," *Observer*, January 30, 2005. As McAlister shows, the equation between Islamic terrorism and "totalitarianism" originated in the late 1970s. McAlister, *Epic Encounters*, 220.

28. John Stuart Mill, "A Few Words on Non-intervention" (1859), in *Essays on Politics and Culture* (Gloucester, MA: Peter Smith, 1973), 377.

29. Elbridge Colby, "How to Fight Savage Tribes," *American Journal of International Law* 221, no. 2 (April 1927): 281.

30. Ibid., 285.

31. Laleh Khalili, *Time in the Shadows: Confinement in Counterinsurgency* (Stanford, CA: Stanford University Press, 2013).

32. John Lewis Gaddis, *Security, Surprise, and the American Experience* (Cambridge, MA: Harvard University Press, 2004), 16, 107.

33. Robert Kaplan, "Supremacy by Stealth," *Atlantic Monthly*, July 2003. Of course, "successful counterinsurgency" included the first concentration camps of the new century, public scandals about U.S. torture, and military atrocities, as well as the largely uncounted Philippine dead. Their numbers have been estimated at between 100,000 and 1 million. See Oscar Camponanes, "Body Count: The War and Its Consequences," in Shaw and Francia, *Vestiges of War*, 138.

34. Michael Rogin, "Liberal Society and the Indian Question," in *Ronald Reagan, the Movie: And Other Episodes in Political Demonology* (Berkeley: University of California Press, 2008).

35. Max Boot, *Savage Wars of Peace: Small Wars and the Rise of American Power* (New York: Basic Books, 2002). See also Agamben, *Homo Sacer*, 10.

36. Langston Hughes, *Langston Hughes and the Chicago Defender: Essays on Race, Politics, and Culture, 1942-1962*, ed. Christopher C. De Santis (Urbana: University of Illinois Press, 1995).

37. Enzo Traverso, *The Origins of Nazi Violence*, trans. Janet Lloyd (New York: New Press, 2003), 2. The use of colonial methods by the Nazis was acutely noted during and after World War II by a wide range of black radicals, and never more eloquently than by Aimé Césaire. See Aimé Césaire, *Discourse on Colonialism* (New York: New York University Press, 2002); see also Nikhil Pal Singh, *Black Is a Country: Race and the Unfinished Struggle for Democracy* (Cambridge, MA: Harvard University Press, 2004).

38. Karl Polanyi, *The Great Transformation: The Political and Economic Origins of Our Time* (Boston: Beacon Press, 1957 [1944]), 120.

39. Ibid., 119-20. Space does not permit me to explore the explicit neoliberal agenda that sought to restructure various sectors of the Iraqi state. One example was Iraqi agriculture. As Iman Khaduri writes, "Paul Bremer updated Iraq's intellectual property law to 'meet current internationally recognized standards of protection.' The updated law made saving seeds for next year's harvest, practiced by 97 percent of Iraqi farmers in 2002, and the standard farming practice

for thousands of years across human civilizations, illegal." Iman Khaduri, "The Ultimate War Crime: Breaking the Agricultural Cycle," Centre for Research on Globalisation, January 25, 2005, www.globalresearch.ca/articles/KHA501A.html, accessed May 23, 2017.

40. Quoted in Sven Lindqvist, *"Exterminate All the Brutes": One Man's Odyssey into the Heart of Darkness and Origins of European Genocide* (New York: Free Press, 1996), 157.

41. Hannah Arendt, "New Preface to Part II" (1967), in *The Origins of Totalitarianism* (New York: Harcourt Brace, 1951), xviii.

42. Ibid., xviii–xxii; see also Pierre Ayconberry, *The Nazi Question: An Essay on Interpretations of National Socialism, 1922–1935* (New York: Pantheon, 1981), 130.

43. Michael Burawoy, "For a Sociological Marxism: The Complementary Convergence of Antonio Gramsci and Karl Polanyi," *Politics and Society* 31, no. 2 (June 2003): 240.

44. Arendt, "New Preface to Part II," 183.

45. Noam Chomsky and Edward Herman, *The Washington Connection and Third World Fascism* (Boston: South End Press, 1979), 41.

46. Anders Stephanson, *Manifest Destiny: American Expansion and the Empire of Right* (New York: Hill and Wang, 1995), 123–25.

47. Walt W. Rostow, *The Stages of Economic Growth: A Non-Communist Manifesto* (Cambridge: Cambridge University Press, 1960).

48. William Westmoreland, quoted in Peter Davis, director, *Hearts and Minds* (1974); LeMay, quoted in Young, *The Vietnam Wars*, 113.

49. See Mamdani, *Good Muslim, Bad Muslim*, 104–5.

50. I am broadly indebted to Colin Dayan for this argument. See Dayan, "Cruel and Unusual," 3. I am also indebted to Kim Gilmore's brilliant "States of Incarceration: Prisoners' Rights and U.S. Prison Expansion after WWII," PhD diss., New York University, 2005.

51. Dayan, "Cruel and Unusual," 6.

52. Evan Horowitz, "What Are Your Chances of Going to Prison?" *Boston Globe*, March 19, 2015, http://www.bostonglobe.com/metro/2015/03/19/what-are-chances-going-prison/n3g84nR4kJriEwM8nbT6ML/story.html; Tracy L. Snell, "Capital Punishment, 2011-Statistical Tables," *U.S. Bureau of Justice Statistics*, revised November 3, 2014, www.bjs.gov/content/pub/pdf/cp11st.pdf; Loïc

Wacquant, "Slavery to Mass Incarceration," *New Left Review*, January-February 2002, 41–60.

53. Jacques Rancière, "Who Is the Subject of the Rights of Man?" *South Atlantic Quarterly* 103, nos. 2–3 (Spring-Summer 2004): 306. The major still-unrealized ambition of those seeking to delimit the scope of rights-based claims is the overturning of a decision that was coterminous with *Furman*, namely *Roe v. Wade* (1973). The effort to advance the personhood of the fetus almost perfectly mirrors the effort to strip rights from existing political subjects, for what is sought is the transmutation of an individual woman's private rights to bodily integrity into sovereign power over life before birth. Although antiabortion discourse often appropriates the rhetoric of abolitionism, it actually represents an effort to extend the frontiers of the biopolitical state, or to further the identification of sovereign power with life itself. This is one reason why the contradiction between opposition to abortion and the defense of capital punishment rarely troubles right-wing judicial activists. The issue is not so much life and death as *whose* life, whose death, and whose power of decision.

54. Bryan Edwards, *The History, Civil and Commercial, of the British West Indies* (1793), quoted in Dayan, "Cruel and Unusual," 5–6.

55. David Bromwich, "Diary," *London Review of Books* 35, no. 13 (2013): 34–35, www.lrb.co.uk/v35/n13/david-bromwich/diary.

56. Thomas Barnett, *The Pentagon's New Map: War and Peace in the Twenty-First Century* (New York: G. P. Putnam's Sons, 2004).

57. Nixon, quoted in Gilmore, "States of Incarceration," 175. One of the many sources for the Kristol quote is Michael Kinsey, "The Evolution of the Neocons," *Los Angeles Times*, April 17, 2005, http://articles.latimes.com/2005/apr/17/opinion/oe-kinsley17.

58. Carl Schmitt, "Definition of Sovereignty," in *Political Theology* (Cambridge, MA: MIT Press, 1985), 5, 11, 13; Schmitt, "Preface to the Second Edition: On the Contradiction between Parliamentarianism and Democracy" (1926), in *The Crisis of Parliamentary Democracy*, trans. Ellen Kennedy (Cambridge, MA: MIT Press, 1985), 12.

59. Schmitt, "Preface," 10.

60. Quoted in Traverso, *The Political Origins of Nazi Violence*, 140, 70.

61. Gaddis, *Security, Surprise, and the American Experience*, 4.

62. Ibid., 16.

63. Seymour Hersh, "The Coming Wars: What the Pentagon Can Now Do in Secret," *New Yorker*, 24–31 January 2005, 40.

64. Paul Gilroy, *Against Race: Imagining Political Culture Beyond the Color Line* (Cambridge, MA: Harvard University Press, 2003), 93.

65. As many observed at the time, the Bush administration appeared to share the viewpoint best articulated by Schmitt: that the state is not the result of a contract but the production of a "homogeneous" form of life. Under its regime, "the unequal, the alien or non-citizen . . . is not helped by the fact that in abstracto he is a person." In this sense, it may be that the religious Right's assertion of a life before birth represents, more than anything else, a new frontier of biopolitics and perhaps the other side, as it were, of the global crusade to inscribe all peoples in a single moral and political order. Schmitt, *Crisis*, 12. "Moment of opportunity" is the Bush administration's own language: see *The National Security Strategy of the United States* (Washington, DC: White House, 2002), www.state.gov/documents/organization/63562.pdf, accessed May 23, 2017.

4. RACIAL FORMATION AND PERMANENT WAR

1. Michael Omi and Howard Winant, *Racial Formation in the United States from the 1960s to the 1980s* (New York: Routledge, 1986), 68.

2. Ange Marie Hancock, *The Politics of Disgust and the Public Identity of the Welfare Queen* (New York: New York University Press, 2004), 58.

3. Mary Dudziak, *Cold War Civil Rights* (Princeton, NJ: Princeton University Press, 2000); Nikhil Pal Singh, *Black Is a Country: Race and the Unfinished Struggle for Democracy* (Cambridge, MA: Harvard University Press, 2004).

4. Stuart Hall, Brian Roberts, John Clarke, Tony Jefferson, and Chas Critcher, *Policing the Crisis: Mugging, the State and Law and Order* (London: Palgrave MacMillan, 1978).

5. Anoop Mirpuri, "Slated for Destruction: Race, Black Radicalism and the Meaning of Captivity in the Postwar Exceptional State," PhD diss., Department of English, University of Washington, 2010.

6. Nikhil Pal Singh, "The Afterlife of Fascism," *South Atlantic Quarterly* 105, no. 1 (Winter 2006): 71–93; Colin Dayan, *The Story of Cruel and Unusual* (Cambridge, MA: MIT Press, 2008).

7. Hall et al., *Policing the Crisis,* chapter 10.

8. For detailed analyses, see Kimberlé Crenshaw, Neil Gotanda, Gary Peller, and Kendall Thomas, *Critical Race Theory: The Key Writings That Formed the Movement* (New York: New Press, 1996). On ballot initiatives, see Daniel Martinez Hosang, *Racial Propositions: Ballot Initiatives and the Making of Postwar California* (Berkeley: University of California Press, 2010).

9. William Julius Wilson, *The Declining Significance of Race: Blacks and Changing America's Institutions* (Chicago: University of Chicago Press, 1980).

10. Lani Guinier and Gerald Torres, *The Miner's Canary: Enlisting Race, Resisting Power, Transforming Democracy* (Cambridge, MA: Harvard University Press, 2003).

11. Adolph Reed Jr. and Kenneth Warren, *Renewing Black Intellectual History: the Ideological and Material Foundations of African American Thought* (New York: Paradigm Publishers, 2010).

12. Naomi Murakawa, "The Origins of the Carceral Crisis: Racial Order as 'Law and Order' in Postwar American Politics," in *Race and American Political Development* (New York: Routledge, 2008), 236.

13. Loïc Wacquant, "From Slavery to Mass Incarceration: Rethinking the 'Race' Question in the United States," *New Left Review* 13 (January–February 2002): 41–60.

14. Ruth Wilson Gilmore, *Golden Gulag: Prisons, Surplus, Crisis and Opposition in Globalizing California* (Berkeley: University of California Press, 2007). See also Étienne Balibar, "Racism and Nationalism," in *Race, Nation, Class: Ambiguous Identities* (London: Verso, 1991).

15. For this phrasing I am indebted to Richard Dyer, *White: Essays on Race and Culture* (New York: Routledge, 1997).

16. Omi and Winant, *Racial Formation,* 64.

17. Michelle Alexander, *The New Jim Crow: Mass Incarceration in an Age of Colorblindness* (New York: New Press, 2010).

18. David Theo Goldberg, *The Threat of Race: Reflections on Racial Neoliberalism* (New York: Wiley-Blackwell, 2008); Arif Dirlik, "Race Talk, Race and Contemporary Racism," *PMLA* 123, no. 5 (2008): 1363–79.

19. Ernest Renan, "What is a Nation?" (1882), in *Becoming National: A Reader,* ed. Geoff Eley and Ronald Grigor Suny (New York: Oxford University Press, 1996), 41–55.

20. LeRoi Jones, "The Changing Same (R&B and New Black Music)" (1966), in Amiri Baraka, *The Leroi Jones/Amiri Baraka Reader* (New York: Thunder's Mouth Press, 1991): 186–210.

21. Anthony Anghie, *Imperialism, Sovereignty and the Making of International Law* (Cambridge: Cambridge University Press, 2007).

22. I am indebted to Gopal Balakrishnan for this formulation. Gopal Balakrishnan, *Antagonistics: Capitalism and Power in an Age of War* (New York: Verso, 2009), 70.

23. Thomas McCarthy, *Race, Empire and the Idea of Human Development* (Cambridge: Cambridge University Press, 2009).

24. While acknowledging the strengths of internal-colonialism perspectives in connecting the national and global dimensions of racial oppression, Omi and Winant suggest that nation-based approaches to racial questions have been politically rather than analytically grounded, and more specifically that they are unable to specify what is national about racial oppression. The remainder of this chapter might be considered a kind of extended answer to this question.

25. H. Barnor Hesse, *Creolizing the Political: A Genealogy of the African Diaspora* (Durham, NC: Duke University Press, forthcoming). See also Anibel Quijano, "Coloniality of Power, Eurocentrism, and Latin America," *Nepantla: Views from South* 1, no. 3 (2000): 533–80.

26. Michael Ignatieff, "The Burden," *New York Times*, January 5, 2003; "Rice, in Alabama, Draws Parallels for Democracy Everywhere," *New York Times*, October 22, 2005; Adam Liptak, "Inmate Count in US Dwarfs Other Nations'," *New York Times*, April 23, 2008.

27. W. E. B. Du Bois, *Black Reconstruction in America, 1860–1880* (New York: Free Press, 1998 [1935]).

28. Quijano, "Coloniality of Power," 566.

29. Edmund Morgan, *American Slavery, American Freedom: The Ordeal of Colonial Virginia* (New York: W. W. Norton, 1975).

30. Thomas Jefferson, *Notes on the State of Virginia* (New York: Penguin, 1999 [1785]).

31. Lisa Ford, *Settler Sovereignty: Jurisdiction and Indigenous People in American and Australia, 1788–1836* (Cambridge, MA: Harvard University Press, 2010).

32. Immanuel Kant, *Metaphysics of Morals* (1797), in Immanuel Kant, *Political Writings* (Cambridge: Cambridge University Press, 1970), 170. See also Ian Baucom, "Cicero's Ghost: The Atlantic, the Enemy and the Laws of War," in *States of Emergency: The Object of American Studies*, ed. Russ Castronovo and Susan Gillman (Chapel Hill: University of North Carolina Press, 2009), 124–43.

33. Stephanie McCurry, *Masters of Small Worlds: Yeoman Households, Gender Relations, and the Political Culture of the Antebellum South Carolina Low Country* (New York: Oxford University Press, 1997).

34. Hannah Rosen, *Terror in the Heart of Freedom: Citizenship, Sexual Violence, and the Meaning of Race in the Post-emancipation South* (Chapel Hill: University of North Carolina Press, 2008); Steven Hahn, *A Nation under Our Feet: Black Political Struggles from Slavery to the Great Migration* (Cambridge, MA: Harvard University Press, 2005).

35. Minnesota Senator William Windon, quoted in Rayford Logan, *The Negro in American Life and Thought: The Nadir, 1877–1901* (New York: Dial Press, 1954); see also Singh, *Black is a Country*, chapter 2.

36. Kahil Gibran Muhammad, *The Condemnation of Blackness: Race, Crime, and the Making of Modern Urban America* (Cambridge, MA: Harvard University Press, 2010), 4.

37. Robert Perkinson, *Texas Tough: The Rise of America's Prison Empire* (New York: Metropolitan Books, 2010).

38. Quoted in Peggy Pascoe, *What Comes Naturally: Miscegenation Law and the Making of Race in America* (New York: Oxford University Press, 2009), 74.

39. Quoted in Brian Wagner, *Disturbing the Peace: Black Culture and the Police Power after Slavery* (Cambridge, MA: Harvard University Press, 2010), 12.

40. Quoted in Dylan Rodriguez, *Forced Passages: Imprisoned Radical Intellectuals and the U.S. Prison Regime* (Minneapolis: University of Minnesota Press, 2006), 20.

41. Dana Priest and William Arkin, "A Hidden World Growing beyond Control," *Washington Post*, July 19, 2010, http://projects.washingtonpost.com/top-secret-america/articles/a-hidden-world-growing-beyond-control/.

42. Robert Kaplan, "The Coming Anarchy," *The Atlantic*, February 1994.

43. Fred Moten, "Black Op," *PMLA* 123, no. 5 (2008): 1743–48.

44. John Lewis Gaddis, *Surprise, Security, and the American Experience* (Cambridge, MA: Harvard University Press, 2004).

45. This is not to say that historic antiblack themes are not present. The right-wing personality Glenn Beck, for example, once described Obama as someone who hates white people and who wants to "settle old racial scores," presumably from the baseline of historically black racial grievances. Dinesh D'Souza and Newt Gingrich sought to "Mau Mau" Obama as a figure of (African) violence and deranged anticolonial and anti-Western grievance. Though the latter cases deploy historically antiblack themes, they also draw from a largely non-U.S. repertoire that in turn reassociates blackness with a sense of threats of the foreign and unfamiliar.

46. This phrase is from Balakrishnan, *Capitalism and Power*, xiv.

5. THE PRESENT CRISIS

1. Nicholas Confessore and Nate Cohn, "Donald Trump's Victory Was Built on a Unique Coalition of White Voters," *New York Times*, November 9, 2016. The *New York Times* piece is not, of course, an endorsement of white supremacy, though it does suggest that whites acted in racial concert, politically. More than half a century ago, the conservative intellectual William F. Buckley illuminated similar logic in defense of white supremacy at the onset of the civil rights movement: "The central question that emerges . . . is whether the White community in the South is entitled to take such measures as are necessary to prevail, politically and culturally, in areas where it does not predominate numerically? The sobering answer is Yes—the White community is so entitled because, for the time being, it is the advanced race." See William F. Buckley, "Why the South Must Prevail," *National Review*, August 24, 1957, 149.

2. Ian Haney López, *Dog Whistle Politics: How Coded Racial Appeals Have Reinvented Racism and Wrecked the Middle Class* (New York: Oxford University Press, 2014).

3. Toni Morrison, "Talk of the Town," *New Yorker*, October 8, 1998, www.newyorker.com/magazine/1998/10/05/comment-6543.

4. Richard Rorty, *Achieving Our Country: Leftist Thought in Twentieth-Century America* (Cambridge, MA: Harvard University Press, 1998), 112.

5. Ibid., 113.

6. In the words of Lee Atwater: "You start out in 1954 by saying, 'Nigger, nigger, nigger.' By 1968 you can't say 'nigger'—that hurts you, backfires. So you

say stuff like, uh, forced busing, states' rights, and all that stuff, and you're getting so abstract. Now, you're talking about cutting taxes, and all these things you're talking about are totally economic things and a byproduct of them is, blacks get hurt worse than whites. . . . 'We want to cut this' is much more abstract than even the busing thing, uh, and a hell of a lot more abstract than 'Nigger, nigger.'" Rick Perlstein, "Exclusive: Lee Atwater's Infamous 1981 Interview; the Southern Strategy," *The Nation,* November 13, 2012, www.thenation.com/article/exclusive-lee-atwaters-infamous-1981-interview-southern-strategy/.

7. The Project for a New American Century was a think tank created in 1997 "to promote American global leadership . . . good for America and good for the world." The idea of an "American century" revived Henry Luce's vision, first put forth in 1941, of projecting American power on the global stage. The organization's principals included Dick Cheney, Paul Wolfowitz, and Donald Rumsfeld, architects of the long war. It shuttered in 2006 and no longer has a public profile. For basic information, see Wikipedia: https://en.wikipedia.org/wiki/Project_for_the_New_American_Century, accessed May 23, 2017.

8. Ron Suskind, "Faith, Certainty and the Presidency of George W. Bush," *New York Times Magazine,* October 17, 2004.

9. Hannah Arendt, "A Special Supplement: Reflections on Violence," *New York Review of Books,* February 29, 1969.

10. George W. Bush quoted in Bob Woodward, *Bush at War* (New York: Simon and Schuster, 2006), 146; John Lewis Gaddis, *Surprise, Security, and the American Experience* (Cambridge, MA: Harvard University Press, 2004).

11. Kate Phillips, "Clinton Touts White Support," *New York Times,* May 8, 2008, https://thecaucus.blogs.nytimes.com/2008/05/08/clinton-touts-white-support/comment-page-61/.

12. "John McCain's Feb. 12 Speech," *New York Times,* February 12, 2008, www.nytimes.com/2008/02/12/us/politics/12text-mccain.html.

13. Courtney Comstock, "Steve Schwarzman on Tax Increases: 'It's Like When Hitler Invaded Poland,'" *Business Insider,* August 16, 2010, www.businessinsider.com/steve-schwarzman-taxes-hitler-invaded-poland-2010-8; James Surowiecki, "Moaning Moguls," *New Yorker,* July 7, 2014, www.newyorker.com/magazine/2014/07/07/moaning-moguls.

14. David Daley, *Ratf**ked: The True Story Behind the Secret Plan to Steal America's Democracy* (New York: Liveright, 2016); Jane Mayer, *Dark Money: The Hidden History of the Billionaires Behind the Rise of the Radical Right* (New York: Doubleday, 2016).

15. "Watch Pres. Obama's Full Response to Trump's Win," *NBC News*, November 9, 2016, www.nbcnews.com/video/watch-pres-obama-s-full-response-to-trump-s-win-804812867679.

16. "Transcript of Barack Obama's Victory Speech," NPR, November 5, 2008, www.npr.org/templates/story/story.php?storyId=96624326.

17. At the time of writing, forty-six bills are under consideration in twenty-one states that will make it harder to vote, ranging from voter ID requirements to limitations on registration and ending early voting. Ari Berman, "The Trump Administration's Lies about Voter Fraud Will Lead to Massive Voter Suppression," *TheNation*, February 13, 2017, www.thenation.com/article/the-trump-administrations-lies-about-voter-fraud-will-lead-to-massive-voter-suppression/.

18. Pierre Dardot and Christian Laval, *The New Way of the World: On Neoliberal Society* (New York: Verso Books, 2014), 4 .

19. Sheldon Wolin, *Democracy Incorporated: Managed Democracy and the Specter of Inverted Totalitarianism* (Princeton, NJ: Princeton University Press, 2008).

20. Brian Bennett, "CIA Director Warns Trump It Would Be the 'Height of Folly' to Scrap Iran Deal," *Los Angeles Times*, November 16, 2016.

21. Mike Lofgren, *The Deep State: The Fall of the Constitution and the Rise of a Shadow Government* (New York: Penguin Random House, 2016). The development of "the deep state" in the United States has not come exclusively or even primarily through unaccountable bureaucracies of the welfare state but rather through the tributaries of the military and security state. This terrain has long been a site of competition between factions of the ruling class and factions within the administrative bureaucracies. What may be new is a breakdown in the long-standing bipartisan consensus on national security and foreign policy.

22. "Steve Bannon Vows 'Economic Nationalist Movement' from White House —'As Exciting as the 1930's, Greater than the Reagan Revolution," Breitbart News, November 18, 2016, accessed May 23, 2017, www.breitbart.com/big-government/2016/11/18/steve-bannon-vows-economic-nationalist-movement-white-house-exciting-1930s-greater-reagan-revolution/.

23. Steven Wertheim, "Quit Calling Donald Trump an Isolationist: He's Worse Than That," *Washington Post*, February 17, 2017, www.washingtonpost .com/posteverything/wp/2017/02/17/quit-calling-donald-trump-an-isolationist-its-an-insult-to-isolationism/?utm_term=.3ad1f7bceb07.

24. Steve Bannon, quoted in Steve Reilly and Brad Heath, "Steve Bannon's Own Words Show Sharp Break on Security Issues," *USA Today*, January 31, 2017, www.usatoday.com/story/news/2017/01/31/bannon-odds-islam-china-decades-us-foreign-policy-doctrine/97292068/. David Remnick, "War without End?" *New Yorker*, April 21, 2003, quotes a senior British official close to the Bush administration as saying, "Everyone wants to go to Baghdad. Real men want to go to Tehran."

25. David Roediger, "2016 and the Little Trumps," Davidroediger.org, February 2, 2017, www.davidroediger.org/?m=201702.

26. Langston Hughes, Langston Hughes and the Chicago Defender: Essays on Race, Politics and Culture, 1942-1962 (Urbana: University of Illinois Press, 1995), 158.

27. Mike Davis, "The Great God Trump and the White Working Class," *Jacobin*, February 7, 2017.

EPILOGUE

1. Barack Obama, *Dreams from My Father* (New York: Crown, 2007).

2. Martin Luther King, Jr., "Beyond Vietnam," speech delivered in New York City, April 4, 1967, http://kingencyclopedia.stanford.edu/encyclopedia /documentsentry/doc_beyond_vietnam/.

3. Ruth Wilson Gilmore, *Golden Gulag: Prisons, Surplus, Crisis and Opposition in Globalizing California* (Berkeley: University of California Press, 2006).

4. Robert McNamara, in *The Fog of War: Eleven Lessons from the Life of Robert S. McNamara*, directed by Errol Morris (Sony Pictures Classics, 2003); quoted in "McNamara's Other War," *Dialog International*, July 11, 2009, accessed May 23, 2017, http://www.dialoginternational.com/dialog_international/2009/07/mcnamaras-other-war.html.

5. King, "Beyond Vietnam." See also Nikhil Pal Singh, *Black Is a Country: Race and the Unfinished Struggle for Democracy* (Cambridge, MA: Harvard University Press, 2005), 1-14.

6. Taylor Branch, *At Canaan's Edge: America in the King Years, 1965-68* (New York: Simon & Schuster, 2006), 596.

7. Karen Yourish, Derek Watkins, Tom Giratikanon, and Jasmine Lee, "How Many People Have Been Killed in ISIS Attacks Around the World?" *New York Times*, July 16, 2016, www.nytimes.com/interactive/2016/03/25/world/map-isis-attacks-around-the-world.htm; Martin Chulov, "Isis: The Inside Story," *Guardian*, December 11, 2014, www.theguardian.com/world/2014/dec/11/-sp-isis-the-inside-story.

8. Charles Tilley, "War Making and State Making as Organized Crime," in *Bringing the State Back In*, ed. Peter Evans, Dietrich Rueschemeyer, and Theda Skocpol (Cambridge: Cambridge University Press, 1985); According to one estimate, over a recent seven-year period in the United States there were approximately ten thousand police homicides, which means that approximately 10 percent of all homicides were committed by police. A staggering one in three Americans killed by people they don't know are killed by police. Patrick Ball, "Violence in Blue: Police Homicides in the United States," *Granta*, March 4, 2016, https://granta.com/violence-in-blue/.

antidiscrimination, 129, 154

antimiscegenation statutes, 144

antipoverty programs, 130. *See also* war on poverty

antiracism, 73, 124–25, 127, 134–35, 145

anti-Semitism, 160–61

Anti-terrorism and Effective Death Penalty Act (1996), 12, 117

appropriation, 34, 76, 77, 84, 91–92, 96. *See also* land appropriation

Arab Mind, The (Patai), 100

Arabs, 13–14, 100–101, 104

Arendt, Hannah, 20, 110–12, 121, 157–58

Armbruster, Frank, 61, 209n67

Asia, 30–31, 50, 61, 138, 156, 170, 171, 180, 184. *See also* Vietnam War

Asians, xii, 13–14, 52, 64, 127, 135

assassinations, x–xi, 32, 61, 69, 161–62

Atlantic slavery, xviii, 85–86, 89, 96, 214n3. *See also* slavery

Atwater, Lee, 130, 156, 231n6

Australia, 50, 51, 56, 140

Ayers, Bill, 160, 179

Balakrishnan, Gopal, 150, 219n42

Baldwin, James, xii, 178

Balibar, Étienne, 100

Baltimore, 56–57

Banaji, Jairus, 84–85

Banfield, Edward, 66–67, 72

Bangladesh, 8

Bannon, Steve, 32, 72, 156, 167, 170, 171, 172

Baptist, Edward, 214n4, 216n11

bare life, 104–5, 109, 113–14, 148, 149

Beck, Glenn, 231n45

Beckert, Sven, 29, 76, 79

Bell, Sean, 22

Benjamin, Walter, 18

Berkeley, Randolph, 62

Berman, Paul, 24

Beyond Entitlement (Mead), 124–25

Bin Laden, Osama, 12, 16

bionatalist state, 121

biopolitics: abortion, 227n65; blackness and, 44, 48, 49, 92; capitalism and, 91, 92; death camps and, 105; Foucault, Michel and, 105, 144, 201n52; homicide and, 120; Nazism and, 105; police power and, 144; preventive war and, 108; race and, 120; religious right and, 227n65; *Roe v. Wade* (1973) and, 226n53

bipartisan consensus, 183–84, 233n21

Birmingham, 57

black freedom movements, xii, 59–60, 124, 126, 138, 181. *See also* civil rights

Black Lives Matter, 72, 165

black nationalists, 160

blackness: biopolitics and, 44, 48, 49, 92; blacks and, 147; capitalism and, 44, 50–51, 94; crime and, 142; democracy and, 143; homicide and, 143; military-police and, 147; Obama, Barack and, 164; police power and, 48, 49, 144–45; policing and, 48–49; security and, 51; settlers and, 27, 143; slavery and, 36, 44, 143; statelessness and, 144–45; United States and, x, 147, 231n45; whiteness and, 94

black power, ix, 5

black radicalism, xiii, 62, 93, 160, 180, 186, 224n37

Black Reconstruction in America (Du Bois), 89, 94

blacks: Asians and, 127; Atwater, Lee and, 231n6; black radicalism, xiii, 93, 180, 186; capitalism and, 82, 96; civil rights and, 126, 128, 144; Civil War and, 21, 51, 143, 187; the Clintons and, 175; colonialism/colonization and, 60, 138–39; commodification and, 92; crime and, 48–49, 58–59, 66, 115, 118, 144, 156; criminalization and, 25, 40, 51, 70–71; democracy and, 131, 181; Dred Scott decision and, 47; Dukakis, Michael and, 130; economics and, xiv, 231n6; felony disfranchisement laws and, 115, 135; Franklin, Benjamin on, 71; frontier wars and, 21; genocide and, 94; great recession of 2008 and, xiv; homicide and, xvii, 141, 144; Hurricane Katrina and, 19; incarceration and, x–xi, xv, xvi, xvii, 7, 115, 128, 135, 139–140, 192n7; Jefferson, Thomas and, 141–42; labor coercion and, 89, 115; Latina/o(s) and, 127; Long Binh stockade (Camp LB) and, 211n80; Louisiana and, 40–41; lynching and, 144; mass/deportations and, x–xi; military and, xvii, 64; militias and, 47; national sovereignty and, 40; *The Negro Family: The Case for National Action* (Moynihan) (1965), 64; neoliberalism and, xiv; Nixon, Richard and, 7; Obama, Barack and, 181; Philippines and, xii, 21; police killings and, xv, 22, 192n9; police/power and, xvii, 48–49, 144–45; policing and, 67, 128; premature death and, 48–49; prisons and, xvii, 17, 131, 135, 144, 187; race war and, 21; racism and, 21–22, 130–31; riots and, 187; Second Amendment and, 47; settlers/sovereignty and, 27, 143; slavery and, 36, 94, 96, 141; social relations and, 143; state violence and, 62, 89; stop-and-frisk and, 70; surveillance and, 54; taxation and, 231n6; torture

and, 14, 17; Trump, Donald and, 163–64, 165, 168; United States and, 22, 25, 187; U.S. foreign policies and, 28–29; Vietnam War and, xii; violence and, 35–36, 48–49, 62, 89, 94, 143, 178–79; wage labor and, 93–94, 95–96; war and, 17, 22; war on drugs and, 187; war on poverty and, 128; welfare state and, 131; whites and, 36, 64, 95–96, 141–42, 143. *See also* African Americans; black freedom movements; blackness; individuals

Blackwater Corporation, 21

Blanco, Kathleen, 20

Bland, Sandra, 181

Blankfein, Lloyd, 160–61, 168

Blood Meridian, or the Evening Redness in the West (McCarthy), 98

Boer War, 108

Boot, Max, 15

borders, 52, 54, 55, 72–73, 120, 172

Branch, Taylor, 187

Brazil, 3

Breitbart News, 167

Bremer, Paul, 224n39

Brennan, John, 169

Brenner, Robert, 213n1

British, the. *See* Great Britain

broken-windows policing, 67

Bromwich, David, 117

Brown, Michael, 181

Brown, Todd, 100

browns, xii, xvii, 7, 59, 89, 156, 157, 187. *See also* Latina/o(s); Muslims

Bryan, William Jennings, 52

Buckley, William F., 231n1

Buffalo soldiers, 21

Bunche, Ralph, 138

Bundy, McGeorge, 64–65

Burge, John, 17, 68–69
Burgess, John, x, 35, 39, 47, 144
Bush, George H. W., 9–10, 11, 130
Bush, George W.: Afghanistan war and, 100, 157; American empire and, 1; cold war and, 2, 13; compassionate conservatism and, 156–57; "A Distinctly American Internationalism" (speech), 1; economics and, 158; fascism and, 106, 223n26; global war on terror and, 13, 30, 31, 106; Hurricane Katrina and, 19, 182; immigration and, 156–57; incarceration and, 157; international law and, 157; Iraq war and, 100–103, 157, 195n6; Kyoto climate-change accords and, 157; long wars and, 2, 157; military and, 9, 13; 9/11 and, 9–10, 98, 101, 121, 157, 158, 195n6; Obama, Barack and, 183; pharmaceuticals and, 157; preemptive war and, 147; preventive war and, 108; Schmitt, Carl and, 227n65; terrorism and, 9, 100–101, 195n6; torture and, 31, 102–3, 157, 158; totalitarianism and, 13, 106; U.S. territorial expansion and, 16, 105; U.S. war crimes and, 102; Vietnam Syndrome and, 22; violence and, 157–58; war and, 161–62
Byrd, Jodi, 33
Byrd, Robert, 223n26

Cambodia, 3, 8
Cambridge Analytica, 166
Camp Bucca, 188
Camp Delta, 117. *See also* Guantanamo Bay
Camp Justice, 117
Canada, 56, 140
Capital, Volume I (Marx), 29, 82, 87, 215n7, 218n23, 218n33

capitalism, 74–97; accumulation and, 50–51, 82–83; American empire and, 29; appropriation and, 76, 77, 84, 91–92; Bannon, Steve and, 170, 171; Beckert, Sven and, 76; biopolitics and, 91, 92; blackness and, 44, 50–51, 94; blacks and, 82, 96; chattel slavery and, 85, 89; class and, xiv–xv, 77, 78, 96; cold war and, 3; colonialism and, xii, 87–88, 214n2; commodification and, 216n13; crime and, 81; criminalization and, 79–80; Douglass, Frederick and, 95; Du Bois, W. E. B. and, 76, 96; ecology and, 182; economics and, xii, 76, 81, 88; English cotton industry and, 90; environment and, 97, 185; Foucault, Michel and, 91; free labor and, 83–84, 88, 91–92; gender and, 76, 84, 86–87, 168; globalization and, 170; global war on terror and, 118; imperialism and, 81, 214n4; Karl Polanyi and, 216n13; labor and, 76, 80, 90, 96, 168, 213n1, 216n13, 217n16; liberalism and, xv–xvi, 29; Marx, Karl and, 29, 75, 76–88, 91, 96; militarization and, 90; military interventions and, 96; Muslims and, 13–14; nationalism and, 81; neoliberalism and, 168; police/power and, 91, 96; premature death and, 76–77, 80–81, 215n7, 218n33; primitive accumulation and, 82–83, 90; private property and, 90; race and, xiv–xv, 29, 30, 75–80, 86, 88, 89–90, 95, 96, 97, 168, 182, 214n4; race war and, 92–93, 158; racial capitalism, 79, 88, 192n10; racism and, 29, 78–79, 89–90, 97; settlers and, 50–51; sexual equity and, 168; social indifference and, 83; the state and, 88; state violence and, 81, 86; Trump, Donald and, 170, 171, 172; United States and, ix, 125; U.S. expansionism and, ix; violence and, 79–80, 82, 86–87, 89–90, 95, 96, 203n71; wage labor and, 75, 80–81, 83, 88; wage slavery and, 82–83; war capitalism, 29, 79, 92; wealth and, 29; whiteness and, 50–51, 78, 94; working class and, 76, 80–81, 168. *See also* slavery and capitalism

capital punishment, 114–15, 226n53

carceral state, the, xiv, xv, xviii, 8, 59, 72–73, 115, 121, 149. *See also* incarceration; prisons; *individual prisons*

Carter, Jimmy, 6

Casey, William, 9, 10–11

Castile, Philando, 181

Central America, 3, 10–11, 171

Central Intelligence Agency. *See* CIA (Central Intelligence Agency)

Central Park Five, 72, 163–64

Chakrabarty, Dipesh, 76

Challenge of Crime in a Free Society, The (study), 209n63

Chaney, James, 126

chattel slavery, 76, 77–78, 80, 85, 89, 214n4, 216n10

Cheney, Dick, 9–11, 20–21, 232n7

Chicago, xvii, 17, 18, 68–69, 126–27, 178

Chicago Tribune, 60

Chile, 3, 8–9, 197n17

China, 5, 10, 171

Chinese, 52

Chomsky, Noam, 112–13

CIA (Central Intelligence Agency), 9–10, 10–11, 57, 60, 62, 102, 108, 169

CI Special Group, 64–65

citizenship, 8, 19, 21, 39, 78, 86, 135–36, 156–57

Citizens United, 161

civilians. *See* noncombatants

Civil Operations and Revolutionary Development Support (CORDS), 61–62

civil rights: African Americans and, 6, 139; blacks and, 126, 128, 144; Chaney, James and, 126; cold war and, xii–xiii; crime and, 59–60, 66; democracy and, 8–9, 114, 139, 182; dogs and, 57; Goldwater, Barry and, 145–46; Goodman, Andrew and, 126; Ignatieff, Michael and, 140; King, Martin Luther, Jr. and, 186; legislation and, xiii; liberalism and, 164; Marx, Karl and, 83; military power and, 114; national security and, 60; neoconservatism and, 118; neoliberalism and, xiv; Obama, Barack and, 139, 149, 150, 164; police power and, 114; race and, ix, 116, 123, 132, 139, 187–88; Reagan, Ronald and, 129; Republican Party and, 154; Rice, Condoleeza and, 139, 140, 182; Schwerner, Michael and, 126; second cold war and, 6; security and, 59–60; state violence and, 59–60; United States and, 114, 139; U.S. Supreme Court and, 115–16, 128; Vietnam War and, 5; violence and, 59–60; whites and, 60, 231n1; World War II and, 54

Civil Rights Congress, 35

Civil War, x, 21, 38, 47, 48, 51, 143, 187

civil wars, 3, 35, 53, 54, 141, 143, 150, 152, 179

class: American empire and, 29; antiracism and, 124; capitalism and, xiv–xv, 77, 78, 96; contempt of elites and, 156; economics and, 213n1; Great Britain and, 75–76, 218n33;

class *(continued)*
    labor coercion and, 89; the Left and, xiv, 176; military and, xiv–xv; police and, xiv–xv; race and, xiv–xv, 78, 96, 131, 140, 186, 192n10; United States and, xiv–xv, 174; violence and, 203n71; whiteness and, 176–77
classical liberalism, 41–43. *See also* liberalism
Clausewitz, Carl von, 22–23, 142–43
climate change, 153–54, 157, 159, 162, 167, 183. *See also* ecology; environment
Clinton, Bill, 12, 117, 146, 154–55, 175
Clinton, Hillary, 153, 159, 166, 169, 173, 174, 175, 183
coerced labor. *See* labor coercion
Colby, Elbridge, 107–8, 111
Colby, William, 62, 108
cold war: Arendt, Hannah and, 112; Bush, George W. and, 2, 13; capitalism and, 3; China and, 171; civil rights and, xii–xiii; communism and, 113; global war on terror and, 13, 18, 117–18; Indian wars and, 24; invasion of Iraq and, 10; long peace and, xviii; long wars and, 2; military and, 3, 10; national security and, 146; 9/11 and, 188; permanent wars and, 30–31; Polanyi, Karl and, 112; Reagan, Ronald and, 11; right wing and, 171; Rumsfeld, Donald and, 2, 9–10; second cold war, 5–6; Stimson, Henry and, 4; United States and, 113; universalism and, 13; U.S. expansionism and, 113; Vietnam War and, 58; whites and, 60. *See also* Soviet Union
Colombia, 16
colonialism: Arendt, Hannah and, 112; blacks and, 60, 138–39; capitalism and, xii, 87–88, 214n2; democracy and, 119; Europe and, 55, 64, 111, 120, 185; fascism and, 109, 110; Gaddis, John Lewis and, 20; global power and, 112; Great Britain and, 214n2; Hitler, Adolf on, 120; homicide and, 137, 184–85; imperialism and, 20; Jacksonianism and, 33; labor coercion and, 81–82, 89; liberal counterinsurgents and, 64–65; liberal democracy and, 112; Marx, Karl and, 82, 218n23; military interventions and, xiii; national sovereignty and, 138; Nazism and, 33, 55, 111, 224n37; *The Negro Family: The Case for National Action* (Moynihan) (1965) and, 64; police and, 69, 144; policing and, 56; preventive war and, 121; race and, xvii, 39, 107, 138, 139, 184, 186, 229n24; race war and, 55; Sepoy Revolt (1857) and, 106–7; slavery and, 82, 87–88; small wars and, 55; "A Special Variety of Colonialism" (O'Dell), 62; United States and, ix, 2–3, 33, 64, 100, 138; U.S. foreign policies and, 170; violence and, 100, 106–7, 142, 144, 185; war and, 54–55, 105–6, 142. *See also* settler colonialism
colonization, 29, 53, 62, 86–87, 99, 107–8, 111, 136, 138
color-blindness, xvii, 115, 123–25, 129, 130, 131, 149, 150, 160, 179
Comey, James, 169
"Coming Anarchy, The" (Kaplan) (essay), 146–47
command and obedience, 118–19
Committee on Present Danger, 10
commodification, 78, 92, 214n3, 216n13
communism: Arendt, Hannah and, 112; Chile and, 197n17; cold war and, 113; counterinsurgency policing and, 63;

economics and, xii; King, Martin Luther, Jr. and, 186; military interventions and, 10; modernization and, 113; Overseas Internal Defense Policy (OIDP) and, 63; Polanyi, Karl and, 112; race and, 5; Rice, Condoleeza and, 19; Rostow, Walt and, 113; slavery and, 125; totalitarianism and, 111; United States and, 10, 19, 113, 138, 170; whites and, 60; World War I and, 21–22

Communist Manifesto (Marx and Engels), 93

compassionate conservatism, 156–57

concentration camps, 105, 108, 224n33

Congo, 3

Congress: Democratic Party and, 161; global war on terror and, 222n15; Medicaid and, 130, 167; military and, 3, 5, 11, 114; Republican Party and, 130, 152, 165, 167; Trump, Donald and, 167; Vietnam War and, 10

conservatives, 66, 146, 160, 174–75. *See also* Republican Party; right wing

CORDS (Civil Operations and Revolutionary Development Support), 61–62

counterinsurgency, 3, 60, 61, 63–67, 69, 109, 112–13, 209n67, 211n88

counterinsurgency wars, xii, 3, 15–16, 23–24, 49, 60–61, 108, 224n33

Creek War (1814), 26

Creveld, Martin Van, 147

crime: arrests and, 72; Banfield, Edward on, 67; blackness and, 142; blacks and, 48–49, 58–59, 66, 115, 118, 144, 156; capitalism and, 81; the carceral state and, 8; *The Challenge of Crime in a Free Society* (study), 209n63; citizenship and, 8; civil rights and, 59–60, 66; Clinton, Bill and, 154; dogs and, 56–57, 211n79; Dukakis,

Michael and, 130; global war on terror and, 128–29; hegemony and, 127; Johnson, Lyndon and, 6; liberalism and, 128–29; Locke, John and, 43; Los Angeles and, 58–59; Mexicans and, 58–59; national security and, 6, 12, 146; national sovereignty and, 142; *The Negro Family: The Case for National Action* (Moynihan) (1965) and, 64; Omnibus Crime Control and Safe Streets Act (1968), 128; policing and, 70; poverty and, 67; race and, xiv–xv, 58–59, 72, 96, 115, 132, 143–44; Republican Party and, 154; settler sovereignty and, 142; slavery and, 144; state violence and, 56; stop-and-frisk and, 70; Thirteenth Amendment and, 115; United States and, 132, 146; Violent Crime and Law Enforcement Act (1994), 12, 117; war and, 117, 128–29, 142, 147; war on drugs and, 128–29; whites and, 156. *See also* war crimes; war on crime

criminalization: arrests and, 72; blacks and, 25, 40, 51, 70–71; capitalism and, 79–80; enemies and, 198n29; immigration and, 7, 72; just wars and, 205n24; Native Americans and, 40; neoliberalism and, xiii; policing and, 73, 128–29; race and, xv, 45, 132, 136; race war and, 142; Reagan, Ronald and, 129; Thatcher, Margaret and, 129; United States and, 72; war and, 54, 142–43

Critchfield, Richard, 63–64

Cruz, Ted, 165

Cuba, 16–17, 23–24, 117, 162

Dardot, Pierre, 168

Dark Continent, 49–50

darker nations, 4, 7, 138

Davis, Mike, 172

Dayan, Colin, 114, 116–17

Deakin, Alfred, 50, 51

death camps, 105. *See also* concentration camps

Declaration of Independence, 27, 40

Deferred Action for Childhood Arrival (DACA), 162

deindustrialization, 155–56

DeMint, Jim, 161

democracy: African Americans and, 139; blackness and, 143; blacks and, 131, 181; civil rights and, 8–9, 114, 139, 182; colonialism and, 119; command and obedience and, 118–19; crisis of democracy, 8–9; economic inequalities and, 38; fascism and, 110; heterogeneity and, 119; Huntington, Samuel and, 8–9, 66; imperialism and, 119; invasion of Iraq and, 125; Iraq war and, 18–19, 100; Obama, Barack and, 164, 181; Panama and, 11; race and, 22, 112; Rice, Condoleeza and, 19–20; Schmitt, Carl on, 119–120; torture and, 109; U.S. foreign policies and, 169–170. *See also* liberal democracy

Democratic Party, 154–55, 159, 161, 173, 175–76

Denning, Michael, 219n47

Department of Health and Human Services, 167

Department of Homeland Security, 21, 70, 167

Department of Justice, 174

deportations. *See* mass/deportations

"Detainee Interrogation in the Global War on terror" (memo), 103, 222n15

Detroit riots (1967), 7, 61

DeVos, Betsy, 167

Diallo, Amadou, 14

dogs, 56–57, 58, 69, 211n79

domestic policies, 4, 61, 69–70, 148–49

domestic terrorism, 128, 154

Dominican Republic, 3

Douglass, Frederick, 74, 75, 78, 93–95, 180, 216n10

Dreams from My Father (Obama), 180

Dred Scott decision, 47

drones, 30, 32, 71, 101, 161–62, 181, 183

drugs, 9, 71, 146, 154, 161–62. *See also* war on drugs

drug wars, 22, 32. *See also* war on drugs

D'Souza, Dinesh, 231n45

Dubber, Marcus, 205n22

Du Bois, W. E. B., x, xii, 21, 35–36, 76, 89, 94, 96, 140

Dukakis, Michael, 130

ecology, 166, 172, 174–75, 182, 183. *See also* environment

economic inequalities, xiv, xv, 38, 134, 173. *See also* wealth

economics: blacks and, xiv, 231n6; Brenner, Robert and, 213n1; Bush, George W. and, 158; capitalism and, xii, 76, 81, 88; class and, 213n1; the Clintons and, 153, 154; communism and, xii; fascism and, 110; globalism and, xii, 2; global power and, 185; Great Depression, 54, 154; imperialism and, 158; Jim Crow and, xv; labor and, 80, 176–77, 213n1; the Left and, 173–74, 176; Marx, Karl and, 216n13; neoliberalism and, xiii, 127, 131, 168, 173; Obama, Barack and, 164, 175; policing and, 9; race and, xvi, 133, 173–74; security state and, xv; sexism and, 173–74; slavery and, 76, 88;

Trump, Donald and, 170, 185–86; United States and, ix, 2, 6, 185, 186; universalism and, 184; whites and, 176, 231n6. *See also* capitalism

Eighth Amendment, 115–16

Ellison, Ralph, xii

empires. *See* American empire

employment, xiii, xiv, 72, 96, 134, 140. *See also* labor; working class

endless war, xv, xviii, 101, 158–59

enemy aliens, 25, 44

enemy combatants, 16–17, 26, 54, 101, 135, 136. *See also* unjust enemies

Englehardt, Tom, 222n15

English, the: capitalism and, 90; class and, 218n33; cotton industry, 215n7; fascism and, 110; industrial revolution, 214n2; Marx, Karl and, 95–96, 215n7, 218n33; migration and, 129; slavery and, 84–85; Thatcher, Margaret, 127, 129; United Kingdom, 127, 129. *See also* Great Britain

English yeomanry, 84

environment, 97, 155, 157, 158–59, 162–63, 177, 185–86. *See also* climate change; ecology

Environmental Protection Agency, 167

Europe: colonialism and, 55, 64, 111, 120, 185; far right and, 171; immigration and, 44, 52, 72; Marx, Karl and, 82, 87; migration and, 147; race and, 52, 184; territorial annexations and, 33; terrorism and, 147, 188; Trump, Donald and, 171; United States and, 170; wage labor and, 215n7

European imperialism, 20

evangelicals, 159, 175. *See also* religious right

expansionism, 120, 171. *See also* U.S. expansionism

Fallujah, 100

far right, 149, 153–54, 165, 167, 171. *See also* right wing; Tea Party

fascism, 21–22, 105–6, 109–13, 120, 121, 170–71, 172, 182, 216n13, 223n26

Faulkner, William, 180

FBI (Federal Bureau of Investigation), 169

Federalist Society, 116

Federal Reserve, 167

felony disfranchisement laws, 115, 135

feminism, 127

Ferguson, Niall, 15

financial deregulation, 154–55, 166, 168

Flynn, Mike, 169

Ford, Gerald, 9–10, 198n21

Ford, Lisa, 142

foreclosures, 161. *See also* home ownership

Foreign Affairs (magazine), 2

Foucault, Michel, 22–23, 38–39, 90, 91, 104–5, 144, 201n52, 220n51

Foundational Constitution (1669), 42

Fourteenth Amendment, 115–16, 135–36

Franklin, Benjamin, 36, 40, 71, 72

Freedomways (journal), 62, 178

free labor, 83–84, 84–85, 87, 88, 91–92, 94, 219n42

free trade, 7, 87–88, 112–13, 154–55, 163, 169–170, 175

Freund, Ernst, 48

Friedman, Thomas, 101

frontier wars, xii, 16, 21, 25–26, 28–29, 30–31, 58, 106, 107–8, 109, 112

Fukuyama, Francis, 170

Furman v. Georgia (1972), 114–15, 226n53

Gaddis, John Lewis, 15, 16, 20, 24, 108, 120, 147, 158

Garner, Jay, 15

Gates, Daryl, 9, 69

gay marriage, 162

gender: capitalism and, 76, 84, 86–87, 168; economic inequalities and, 173; neoliberalism and, 165; Obama, Barack and, 164; race and, xvi, 135; sexuality and, 127; slavery and, 77, 86–87; Trump, Donald and, 165; United States and, 112. *See also* chattel slavery; sexism; women

Geneva Conventions, 16, 33, 102, 209n67

genocide, 12, 43, 82, 91, 94, 111, 122. *See also* homicide

Georgia, 35–36

Georgia General Assembly, 35, 46

German war crimes, 55

ghettos, 62, 67, 109, 186. *See also* Detroit riots (1967); Watts riots

Gilmore, Ruth Wilson, 8, 132–33, 197n16

Gilroy, Paul, 121

Gingrich, Newt, 130, 152, 231n45

globalism, xii, 2, 14, 155, 170, 171. *See also* global power

globalization, 6, 154–55, 155–56, 163, 170

global leadership, 4, 157, 232n7

global power: Arendt, Hannah on, 111, 112; colonialism and, 112; domestic politics and, 8; economics and, 185; emancipatory narrative and, 25–26; human rights and, 114; Indian wars and, 25–26; Jim Crow and, 25; race and, xii, xiii, 4–5, 138; slavery and, 25–26; Trump, Donald and, 170; United States and, xii, xiii, 2, 25; universalism and, 4; violence and, 185

global war on terror: Afghanistan war and, 1, 16; Bush, George W. and, 13, 30, 31, 106; capitalism and, 118; cold war and, 13, 18, 117–18; Congress and, 222n15; crime and, 128–29; "Detainee Interrogation in the Global War on terror" (memo), 103, 222n15; drones and, 71; fascism and, 106; imperialism and, 18; incarceration and, 117; inequality and, xiii; internationalism and, 18, 31–32; as long war, 117–18; Muslims and, 13; Native Americans and, 16; Obama, Barack and, 31–32, 182; policing and, 53–54; race and, 149; racism and, 18; right-wing jurisprudence and, 119; Sunni Muslims and, 16; torture and, 33, 222n16; United States and, 1–2; violence and, 31–32; war and, 128–29. *See also* 9/11

Goldman Sachs, 160–61, 168–69

Goldwater, Barry, 145–46

Goodman, Andrew, 126

good wars. *See* just wars

GOP. *See* Republican Party

Göring, Hermann, 223n26

Great Britain: Camp Justice and, 117; class and, 75–76, 218n33; Colby, Elbridge and, 107, 108; colonialism and, 214n2; domestic terrorism and, 128; free trade and, 87; incarceration and, 140; industrial revolution and, 214n2; migration and, 129; Native Americans and, 40; Nazism and, 120; neoliberalism and, 127; policing and, 128; prisons and, 140; race and, 129; slavery and, 40, 87, 214n2; torture and, 222n16; voting rights and, 119. *See also* English, the

Great Depression, 54, 154

Great Society, 22, 130

great transformation, 125

Greece, 3

Grenada, 3

Grenier, John, 26

Grotius, Hugo, 92–93

Korea, 3, 171
Kristol, Irving, 118
Ku Klux Klan, 57
Kweli, Talib, 14
Kyoto climate-change accords, 157

labor: capitalism and, 44, 76, 80, 90, 96,
    168, 213n1, 216n13, 217n16; Douglass,
    Frederick and, 93; economics and,
    80, 176–77, 213n1; fascism and, 110;
    Fourteenth Amendment and, 116;
    globalization and, 155–56; liberals
    and, 175; Marx, Karl and, 81–82, 84,
    85; Obama, Barack and, 161, 164, 180;
    primitive accumulation and, 29; race
    and, ix, 93–94; racism and, 89, 135;
    slavery and, 36, 44, 76; Trump,
    Donald and, 167; violence and,
    89–90; whiteness and, 140. See also
    free labor; Marx, Karl; wage labor
labor coercion, 81–82, 89, 90, 92, 115
labor movements, 85
Lakota Sioux, 51–52
land appropriation, 36–37, 40, 43, 44, 55.
    See also U.S. territorial expansion
Laos, 3
Latina/o(s), 70, 127, 135, 192n9
Laval, Christian, 168
law-and-order, 128. See also policing
laws of war, 33, 103, 107, 184. See also
    international law; war crimes
Lebanon, 3
Left, the, xiv, 124, 152, 156, 158, 168,
    173–74, 175–76. See also Democratic
    Party; liberals
LeMay, Curtis, 113
Lewis, Bernard, 100, 147
LGBT, 127, 153, 162
liberal democracy, 6, 109–10, 112, 120,
    121–22, 181, 183, 184–85

liberalism: abolitionism and, 164; Arendt,
    Hannah and, 112; capitalism and,
    xv–xvi, 29; civil rights and, 164;
    crime and, 128–29; fascism and, 110;
    Losurdo, Domenico and, 205n23;
    national sovereignty and, 119; New
    Deal liberalism, 112; Polanyi, Karl
    and, 112; race and, 130; Schmitt, Carl
    and, 119–120; social justice and, 173;
    United States and, 118, 125; U.S.
    expansionism and, 109; war and,
    128–29. See also racial liberalism
liberals, 156, 158, 160, 165, 171, 174–75. See
    also Left, the
Life magazine, 60–61
Liptak, Adam, 139–140
Locke, Alain, 4
Locke, John, 41, 42, 43, 64, 66, 92–93,
    206n26
Lodge, Henry Cabot, 4
Logan (Indian chief), 23
Logan, Rayford, 144
long wars: Bush, George W. and, 157;
    clash of civilizations and, 15;
    duration and, 121; global leadership
    and, 157; global war on terror as,
    117–18; Iraq war as, 102; 9/11 and, 30,
    188; normalcy and, 30–31; Obama,
    Barack and, 32, 149, 161–62; race and,
    xviii; race war and, 15; Rumsfeld,
    Donald and, 2; state racism and, 31;
    terrorism and, 150–51; Trump,
    Donald and, 159. See also permanent
    wars; individual wars
Los Angeles, 58–59, 60, 65, 69, 146,
    209n68
Los Angeles Police Department, 9
Losing Ground (Murray), 124–25
Losurdo, Domenico, 205n23
Louima, Abner, 14

Louisiana, 40–41
Lowe, Lisa, 58
Luce, Henry, 232n7
Luxemburg, Rosa, 90
lynching, xiv, 17, 35, 51, 89, 144

MacArthur, Douglas, 171
Madison, James, 36
Mahan, Alfred Thayer, 50
Malayan counterinsurgency, 63–64
Manhattan Institute (think tank), 9
Manifest Destiny, 193n11
manufacturing, 154–56, 166–67. *See also*
    free trade
markets, xiii, xiv, 76, 91, 110, 112, 216n13.
    See also capitalism; neoliberalism
Martin, Trayvon, 181
Marx, Karl, 74–92; abolitionism and,
    87–88, 219n42; *Black Reconstruction in
    America* (Du Bois) and, 89; capitalism
    and, 29, 75, 76–88, 91, 96; chattel
    slavery and, 80; civil rights and,
    83; colonialism and, 82, 218n23;
    Communist Manifesto (Marx and
    Engels), 93; economics and, 216n13;
    the English and, 84–85, 95–96, 215n7,
    218n33; Europe and, 82, 87; fascism
    and, 110; genocide and, 82, 91;
    Grundrisse, 75, 83; labor and, 81–82,
    84, 85; Luxemburg, Rosa and, 90;
    primitive accumulation and, 92,
    216n12; proletariats and, 81; race and,
    79; Schlesinger, Arthur, Jr. and, 66;
    slavery and, 75, 76–77, 78, 80–88; on
    social relations, 74–75; violence and,
    82, 91. *See also Capital, Volume I* (Marx)
mass deportations: blacks and, x–xi;
    Clinton, Bill and, 154; Great
    Depression and, 54; Immigration and
    Customs Enforcement (ICE) and,
    72–73; liberal democracy and, 121–22;
    Obama, Barack and, 32, 162, 164;
    race and, 101; Trump, Donald and,
    32, 162; United States and, x–xi, xvii,
    25, 121–22, 135, 158–59, 177; war and,
    25; World War II and, 54
mass detentions, 61–62, 73
mass surveillance, 54, 161–62, 183
McCain, John, 159–160, 179–180, 183
McCarthy, Cormac, 98
McCone, John, 60
McCoy, Alfred, 49
McFarland, Howard, xii
McNamara, Robert, 184
McWilliams, Carey, 52
Mead, Laurence, 124–25
Medicaid, 130, 167
Mercer, Robert and Rebekah, 165
Metaphysics (Kant), 142–43
Mexicans, 52, 58–59
Mexico, 7, 30–31, 98–99, 156
Michaels, Walter Benn, 156
Michigan State University Group (MSUG),
    57
Middle East, 3, 15, 188. *See also* Afghani-
    stan war; Iraq war
Midwest, 153, 155, 175
migrants, xv, xvi, 32, 52, 92, 129, 154,
    156–57, 162, 166
migration, 129, 147. *See also* immigration
militarism, 181
militarization, 35, 53–54, 90, 112–13,
    128–29
military: American empire and, 2, 3–4,
    14, 17, 27–28; appropriation and, 92;
    blacks and, xvii, 64; borders and, 54;
    Bush, George W. and, 9, 13; class and,
    xiv–xv; cold war and, 3, 10; Congress
    and, 3, 5, 11, 114; deep state and,
    233n21; homicide and, 188; Indian

military *(continued)*
    wars and, 24, 26; Muslims and, 135;
    national sovereignty and, 2, 3–4;
    Obama, Barack and, 159, 162–63;
    police and, 7, 27, 67, 143, 145; police
    power and, xx, 6, 50; policing and, 9,
    61, 146; prisons and, 180; Roosevelt,
    Theodore and, 50; torture and, 17;
    United States and, x–xi; U.S.
    expansionism and, 113; U.S. foreign
    policies and, 28–29, 187; violence
    and, 18, 30; war and, 54, 67, 188; war
    on drugs and, 7
military actions, x–xi, 5, 67, 69, 99,
    107–8, 128–29, 205n24
military atrocities, 8, 224n33. *See also* war
    crimes
Military Establishment, The (study), 67
military interventions: American empire
    and, 3–4, 17; capitalism and, 96;
    China and, 10; cold war and, 10;
    colonialism and, xiii; communism
    and, 10; counterinsurgency policing
    and, 63; international law and, 3;
    Iran and, 3; police actions and, 54;
    race and, xiii; state violence and, 29;
    United States and, 3–4, 54, 170; U.S.
    foreign policies and, 28–29; Vietnam
    War and, 3–4, 10; violence toll and, 3;
    war and, 54
military power, 2, 3, 6, 11–12, 13, 14, 60,
    114, 172, 187
militias, 27, 45, 47, 143
Mill, John Stuart, 106–7, 111, 121
Miller, Geoffrey, 222n18
Miller, Stephen, 167
minimum wage, 177
Mnuchin, Steve, 168–69
modernization, 112, 113
Modoc Indian prisoners, 33

Moore, Jason W., 91–92
Morgan, Edmund, 141
Morgan, Jennifer, xix, 77–78
Morrison, Toni, 155
Moten, Fred, 147
Moynihan, Daniel Patrick, 64, 66, 198n21
Muhammad, Khalil Gibran, 144
multiculturalism, 131, 156, 159, 160, 174
Murakawa, Naomi, 59, 132
Murray, Anna, 95
Murray, Charles, 66–67, 124–25
Muslims: global war on terror and, 13;
    immigration and, 13–14, 72; Iraq war
    and, 100, 101; military and, 135;
    Obama, Barack as, xvii, 160, 164;
    racial profiling and, 13–14; state
    violence and, 104; Sunni Muslims,
    15, 16, 188; terrorism and, 101;
    Trump, Donald and, 32, 165, 167
Myrdal, Gunnar, 4, 138

NAFTA (North American Free Trade
    Agreement), 7, 175
Nagasaki, 4
Namibia, 111
Narrative of the Life of Frederick Douglass
    (Douglass), 74, 94
nation, the, 136–37, 229n24. *See also*
    national sovereignty; state, the;
    United States
National Guard, 7, 20
nationalism, 33–34, 81, 99–100, 106,
    136–37, 139, 180, 183
nationality, 8, 135, 140–41
national security: bipartisan consensus
    and, 183–84, 233n21; civil rights and,
    60; Clinton, Hillary and, 169; cold
    war and, 146; crime and, 6, 12, 146;
    enemy aliens and, 44; hegemony
    and, 127; invasion of Iraq and, 10;

neoliberalism: blacks and, xiv; capitalism and, 168; the carceral state and, xiv; civil rights and, xiv; Clinton, Hillary and, 174; criminalization and, xiii; economics and, xiii, 127, 131, 168, 173; finance and, 154–55; gender and, 165; Great Britain and, 127; incarceration and, 118, 131; Iraqi agriculture and, 224n39; the Left and, xiv, 168; markets and, xiv; Obama, Barack and, 150, 162–63, 174; race and, xiii–xiv, 131, 160; Reagan, Ronald and, 127; social justice and, 168; Thatcher, Margaret and, 127; trade and, 154–55; Trump, Donald and, 168–69; United Kingdom and, 127; United States and, 127; welfare state and, xiii, 9, 173; workfare and, 154–55

New Deal liberalism, 112

new Jim Crow, 8. *See also* Jim Crow

New Orleans. *See* Hurricane Katrina

New York City, 130

New York City Police Department (NYPD), 14, 70

New York Times, 2, 14, 101, 139–140, 152, 153, 163–64, 181, 231n1

Ngo, Dinh Diem, 57

Nicaragua, 3

9/11: Afghanistan war and, 1; Bush, George W. and, 9–10, 98, 101, 121, 157, 158, 195n6; Gaddis, John Lewis and, 120, 147; Iraq war and, 101, 102; long wars and, 30, 188; race and, 14, 147; security state and, xv. *See also* global war on terror; terrorism

Nixon, Richard, 4–5, 6–7, 8, 118, 197n17

noncombatants, 54, 107, 108, 184. *See also* violence toll

Noriega, Manuel, 11

normalcy, 30–31, 73

North American Free Trade Agreement (NAFTA), 7, 175

Notes on the State of Virginia (1787) (Jefferson), 23

nuclear weapons, 4, 6, 112–13, 162–63, 184, 195n6

Nuremberg laws, 33. *See also* international law

Nyquist, Mary, 86

Obama, Barack, 159–165, 178–181; Afghanistan war and, 182–83; Africa and, 180, 184; African Americans and, 149; Asia and, 180, 184; assassinations and, 32; blackness and, 164; blacks and, 181; Bush, George W. and, 183; citizenship and, 135–36; civil rights and, 139, 149, 150, 164; civil wars and, 179; class and, 174; climate change and, 162; Clinton, Hillary and, 159, 183; color-blindness and, 149, 150, 179; Cuba and, 162; Deferred Action for Childhood Arrival (DACA), 162; democracy and, 164, 181; drones and, 32, 181, 183; drug wars and, 32; economics and, 164, 175; environment and, 162–63; far right and, 149; financial collapse (2008) and, 162; Fourteenth Amendment and, 135–36; gender/discrimination and, 164; global war on terror and, 31–32, 182; Guantanamo Bay and, 162, 182; health care and, 161, 162–63; Holder, Eric and, 71; immigration and, 162–63; incarceration and, 32, 161–62, 180; Iran and, 162; Iraq war and, 18–19; King, Martin Luther, Jr. and, 179, 186; labor and, 161, 164, 180; LGBT and, 162; liberal reformism and, 161, 164;

long wars and, 32, 149, 161–62; mass/
deportations and, 32, 162, 164;
McCain, John and, 183; migrants and,
32, 162; military and, 159, 162–63;
multiculturalism and, 159, 174; as
Muslim, xvii, 160, 164; national
security and, 183; neoliberalism and,
150, 162–63, 174; *New York Times* and,
181; noncombatants and, 184;
populism and, 159, 160; prisons and,
180; race and, 19, 160, 162–63, 164,
175, 180–81, 182, 187; racism and, xvii,
149–150; Rice, Condoleeza and, 182;
right wing and, 161, 231n45; sexual
discrimination and, 164; taxation
and, 160; Tea Party and, 149, 160;
terrorism and, 161–62; torture and,
162, 182; totalitarianism and, 160;
Trump, Donald and, 149, 150, 162,
163–64, 175, 183; violence and, 180;
Wall Street and, 160–61; war and, 164,
180–81, 182–83; war on drugs and, 32;
wealth inequality and, 164; whites
and, 231n45; white supremacy and,
150; women and, 162, 180
O'Dell, Jack, 22, 62
OIDP. *See* Overseas Internal Defense
Policy (OIDP)
Omi, Michael, 123–24, 125, 229n24
Omnibus Crime Control and Safe Streets
Act (1968), 128
Operation Ceasefire, 71
Operation Infinite Justice, 13. *See also*
global war on terror
Operation Iraqi Freedom, 195n6. *See also*
Iraq war
Operation Just Cause, 11
Operation Phoenix, 61–62, 108, 209n67
Origins of Totalitarianism, The (Arendt),
111–12

O'Sullivan, John, 98–99
Overseas Internal Defense Policy (OIDP),
63, 65

Paine, Thomas, 40
Pakistan, 8, 181
Palin, Sarah, 160
Panama, 11
Panama Canal, 171
Parker, William, 58–59, 60, 65, 210n74
Parker on Police (Parker), 210n74
Patai, Raphael, 100
Pearl Harbor, 30–31
Pelican Bay (prison), 117
penal labor, 89
permanent wars, 2, 30–31, 136
Philippines: American empire and, 15;
blacks and, xii, 21; Colby, Elbridge
and, 108; counterinsurgency wars
and, xii, 3, 23–24, 49, 108, 224n33;
Indian wars and, 24; Iraq war and,
158; Native Americans and, 16;
permanent wars and, 30–31;
United States and, 49, 99, 224n33;
U.S.-Philippine war (1898), xii, 15,
49, 99, 108; U.S. territorial expansion
and, 99
Philippines War of 1898. *See*
U.S.-Philippine war (1898)
Phillips, Kevin, 156
Phillips, U.B., 47
Plessy v. Ferguson (1896), 49, 144
Polanyi, Karl, 110, 112, 216n13
police: appropriation and, 92; assassinations and, 69; blacks and, xvii,
48–49, 144–45; capitalism and,
91, 96; Civil War and, 143; class
and, xiv–xv; colonialism and, 69,
144; counterinsurgency and, 69;
Department of Justice and, 174; dogs

Vietnam War and, 61–62; violence and, 48, 73; war and, 45, 55–56, 67–68, 71, 73; war on crime/drugs/ poverty and, 53–54; whiteness and, 50. *See also* law-and-order

Policing the Crisis (Hall), 128

populism, 159, 160, 165, 167, 170

Postlethwayt, Malachy, 87

poverty, xiv, 7, 9, 53–54, 67, 81. *See also* war on poverty

Powell, Colin, 12

preemptive war, 147, 158

premature death, 48–49, 76–77, 80–81, 132–33, 149, 177, 179, 197, 215n7, 218n33. *See also* homicide

preventive war, 108, 121

Price, Mike, 167

primitive accumulation, 29, 82–83, 90, 92, 216n12

prisons: Agamben, Giorgio and, 105; appropriation and, 92; blacks and, xvii, 17, 131, 135, 144, 187; Clinton, Bill and, 155; fascism and, 109; Great Britain and, 140; homicide and, 144; liberal democracy and, 121–22; Long Binh stockade (Camp LB), 211n80; military and, 180; Obama, Barack and, 180; police and, 17; race and, 115, 139–140; slavery and, 116; United States and, 117, 121–22; U.S. Supreme Court and, 115, 116; Vietnam War and, 61–62; war on drugs and, 117. *See also* carceral state, the; incarceration; *individual prisons*

private property, 37–38, 39, 43, 47, 90, 172

Project for a New American Century, 12–13, 232n7

proletariats, 81, 219n47

property, 26, 29, 30, 36, 37, 41, 76, 78, 110. *See also* private property

proxy wars, 3, 11, 112–13

Pruitt, Scott, 167

public education, 159, 167, 174

race: Abu Ghraib prison and, xvii; Afghanistan war and, 15; American empire and, xii, 5, 29–30; antimiscegenation and, 144; antiracism and, 73; Atwater, Lee and, 130; Australia and, 50; Bannon, Steve and, 72; biopolitics and, 120; Burgess, John and, x; capitalism and, xiv–xv, 29, 30, 75–80, 86, 88, 89–90, 95, 96, 97, 168, 182, 214n4; the carceral state and, 115, 121, 149; civil exclusion and, 148; civil rights and, ix, 116, 123, 132, 139, 187–88; class and, xiv–xv, 78, 96, 131, 140, 186, 192n10; Clinton, Hillary and, 153; colonialism and, xvii, 39, 107, 138, 139, 184, 186, 229n24; colonization and, 99, 136, 138; color-blindness and, xvii, 123–25, 131, 160; communism and, 5; conservatives and, 146, 160; counterinsurgency and, 64, 65; crime and, xiv–xv, 58–59, 72, 96, 115, 132, 143–44; criminality and, 35, 146; criminalization and, xv, 45, 132, 136; Deakin, Alfred and, 50, 51; democracy and, 22, 112; domestic policies and, 69–70, 148–49; Douglass, Frederick and, 93, 94, 95; Du Bois, W. E. B. and, x, 96; economics and, xvi, 133, 173–74; employment and, 140; enemy aliens and, 44; Europe and, 52, 184; Foucault, Michel on, 22–23; frontier wars and, xii, 108; gender and, xvi, 135; globalism and, xii; global power and, xii, xiii, 4–5, 138; global war on terror and, 149;

race *(continued)*
Great Britain and, 129; Guantanamo Bay and, xvii; hegemony and, 127; heterogeneity and, xv–xvi; human rights and, 50; Hurricane Katrina and, 200n47; ideologies and, 133–35; immigration and, ix, 39–40, 52, 135–36; imperialism and, xvii, 50, 111, 186; incarceration and, xvii, 139–140; Indian wars and, xvii–xviii; institutions and, 133–35, 136, 140; Japan and, 184; Jim Crow and, xvi, 149; jurisprudence and, 129; King, Martin Luther, Jr. and, 181, 186; labor and, ix, 93–94; labor coercion and, 82, 89; the Left and, 124, 174; liberal counterinsurgents and, 64–65; liberal democracy and, 112; liberalism and, 130; liberals and, 160; long wars and, xviii; Los Angeles and, 58–59; Marx, Karl and, 79; mass/deportations and, 101; military interventions and, xiii; multiculturalism and, 131, 160; national sovereignty and, 137–38; the nation and, 136–37, 229n24; neoliberalism and, xiii–xiv, 131, 160; *New York Times* and, 153; 9/11 and, 14, 147; Nixon, Richard and, 4–5; Obama, Barack and, 19, 160, 162–63, 164, 175, 180–81, 182, 187; Omi, Michael and, 123–24; permanent wars and, 136; police killings and, 165; police/power and, 43, 45, 49, 59, 70, 144, 165; policing and, 35–36, 45–46, 48, 56, 60, 67–68, 128; prisons and, 115, 139–140; racial differentiation and, 132; *Racial Formation in the United States from the 1960s to the 1980s* (Omi and Winant) and, 123–25, 127, 131–32, 134, 136,

147–49; racial inequality and, 134; racism and, xvi, 133, 134–35, 149; Reagan, Ronald and, 126, 129–130; Republican Party and, 129–130, 153–54; Rice, Condoleeza and, 19–20; right wing and, 126, 171, 172; Sanders, Bernie and, 173; security and, x–xi, xv, 27, 52, 131–32; settler colonialism and, 140, 148–49; settlers and, xvii, 50, 72, 99; slavery and, xvii–xviii, 77, 136, 182; social authorship and, xvii; social relations and, 134, 136, 141; sovereignty and, 147; the state and, xv, 131–32, 137, 148; state violence and, 132–33, 136, 140–41, 149, 182; stop-and-frisk and, 70; torture and, xvii; Trump, Donald and, 72, 130, 168, 170, 179, 183; United States and, ix, 4–5, 52–53, 112, 123–27, 135–36, 138, 140, 145, 148–49, 174, 186; universal human rights and, 2–3; universalism and, 4; U.S. foreign policies and, 25, 139, 148–49, 187; U.S.-Philippine war (1898) and, 49; U.S. Supreme Court and, 179; U.S. territorial expansion and, 99; Vietnam War and, 6, 58; violence and, xiii, 46, 69–70, 72, 82, 87, 109, 136, 142, 144, 149, 178–79, 186–87, 189, 203n71; Virginia and, 141; war and, xi–xii, 21–23, 31, 45, 67–68, 73, 136, 142, 182, 189; war on drugs and, 115, 117; whiteness and, 38, 94, 95, 140; whites and, 37, 45, 50, 156; white supremacy and, xiv–xv, 130, 149; Winant, Howard and, 123–24; Wolfe, Patrick and, 79; working class and, 156; World Wars and, xii. *See also* racial liberalism

race war: Afghanistan war as, 158; blacks and, 21; capitalism and, 92–93, 158;

Rainbow Coalition, 126–27
Rand Corporation, 65, 67
Reagan, Ronald, 6, 7, 9, 10–11, 117, 124,
    126, 127, 129–130, 170
Rector, Ricky Ray, 154
Reed, Adolph, 131
Rehnquist, William, 115–16
religion, xvi, 121–22. *See also* Islam
religious right, 159, 175, 227n65. *See also*
    far right
Renan, Ernest, 136
reproductive rights, 154, 162, 172. *See also*
    abortion
republicanism, 206n31
Republican Party, 129–130, 152, 153–54,
    161, 165, 166, 167, 175
Revolutionary War, 21
Rice, Condoleeza, 19–20, 139, 140, 182,
    195n6
Rice, Tamir, 181
Right, the. *See* conservatives; far right;
    Republican Party; Tea Party
right wing: Asia and, 171; Central America
    and, 171; Clinton, Bill and, 154; cold
    war and, 171; command and
    obedience and, 118–19; Cruz, Ted
    and, 165; Europe and, 171; expan-
    sionism and, 172; Iran and, 171; Iraq
    war and, 171; jurisprudence and, 119;
    Obama, Barack and, 161, 231n45;
    Panama Canal and, 171; race and, 126,
    171, 172; racism and, 154; religious
    right, 159, 175, 227n65; Republican
    Party as, 153–54; sovereignty and,
    172; taxation and, 155–56; Trump,
    Donald and, 167–68, 171; United
    States and, 171, 172; Vietnam War
    and, 171; whites and, 156; World War
    II and, 171. *See also* individuals
riots, 7, 9, 22, 61, 69, 130, 146, 187

Robinson, Cedric, 79, 88
Roe v. Wade (1973), 226n53
Rogin, Michael, 109, 203n71
Romney, Mitt, 160
Roosevelt, Theodore, 23–24, 48, 50
Rorty, Richard, 155–56, 158, 159
Rostow, Walt, 61, 113
Rumsfeld, Donald, 1, 2, 9–11, 198n21, 232n7
Russian interference, 169
Rust Belt, 163. *See also* Midwest
Rwanda, 12

Sanders, Bernie, 173, 176
Scheindlin, Shira A., 70
Schlesinger, Arthur, Jr., 66, 156
Schmitt, Carl, 54–55, 104, 119–120, 121,
    171, 205n24, 227n65
school integration, 125, 179
Schwerner, Michael, 126
Scott, Walter, 181
Seal Team 6, 16
Seattle protests, 155
Second Amendment, 47
second cold war, 5–6. *See also* cold war
Second Treatise on Civil Government (Locke),
    41
security: blackness and, 51; civil rights
    and, 59–60; deep state and, 233n21;
    enemy aliens and, 25; police and, 72;
    policing and, 60; race and, x–xi, xv,
    27, 52, 131–32; the state and, xv,
    131–32; violence and, 43, 181. *See also*
    national security
Seminole War, 33
Serbia, 12
Sessions, Jeff, 168, 172, 174
settler colonialism, xviii, 24–25, 79,
    105–6, 120, 140, 148–49, 185
settlers: American federalism and, 45;
    blackness and, 27; blacks and, 27;

torture *(continued)*
    universal human rights and, 103;
    U.S. war crimes and, 102–3; war and,
    68–69; war on drugs and, 117; Yoo,
    John and, 33. *See also* Guantanamo Bay
totalitarianism, 13, 106, 109, 110, 111–12,
    121, 160, 169
trade, 2, 7, 154–55, 175. *See also* free trade
Trans-Pacific Partnership free-trade
    agreement, 163
tribal sovereignty, 45, 142
Trietschke, Heinrich von, 111
Trop v. Dulles (1958), 114–15
Truman, Harry, 59
Trump, Donald, 165–176; abortion and,
    165; anti-Semitism and, 160–61;
    Bannon, Steve and, 167; blacks and,
    163–64, 165, 168; borders and, 172;
    Cambridge Analytica and, 166;
    capitalism and, 170, 171, 172; China
    and, 171; CIA and, 169; civil wars and,
    150; climate change and, 159, 183;
    Clinton, Hillary and, 166, 183;
    Comey, James and, 169; Congress
    and, 167; conservatives and, 174–75;
    corporate America and, 168–69;
    Democratic Party and, 175–76;
    ecology and, 183; economics and,
    170, 185–86; election of, 152–53;
    environment and, 159, 185–86;
    Europe and, 171; fascism and, 170–71;
    FBI and, 169; financial deregulation
    and, 166, 168; gender and, 165;
    globalism and, 171; global power and,
    170; Guantanamo Bay and, 102;
    health care and, 162; Hitler, Adolf
    and, 169; immigration and, 72, 168;
    imperialism and, 32; Iran and, 171;
    Iraq war and, 32; Jackson, Andrew
    and, 32; kleptocracy and, 168; labor
    and, 167; the Left and, 152, 175–76;
    liberals and, 174–75; long wars and,
    159; mass/deportations and, 32, 162;
    media and, 166; migrants and, 166;
    military power and, 172; Muslims
    and, 32, 165, 167; national security
    and, 159, 169; neoliberalism and,
    168–69; Obama, Barack and, 149,
    150, 162, 163–64, 175, 183; police and,
    72; police power and, 72, 172–73;
    populism and, 165, 167, 170; private
    property and, 172; public education
    and, 159, 167; race and, 72, 130, 168,
    170, 179, 183; racial profiling and, 32;
    racism and, ix–x, 153, 159, 163–64,
    165, 171–72, 173–74, 183, 185–86;
    Reagan, Ronald and, 170; reproduc-
    tive rights and, 172; Republican Party
    and, 153, 165, 167, 175; right wing
    and, 167–68, 171; Russian interference
    and, 169; sadism and, 165; sexism
    and, 173–74; social Darwinism and,
    170–71; taxation and, 166, 168;
    terrorism and, 165; torture and, 165;
    totalitarianism and, 169; U.S. foreign
    policies and, 32, 165, 169; violence
    and, 166; war and, 171; whites and,
    172, 175; white supremacy and, 159,
    163–64, 170–71; women and, 165, 166,
    168; working class and, 175
Tuck, Richard, 206n26
Turner, Frederick Jackson, 26
Twentieth-Century Fund, 67

United Kingdom, 127, 129. *See also*
    English, the; Great Britain
United Nations, 2, 3, 198n21
United States: abolitionism and, 25–26;
    antiracism and, 124–25; Asia and,
    170; assassinations and, x–xi; black

freedom movements and, 126, 138, 181; blackness and, x, 147, 231n45; blacks and, 22, 25, 187; borders and, 55; capitalism and, ix, 125; capital punishment and, 114–15; civil rights and, 114, 139; civil wars and, 3; class and, xiv–xv, 174; cold war and, 113; colonialism and, ix, 2–3, 33, 64, 100, 138; colonization and, 138; communism and, 10, 19, 113, 138, 170; counterinsurgencies and, 3; crime and, 132, 146; criminalization and, 72; darker nations and, 138; deep state and, 233n21; economics and, ix, 2, 6, 185, 186; enemy aliens and, 25; environment and, 158–59; Europe and, 170; fascism and, 106, 109, 112–13, 172, 182; free trade and, 112–13, 154–55; frontier wars and, 25–26; genocide and, 122; globalism and, xii, 14; globalization and, 170; global leadership and, 4; global war on terror and, 1–2; hegemony and, 5–6; homicide and, 181, 185, 235n8; homogeneity and, 146; human rights and, 5, 6, 114; immigration and, 25; imperialism and, ix, 2–3, 27–28, 28–29, 99–100, 111, 114; incarceration and, 117, 121–22, 139–140, 158–59; international law and, 2, 222n16; invasion of Iraq and, 1–2, 125; Japan and, 170; Jim Crow and, ix; land appropriation and, 40; Latina/o(s) and, 135; liberalism and, 125; liberalism and, 118; mass/deportations and, x–xi, xvii, 25, 121–22, 135, 158–59, 177; Mexico and, 98–99; military and, x–xi, 3–4, 54, 170; military power and, 2, 11–12, 187; nationalism and, 183; national security and, 54; Native Americans and, ix, 20, 24, 26, 36–37; neoliberalism and, 127; nuclear weapons and, 184; permanent wars and, 2; Philippines and, 49, 99, 224n33; police/power and, 52–53, 55, 172–73, 235n8; policing and, 128, 170; postslavery and, 51; poverty and, xiv; prisons and, 117, 121–22; property ownership and, 29; proxy wars and, 3; race and, ix, 4–5, 52–53, 112, 123–27, 135–36, 138, 140, 145, 148–49, 174, 186; racial differentiation and, 39; racial exclusion and, 187–88; racial liberalism and, 125, 131; racism and, x, 33–34, 106, 114, 125, 163–64; right wing and, 171, 172; slavery and, ix, 25–26, 36, 40, 122; sovereign violence and, 148; terrorism and, 1–2, 100–101, 188; torture and, 109, 121–22, 158–59, 222n16, 224n33; universal human rights and, 2–3; Vietnam War and, 3–4, 5–6; violence and, 22, 24, 28, 30, 100, 104, 114, 186; war and, 52–53, 55, 123, 158–59, 189; war on crime and, 6–7; whites and, 126, 141; white supremacy and, 138, 163–64, 188. *See also* American empire; global power; liberal democracy

universal human rights, 2–3, 6, 103, 113. *See also* human rights

universalism, 4, 13, 18, 112, 118, 137, 172, 180, 184

universal rights, 113, 114, 119

unjust enemies, 142–43

U.S. Agency for International Development, 209n67

USA Patriot Act (2001), 117

U.S. Congress. *See* Congress

U.S. Constitution, 46–47, 71, 111. *See also individual Amendments*

U.S. domestic policies, 4, 61, 69–70, 148–49

U.S. expansionism, ix, 53, 99, 108–9, 113, 122, 172, 182, 184

U.S. foreign policies: bipartisan consensus and, 233n21; black freedom movements and, 138; blacks and, 28–29; Bundy, McGeorge on, 64–65; Clinton, Hillary and, 159; colonialism and, 170; democracy and, 169–170; free trade and, 169–170; frontier wars and, 28–29; human rights and, 5; immigration and, 28–29; King, Martin Luther, Jr. and, 186; military and, 28–29, 187; Moynihan, Daniel Patrick and, 198n21; national belonging and, 28–29; national sovereignty and, 169–170; Overseas Internal Defense Policy (OIDP) and, 63; race and, 25, 139, 148–49, 187; Reagan, Ronald and, 6; slavery and, 170; state violence and, 28–29; Trump, Donald and, 32, 165, 169; Vietnam War and, 61, 187; violence and, 7, 69–70; war and, 187; World War II and, 169–170

U.S. foreign relations, 25, 28

U.S. immigration policy, 6. *See also* immigration

U.S. military. *See* military

U.S. military interventions. *See* military interventions

U.S. military power. *See* military power

U.S.-Philippine war (1898), xii, 15, 49, 99, 108. *See also* Philippines: counterinsurgency wars and the

U.S.-Soviet nuclear arms control agreement, 6

U.S. State Department, 57, 125

U.S. Supreme Court, 49, 52, 114–15, 115–16, 128, 161, 166, 179. *See also individual decisions*

U.S. territorial expansion: Bush, George W. and, 16, 105; Gaddis, John Lewis and, 16, 24; Haiti and, 99; Indian wars and, 26–27; Jackson, Andrew and, 99; Jacksonianism and, 32–33, 203n71; military actions and, 99; O'Sullivan, John and, 98–99; Philippines and, 99; race and, 99; settlers and, 39, 204n4; totalitarianism and, 109; Vietnam War and, 99; violence and, 28, 109, 203n71; war and, 26, 99; Wilson, Woodrow and, 99; Wolfe, Patrick and, 24–25. *See also* U.S. expansionism

U.S. war crimes, 5, 102–3, 104

Viet Minh, 63–64

Vietnam, 3

Vietnam War: Asia and, 61; Baldwin, James and, xii; bare life and, 113–14; black power and, 5; blacks and, xii; Civil Operations and Revolutionary Development Support (CORDS) and, 61–62; civil rights and, 5; Colby, William and, 108; cold war and, 58; Congress and, 10; counterinsurgency and, 69, 209n67; criminality and, 184; global ideals and, 8; Huntington, Samuel on, 66; imperialism and, 6; Indian wars and, 24; invasion of Iraq and, 11; Iraq war and, 158; Johnson, Lyndon and, 99; King, Martin Luther, Jr. and, xiii, 22, 186, 187; LeMay, Curtis and, 113; liberals and, 171; Long Binh stockade (Camp LB), 211n80; McNamara, Robert and, 184;

military interventions and, 3–4, 10; national sovereignty and, 3–4; neoconservatism and, 118; Operation Phoenix and, 61–62; peace movements and, 5; permanent wars and, 30–31; police and, 57, 58, 69, 209n67; policing and, 61–62; prisons and, 61–62; race and, 6, 58; right wing and, 171; Rostow, Walt on, 61; Sloane, Charles F. and, 57–58; state violence and, 70; United States and, 3–4, 5–6; U.S. foreign policies and, 61, 187; U.S. territorial expansion and, 99; war on poverty and, 128; Westmoreland, William and, 113

violence: Abu Ghraib prison and, 100; American empire and, 29–30, 109; appropriation and, 91–92; Bannon, Steve and, 72; blacks and, 35–36, 48–49, 62, 89, 94, 143, 178–79; Bush, George W. and, 157–58; capitalism and, 79–80, 82, 86–87, 89–90, 95, 96, 97, 203n71; centralized authority and, 172; chattel slavery and, 85, 89; civil rights and, 59–60; Civil War and, 143; class and, 203n71; colonialism and, 100, 106–7, 142, 144, 185; colonization and, 107–8, 138; criminality and, 73; Dark Continent and, 49–50; Douglass, Frederick and, 95; expansionism and, 157–58, 184; Fallujah and, 100; fascism and, 110; Foucault, Michel and, 91; frontier wars and, 106; Gaddis, John Lewis on, 158; ghettos and, 186; global power and, 185; global war on terror and, 31–32; Guantanamo Bay and, 100; Hofstadter, Richard and, 202n64; imperialism and, 114, 185; interna-

tional law and, 43; King, Martin Luther, Jr. on, 62, 186; labor and, 89–90; the Left and, 174; liberal democracy and, 183, 185; Marx, Karl and, 91; military/actions and, 18, 30, 107–8; *The Military Establishment* (study) on, 67; Native Americans and, 25, 26–27; Nazism and, 105, 220n51; *The Negro Family: The Case for National Action* (Moynihan) (1965) and, 64; normalcy and, 73; Obama, Barack and, 180; Operation Ceasefire and, 71; Overseas Internal Defense Policy (OIDP) and, 63, 65; police brutality, 60, 68–69; police/power and, 49–50, 67–68, 143, 144; policing and, 48, 73; property ownership and, 29; race and, xiii, 46, 69–70, 72, 82, 87, 109, 136, 142, 144, 149, 178–79, 186–87, 189, 203n71; race war and, 23; racial differentiation and, xvi, 46, 96, 149, 188–89; racism and, x, 179; security and, 43, 181; settler colonialism and, 185; settlers and, 45, 142; slavery and, 45, 46, 77, 78, 89, 94, 95, 97, 109; Sloane, Charles F. on, 56; sovereignty and, 145; the state and, 150–51; Trump, Donald and, 166; United States and, 22, 24, 28, 30, 100, 104, 114, 186; U.S. expansionism and, 108–9; U.S. foreign policies/relations and, 7, 28, 69; U.S. territorial expansion and, 28, 109, 203n71; wage labor and, 81; war and, 53, 54, 56, 71; white supremacy and, 71; whites/whiteness and, 95, 143; Wilderson, Frank and, 216n11; World War II and, 184, 185. *See also* homicide; police killings; state violence

violence toll, 3, 12, 32, 71, 201n52

white supremacy: Africa and, 138; anticommunism and, 113; antiracism and, 135; Asia and, 138; civil rights and, 231n1; Civil War and, x, 47, 48, 51; colonization and, 99; Du Bois, W. E. B. and, 140; great transformation and, 125; King, Martin Luther, Jr. and, 186; McCain, John and, 180; national sovereignty and, 150; *New York Times* and, 231n1; Obama, Barack and, 150; police power and, 47, 48, 145; postslavery U.S. and, 51; race and, xiv–xv, 130, 149; Rice, Condoleeza and, 20; slavery and, x; Trump, Donald and, 159, 163–64, 170–71; United States and, 138, 163–64, 188; violence and, 71; World War II and, 138. *See also* individuals

Wilderson, Frank, 216n11

Williams, Eric, 85, 214n4

Wilson, James Q., 66–67

Wilson, O. W., 210n74

Wilson, Woodrow, 52, 99

Winant, Howard, 123–24, 125, 229n24

Wolfe, Patrick, 24–25, 79

Wolfowitz, Paul, 9–10, 11, 12, 195n6, 232n7

Wolin, Sheldon, 169, 223n26

women: Clinton, Hillary and, 153; Fourteenth Amendment and, 116; free labor and, 92; Obama, Barack and, 162, 180; Republican Party and, 154; Rorty, Richard and, 156; slavery and capitalism and, 78, 89; Trump, Donald and, 165, 166, 168; working class and, 177. *See also* abortion; gender; reproductive rights

Wood, Ellen Meiskins, 214n2

workfare, 154–55

working class: capitalism and, 76, 80–81, 168; Clinton, Hillary and, 159; eight-hour day and, 85; globalism and, 170; liberals and, 156; race and, 156; racism and, 176–77; Rorty, Richard on, 155; slavery and, 217n20; Trump, Donald and, 175; whites and, 176–77; women and, 177

World Trade Organization, 155

World War I, xii, 21–22, 52, 53, 55, 111

World War II: African Americans and, 21–22; civil rights and, 54; fascism and, 21–22, 106, 110; German war crimes, 55; global leadership and, 4; great transformation and, 125; imperialism and, 111; Indian wars and, 24, 193n11; Kaplan, Robert on, 193n11; long peace and, xviii; mass/deportations and, 54; noncombatants and, 108; peace and, 53; permanent wars and, 30–31; police power and, 55; race and, xii; race war and, 53; racism and, 21–22; right wing and, 171; slavery and, 193n11; territorial annexations and, 33; universalism and, 184; U.S. expansionism and, 184; U.S. foreign policies and, 169–170; violence and, 184, 185; white supremacy and, 138

Wounded Knee, 30–31, 51–52

Wright, Jeremiah, 160, 179

Yarmolinsky, Adam, 65, 67

yellow peril, 50

Yette, Samuel, 62

Yoo, John, 33

Zuley, Richard, 17, 69